Introduction
to
Nanotechnology

Introduction to Nanotechnology

Editor

B.K. Parthasarathy

ISHA

ISHA BOOKS

Delhi-110009

Introduction to Nanotechnology

ISBN: 81-8205-436-2

Published in 2007 in India by
ISHA Books
B-63, 1st Floor, New Gupta Colony,
Near DDA Market,
Delhi-110009
Phone: 9212142040
ishabooks@hotmail.com

Laser Type Setting by: Rudra Computer Graphics, Delhi
Printed at: Salasar Imaging System, Delhi

Preface

Amongst the most fascinating and promising scientific fields to emerge in the 21st century has been that of nanotechnology. A form of micromechanics, the premise of this science rests on the control of matter ranging in size from 1 to 100 micrometers, or nanometeres (1 billionth of a metre) and the fabrication of devices along the same size range. A highly multidisciplinary field, nanotechnology derives its study and practice from fields as varied as colloidal science, supramolecular chemistry and device physics. One can often view this science as the moulding of the existing sciences into the nanoscale. Adhering to the adage"small is beautiful", this science truly holds the potential to revolutionise science and life, and is already being heralded as a precursor to the next Industrial Revolution.

This book takes an in-depth approach towards understanding nanotechnology, seeking to provide readers with a one-stop manual on the subject. It explores comprehensively the hype behind the science, the potential that it offers, and the whole rigmarole that comes with it. U. S. scientists have already etched from silicon an electronic motor that is smaller than .1mm wide and have made workable gears with a diamter less than a human hair. Further devices have resulted in the manipulation of electrons and individual atoms. The book expounds the history, techniques, principles, devices and the future of nanotechnology, with insights being also given on the scope, challenges, opportunities and the advent of this science in our daily life. The effort is to equip readers with an insightful and informative manual, and it is hoped that the endeavour bears fruit by proving highly useful to readers.

Editor

Contents

1

Introduction

The new technology will handle individual atoms and molecules with control and precision; call it molecular technology. It will change our world in more ways than we can imagine. Microcircuits have parts measured in micrometers—that is, in millionths of a meter—but molecules are measured in nanometers. We can use the terms "nanotechnology" and "molecular technology" interchangeably to describe the new style of technology. The engineers of the new technology will build both nanocircuits and nanomachines.

One dictionary definition of a machine is "any system, usually of rigid bodies, formed and connected to alter, transmit, and direct applied forces in a predetermined manner to accomplish a specific objective, such as the performance of useful work."

Molecular machines fit this definition quite well. To imagine these machines, one must first picture molecules. We can picture atoms as beads and molecules as clumps of beads, like a child's beads linked by snaps. In fact, chemists do sometimes visualise molecules by building models from plastic beads.

Atoms are rounded like beads, and although molecular bonds are not snaps. If an atom were the size of a small marble, a fairly complex molecule would be the size of your fist. This makes a useful mental image, but atoms are really about 1/10,000 the size of bacteria, and bacteria are about 1/10,000 the size of mosquitoes.

The things around us act as they do because of the way their molecules behave. Air holds neither its shape nor its volume because its molecules move freely, bumping and ricocheting through open space. Water molecules stick together as they move about, so water holds a constant volume as it changes shape. Copper holds its shape because its atoms stick together in regular patterns; we can bend it and hammer it because its atoms can slip over one another while remaining bound together.

Glass shatters when we hammer it because its atoms separate before they slip. Rubber consists of networks of kinked molecules, like a tangle of springs. When stretched and released, its molecules straighten and then coil again. These simple molecular patterns make up passive substances. More complex patterns make up the active nanomachines of living cells. Biochemists already work with these machines, which are chiefly made of protein, the main engineering material of living cells.

These molecular machines have relatively few atoms, and so they have lumpy surfaces, like objects made by gluing together a handful of small marbles. Also, many pairs of atoms are linked by bonds that can bend or rotate, and so protein machines are unusually flexible. But like all machines, they have parts of different shapes and sizes that do useful work. All machines use clumps of atoms as parts. Protein machines simply use very small clumps.

Biochemists dream of designing and building such devices, but there are difficulties to be overcome. Engineers use beams of light to project patterns onto silicon chips, but chemists must build much more indirectly than that. When they combine molecules in various sequences, they have only limited control over how the molecules join. When biochemists need complex molecular machines, they still have to borrow them from cells.

Nevertheless, advanced molecular machines will eventually let them build nanocircuits and nanomachines as easily and directly as engineers now build microcircuits or washing machines. Then progress will become swift and dramatic. Genetic engineers are already showing the way. Ordinarily, when chemists make molecular chains - called "polymers" - they dump molecules into a vessel where they bump and snap together haphazardly in a liquid. The resulting chains have varying lengths, and the molecules are strung together in no particular order. But in modern gene synthesis machines, genetic engineers build more orderly polymers - specific DNA molecules - by combining molecules in a particular order.

These molecules are the nucleotides of DNA (the letters of the genetic alphabet) and genetic engineers don't dump them all in together. Instead, they direct the machine to add different nucleotides in a particular sequence to spell out a particular message. They first bond one kind of nucleotide to the chain ends, then wash away the leftover material and add chemicals to prepare the chain ends to bond the next nucleotide. They grow chains as they bond on nucleotides, one at a time, in a programmed sequence. They anchor the very first nucleotide in each chain to a solid surface to keep the chain from washing away with its chemical bathwater. In this way, they have a big clumsy machine in a cabinet assemble specific molecular structures from parts a hundred million times smaller than itself. But this blind assembly process accidentally omits nucleotides from some chains.

The likelihood of mistakes grows as chains grow longer. Like workers discarding bad parts before assembling a car, genetic engineers reduce errors by discarding bad chains. Then, to join these short chains into working genes, they turn to molecular machines found in bacteria. These protein machines, called restriction enzymes, "read" certain DNA sequences as "cut here." They read these genetic patterns by touch, by sticking to them, and they cut the chain by rearranging a few atoms.

Other enzymes splice pieces together, reading matching parts as "glue here" - likewise "reading" chains by selective stickiness and splicing chains by rearranging a few atoms. By using gene machines to write, and restriction enzymes to cut and paste, genetic engineers can write and edit whatever DNA messages they choose. But by itself, DNA is a fairly worthless molecule. It is neither strong like Kevlar, nor colourful like a dye, nor active like an enzyme, yet it has something that industry is prepared to spend millions of dollars to use: the ability to direct molecular machines called ribosomes. In cells, molecular machines first transcribe DNA, copying its information to make RNA "tapes." Then, much as old numerically controlled machines shape metal based on instructions stored on tape, ribosomes build proteins based on instructions stored on RNA strands.

And proteins are useful. Proteins, like DNA, resemble strings of lumpy beads. But unlike DNA, protein molecules fold up to form small objects able to do things. Some are enzymes, machines that build up and tear down molecules. Other proteins are hormones, binding to yet other proteins to signal cells to change their behaviour. Genetic engineers can produce these objects cheaply by directing the cheap and efficient molecular machinery inside living organisms to do the work. Whereas engineers running a chemical plant must work with vats of reacting chemicals, engineers working with bacteria can make them absorb chemicals, carefully rearrange the atoms, and store a product or release it into the fluid around them.

Genetic engineers have now programmed bacteria to make proteins ranging from human growth hormone to rennin, an enzyme used in making cheese. The pharmaceutical company Eli Lilly (Indianapolis) is now marketing Humulin, human insulin molecules made by bacteria.

Protein Machines

These protein hormones and enzymes selectively stick to other molecules. An enzyme changes its target's structure, then moves on; a hormone affects its target's behaviour only so long as both remain stuck together. Enzymes and hormones can be described in mechanical terms, but their behaviour is more often described in chemical terms. But other proteins serve basic mechanical functions. Some push and pull, some act as cords or struts, and parts of some molecules make excellent bearings.

The machinery of muscle, for instance, has gangs of proteins that reach, grab a "rope" (also made of protein), pull it, then reach out again for a fresh grip; whenever you move, you use these machines. Amoebas and human cells move and change shape by using fibres and rods that act as molecular muscles and bones. A reversible, variable-speed motor drives bacteria through water by turning a corkscrew shaped propeller. If a hobbyist could build tiny cars around such motors, several billions of billions would fit in a pocket, and 150-lane freeways could be built through your finest capillaries.

Simple molecular devices combine to form systems resembling industrial machines. In the 1950s engineers developed machine tools that cut metal under the control of a punched paper tape. A century and a half earlier, Joseph-Marie Jacquard had built a loom that wove complex patterns under the control of a chain of punched cards. Yet over three billion years before Jacquard, cells had developed the machinery of the ribosome. Ribosomes are proof that nanomachines built of protein and RNA can be programmed to build complex molecules. Then consider viruses. One kind, the T4 phage, acts like a spring-loaded syringe and looks like something out of an industrial parts catalogue. It can stick to a bacterium, punch a hole, and inject viral DNA. Like a conqueror seizing factories to build more tanks, this DNA then directs the cell's machines to build more viral DNA and syringes. Like all organisms, these viruses exist because they are fairly stable and are good at getting copies of themselves made.

Whether in cells or not, nanomachines obey the universal laws of nature. Ordinary chemical bonds hold their atoms together, and ordinary chemical reactions assemble them. Protein molecules can even join to form machines without special help, driven only by thermal agitation and chemical forces. By mixing viral proteins (and the DNA they serve) in a test tube, molecular biologists have assembled working T4 viruses.

This ability is surprising: imagine putting automotive parts in a large box, shaking it, and finding an assembled car when you look inside! Yet the T4 virus is but one of many self-assembling structures. Molecular biologists have taken the machinery of the ribosome apart into over fifty separate protein and RNA molecules, and then combined them in test tubes to form working ribosomes again. To see how this happens, imagine different T4 protein chains floating around in water. Each kind folds up to form a lump with distinctive bumps and hollows, covered by distinctive patterns of oiliness, wetness, and electric charge.

Picture them wandering and tumbling, jostled by the thermal vibrations of the surrounding water molecules. From time to time two bounce together, then bounce apart. Sometimes, though, two bounce together and fit, bumps in hollows, with sticky patches matching; they then pull together and stick. In this way protein adds to protein to make sections of the virus, and sections assemble to form the whole. Protein engineers will not need nanoarms and nanohands to assemble complex nanomachines.

Still, tiny manipulators will be useful and they will be built. Just as today's engineers build machinery as complex as player pianos and robot arms from ordinary motors, bearings, and moving parts, so tomorrow's biochemists will be able to use protein molecules as motors, bearings, and moving parts to build robot arms which will themselves be able to handle individual molecules.

Second Generation Nanotechnology

Despite its versatility, protein has shortcomings as an engineering material. Protein machines quit when dried, freeze when chilled, and cook when heated. We do not build machines of flesh, hair, and gelatin; over the centuries, we have learned to use our hands of flesh and bone to build machines of wood, ceramic, steel, and plastic. We will do likewise in the future. We will use protein machines to build nanomachines of tougher stuff than protein. As nanotechnology moves beyond reliance on proteins, it will grow more ordinary from an engineer's point of view.

Molecules will be assembled like the components of an erector set, and well-bonded parts will stay put. Just as ordinary tools can build ordinary machines from parts, so molecular tools will bond molecules together to make tiny gears, motors, levers, and casings, and assemble them to make complex machines. Parts containing only a few atoms will be lumpy, but engineers can work with lumpy parts if they have smooth bearings to support them.

Conveniently enough, some bonds between atoms make fine bearings; a part can be mounted by means of a single chemical bond that will let it turn freely and smoothly. Since a bearing can be made using only two atoms, nanomachines can indeed have mechanical components of molecular size. How will these better machines be built? Over the years, engineers have used technology to improve technology. They have used metal tools to shape metal into better tools, and computers to design and programme better computers. They will likewise use protein nanomachines to build better nanomachines. Enzymes show the way: they assemble large molecules by "grabbing" small molecules from the water around them, then holding them together so that a bond forms.

Enzymes assemble DNA, RNA, proteins, fats, hormones, and chlorophyll in this way - indeed, virtually the whole range of molecules found in living things. Biochemical engineers, then, will construct new enzymes to assemble new patterns of atoms. For example, they might make an enzyme-like machine which will add carbon atoms to a small spot, layer on layer.

If bonded correctly, the atoms will build up to form a fine, flexible diamond fiber having over fifty times as much strength as the same weight of aluminum. Aerospace companies will line up to buy such fibres by the ton to make advanced composites. But the great advance will come when protein machines are able to make structures more complex than mere fibres.These programmable protein machines will resemble ribosomes programmed by RNA, or the older generation of automated machine tools programmed by punched tapes. They will open a new world of possibilities, letting engineers escape the limitations of proteins to build rugged, compact machines with straightforward designs.

Engineered proteins will split and join molecules as enzymes do. Existing proteins bind a variety of smaller molecules, using them as chemical tools; newly engineered proteins will use all these tools and more. Further, organic chemists have shown that chemical reactions can produce remarkable results even without nanomachines to guide the molecules. Chemists have no direct control over the tumbling motions of molecules in a liquid, and so the molecules are free to react in any way they can, depending on how they bump together.

Yet chemists nonetheless coax reacting molecules to form regular structures such as cubic and dodecahedral molecules, and to form unlikely-seeming structures such as molecular rings with highly strained bonds. Molecular machines will have still greater versatility in bondmaking, because they can use similar molecular motions to make bonds, but can guide these motions in ways that chemists cannot. Indeed, because chemists cannot yet direct molecular motions, they can seldom assemble complex molecules according to specific plans.

The largest molecules they can make with specific, complex patterns are all linear chains. Chemists form these patterns by adding molecules in sequence, one at a time, to a growing chain. With only one possible bonding site per chain, they can be sure to add the next piece in the right place. But if a rounded, lumpy molecule has a hundred hydrogen atoms on its surface, how can chemists split off just one particular atom to add something in its place? Stirring simple chemicals together will seldom do the job, because small molecules can seldom select specific places to react with a large molecule. But protein machines will be more choosy.

A flexible, programmable protein machine will grasp a large molecule (the workpiece) while bringing a small molecule up against it in just the right place. Like an enzyme, it will then bond the molecules together. By bonding molecule after molecule to the workpiece, the machine will assemble a larger and larger structure while keeping complete control of how its atoms are arranged. This is the key ability that chemists have lacked. Like ribosomes, such nanomachines can work under the direction of molecular tapes. Unlike ribosomes, they will handle a wide variety of small molecules and will join them to the workpiece anywhere desired, not just to the end of a chain.

Protein machines will thus combine the splitting and joining abilities of enzymes with the programmability of ribosomes. But whereas ribosomes can build only the loose folds of a protein, these protein machines will build small, solid objects of metal, ceramic, or diamond - invisibly small, but rugged. Where our fingers of flesh are likely to bruise or burn, we turn to steel tongs. Where protein machines are likely to crush or disintegrate, we will turn to nanomachines made of tougher stuff.

Promises of Nano Technology

Benjamin Franklin wanted a procedure for stopping and restarting metabolism, but none was then known. We can stop metabolism in many ways, but biostasis, to be of use, must be reversible. This leads to a curious situation. Whether we can place patients in biostasis using present techniques depends entirely on whether future techniques will be able to reverse the process.

The procedure has two parts, of which we must master only one. If biostasis can keep a patient unchanged for years, then those future techniques will include sophisticated cell repair systems. We must therefore judge the success of present biostasis procedures in light of the ultimate abilities of future medicine. Before cell repair machines became a clear prospect, those abilities - and thus the requirements for successful biostasis - remained grossly uncertain. Now, the basic requirements seem fairly obvious. Molecular machines can build cells from scratch, as dividing cells demonstrate. They can also build organs and organ systems from scratch, as developing embryos demonstrate.

Physicians will be able to use cell repair technology to direct the growth of new organs from a patient's own cells. This gives modern physicians great leeway in biostasis procedures: even if they were to damage or discard most of a patient s organs, they would still do no irreversible harm. Future colleagues with better tools will be able to repair or replace the organs involved. Most people would be glad to have a new heart, fresh kidneys, or younger skin. But the brain is another matter.

A physician who allows the destruction of a patient's brain allows the destruction of the patient as a person, whatever may happen to the rest of the body. The brain holds the patterns of memory, of personality, of self. Stroke patients lose only parts of their brains, yet suffer harm ranging from partial blindness to paralysis to loss of language, lowered intelligence, altered personality, and worse.

The effects depend on the location of the damage. This suggests that total destruction of the brain causes total blindness, paralysis, speechlessness, and mindlessness, whether the body continues to breathe or not. As Voltaire wrote, "To rise again - to be the same person that you were - you must have your memory perfectly fresh and present; for it is memory that makes your identity. If your memory be lost, how will you be the same man?"

Anesthesia interrupts consciousness without disrupting the structure of the brain, and biostasis procedures must do likewise, for a longer time. This raises the question of the nature of the physical structures that underlie memory and personality. Neurobiology, and informed common sense, agree on the basic nature of memory. As we form memories and develop as individuals, our brains change. These changes affect the brain's function, changing its pattern of activity: When we remember, our brains do something; when we act, think, or feel, our brains do something.

Brains work by means of molecular machinery. Lasting changes in brain function involve lasting changes in this molecular machinery - unlike a computer's memory, the brain is not designed to be wiped clean and refilled at a moment's notice. Personality and long-term memory are durable. Throughout the body, durable changes in function involve durable changes in molecular machinery. When muscles become stronger or swifter, their proteins change in number and distribution. When a liver adapts to cope with alcohol, its protein content also changes. When the immune system learns to recognise a new kind of influenza virus, protein content changes again. Since protein-based machines do the actual work of moving muscles, breaking down toxins, and recognising viruses, this relationship is to be expected. In the brain, proteins shape nerve cells, stud their surfaces, link one cell to the next, control the ionic currents of each neural impulse, produce the signal molecules that nerve cells use to communicate across synapses, and much, much more. When printers print words, they put down patterns of ink; when nerve cells change their behaviour, they change their patterns of protein.

Printing also dents the paper, and nerve cells change more than just their proteins, yet the ink on the paper and the proteins in the brain are enough to make these patterns clear. The changes involved are far from subtle. Researchers report that long-term changes in nerve cell behaviour involve "striking morphological changes" in synapses: they change visibly in size and structure. It seems that long-term memory is not some terribly delicate pattern, ready to evaporate from the brain at any excuse. Memory and personality are instead firmly embodied in the way that brain cells have grown together, in patterns formed through years of experience.

Memory and personality are no more material than the characters in a novel; yet like them they are embodied in matter. Memory and personality do not waft away on the last breath as a patient expires. Indeed, many patients have recovered from so-called "clinical death," even without cell repair machines to help. The patterns of mind are destroyed only when and if the attending physicians allow the patient's brain to undergo dissolution. This again allows physicians considerable leeway in biostasis procedures: typically, they need not stop metabolism until after vital functions have ceased. It seems that preserving the cell structures and protein patterns of the brain will also preserve the structure of the mind and self. Biologists already know how to preserve tissue this well. Resuscitation technology must await cell repair machines, but biostasis technology seems well in hand.

Reversing biostasis

Imagine that a patient has expired because of a heart attack. Physicians attempt resuscitation but fail, and give up on restoring vital functions. At this point, though, the patient's body and brain are just barely nonfunctional - most cells and tissues, in fact, are still alive and metabolising. Having made arrangements beforehand, the patient is soon placed in biostasis to prevent irreversible dissolution and await a better day. Years pass. The patient changes little, but technology advances greatly. Biochemists learn to design proteins. Engineers use protein machines to build assemblers, then use assemblers to build a broad-based nanotechnology.

With new instruments, biological knowledge explodes. Biomedical engineers use new knowledge, automated engineering, and assemblers to develop cell repair machines of growing sophistication. They learn to stop and reverse aging. Physicians use cell repair technology to resuscitate patients in biostasis - first those placed in biostasis by the most advanced techniques, then those placed in biostasis using earlier and cruder techniques.

Finally, after the successful resuscitation of animals placed in biostasis using the old techniques of the 1980s, physicians turn to our heart-attack patient. In the first stage of preparation, the patient lies in a tank of liquid nitrogen surrounded by equipment. Glassy protectant still locks each cell's molecular machinery in a firm embrace. This protectant must be removed, but simple warming might allow some cell structures to move about prematurely. Surgical devices designed for use at low temperatures reach through the liquid nitrogen to the patient's chest. There they remove solid plugs of tissue to open access to major arteries and veins. An army of nanomachines equipped for removing protectant moves through these openings, clearing first the major blood vessels and then the capillaries.

This opens paths throughout the normally active tissues of the patient's body. The larger surgical machines then attach tubes to the chest and pump fluid through the circulatory system. The fluid washes out the initial protectant-removal machines. Now the machines pump in a milky fluid containing trillions of devices that enter cells and remove the glassy protectant, molecule by molecule. They replace it with a temporary molecular scaffolding that leaves ample room for repair ma nes to work.

As these protectantremoval machines uncover biomolecules, including the structural and mechanical components of the cells, they bind them to the scaffolding with temporary cross-links. When molecules must be moved aside, the machines label them for proper replacement. Like other advanced cell repair machines, these devices work under the direction of on-site nanocomputers. When they finish, the low-temperature machines withdraw.

Through a series of gradual changes in composition and temperature, a water-based solution replaces the earlier cryogenic fluid and the patient warms to above the freezing point. Cell repair machines are pumped through the blood vessels and enter the cells. Repairs commence. Small devices examine molecules and report their structures and positions to a larger computer within the cell. The computer identifies the molecules, directs any needed molecular repairs, and identifies cell structures from molecular patterns.

Where damage has displaced structures in a cell, the computer directs the repair devices to restore the molecules to their proper arrangement, using temporary cross-links as needed. Meanwhile, the patient's arteries are cleared and the heart muscle, damaged years earlier, is repaired. Finally, the molecular machinery of the cells has been restored to working order, and coarser repairs have corrected damaged patterns of cells to restore tissues and organs to a healthy condition.

The scaffolding is then removed from the cells, together with most of the temporary cross-links and much of the repair machinery. Most of each cell's active molecules remain blocked, though, to prevent premature, unbalanced activity. Outside the body, the repair system has grown fresh blood from the patient's own cells. It now transfuses this blood to refill the circulatory system, and acts as a temporary artificial heart.

The remaining devices in each cell now adjust the concentration of salts, sugars, ATP, and other small molecules, largely by selectively unblocking each cell's own nanomachinery. With further unblocking, metabolism resumes step by step; the heart muscle is finally unblocked on the verge of contraction. Heartbeat resumes, and the patient emerges into a state of anesthesia. While the attending physicians check that all is going well, the repair system closes the opening in the chest, joining tissue to tissue without a stitch or a scar. The remaining devices in the cells disassemble one another into harmless waste or nutrient molecules.

As the patient moves into ordinary sleep, certain visitors enter the room, as long planned. At last, the sleeper wakes refreshed to the light of a new day - and to the sight of old friends. Before considering resuscitation, however, some may ask what becomes of the soul of a person in biostasis. Some people would answer that the soul and the mind are aspects of the same thing, of a pattern embodied in the substance of the brain, active during active life and quiescent in biostasis. Assume, though, that the pattern of mind, memory, and personality leaves the body at death, carried by some subtle substance.

The possibilities then seem fairly clear. Death in this case has a meaning other than irreversible damage to the brain, being defined instead by the irreversible departure of the soul. This would make biostasis a pointless but harmless gesture - after all, religious leaders have expressed no concern that mere preservation of the body can somehow imprison a soul. Resuscitation would, in this view, presumably require the cooperation of the soul to succeed. The act of placing patients in biostasis has in fact been accompanied by both Catholic and Jewish ceremonies. With or without biostasis, cell repair cannot bring immortality.

Physical death, however greatly postponed, will remain inevitable for reasons rooted in the nature of the universe. Biostasis followed by cell repair thus seems to raise no fundamental theology. It resembles deep anesthesia followed by life-saving surgery: both procedures interrupt consciousness to prolong life. To speak of "immortality" when the prospect is only long life would be to ignore the facts or to misuse words.

The prospect of biostasis seems tailor-made to cause future shock. Most people find today's accelerating change shocking enough when it arrives a bit at a time. But the biostasis option is a present-day consequence of a whole series of future breakthroughs. This prospect naturally upsets the difficult psychological adjustments that people make in dealing with physical decline. As molecular technology advances, understanding of cell repair will spread through the popular culture.

Expert opinion will increasingly support the idea. Biostasis will grow more common, and its costs will fall. It seems likely that many people will eventually consider biostasis to be the norm, to be a standard lifesaving treatment for patients who have expired. But until cell repair machines are demonstrated, the all too human tendency to ignore what we haven't seen will slow the acceptance of biostasis. Millions will no doubt pass from expiration to irreversible dissolution because of habit and tradition, supported by weak arguments. The importance of clear foresight in this matter makes it important to consider possible arguments before leaving the topic of life extension and moving on to other matters. Whether people choose to use biostasis will depend on whether they see it as worth the gamble.

This gamble involves the value of life (which is a personal matter), the cost of biostasis (which seems reasonable by the standards of modern medicine), the odds that the technology will work (which seem excellent), and the odds that humanity will survive, develop the technology, and revive people. This final point accounts for most of the overall uncertainty. Assume that human beings and free societies will indeed survive. If so, then technology will continue to advance. Developing assemblers will take years. Studying cells and learning to repair the tissues of patients in biostasis will take still longer.

At a guess, developing repair systems and adapting them to resuscitation will take three to ten decades, though advances in automated engineering may speed the process. The time required seems unimportant, however. Most resuscitated patients will care more about the conditions of life - including the presence of their friends and family—than they will care about the date on the calendar. With abundant resources, the physical conditions of life could be very good indeed. The presence of companions is another matter. Techniques for placing patients in biostasis are already known, and the costs could become low, at least compared to the costs of major surgery or prolonged hospital care.

Resuscitation technology, though, will be complex and expensive to develop. Will people in the future bother? It seems likely that they will. They may not develop nanotechnology with medicine in mind - but if not, then they will surely develop it to build better computers. They may not develop cell repair machines with resuscitation in mind, but they will surely do so to heal themselves. They may not programme repair machines for resuscitation as an act of impersonal charity, but they will have time, wealth, and automated engineering systems, and some of them will have loved ones waiting in biostasis. Resuscitation techniques seem sure to be developed.

With replicators and space resources, a time will come when people have wealth and living space over a thousandfold greater than we have today. Resuscitation itself will require little energy and material even by today's standards. Thus, people contemplating resuscitation will find little conflict between their self-interest and their humanitarian concerns.

Common human motives seem enough to ensure that the active population of the future will awaken those in biostasis. The first generation that will regain youth without being forced to resort to biostasis may well be with us today. The prospect of biostasis simply gives more people more reason to expect long life - it offers an opportunity for the old and a form of insurance for the young.

As advances in biotechnology lead toward protein design, assemblers, and cell repair, and as the implications sink in, the expectation of long life will spread. By broadening the path to long life, the biostasis option will encourage a more lively interest in the future. And this will spur efforts to prepare for the dangers ahead.

Dangers of Nanotechnology

Thinking machines and replicating assemblers pose basic threats to people and to life on Earth. Today's organisms have abilities far from the limits of the possible, and our machines are evolving faster than we are. Within a few decades they seem likely to surpass us. Unless we learn to live with them in safety, our future will likely be both exciting and short. We cannot hope to foresee all the problems ahead, yet by paying attention to the big, basic issues, we can perhaps foresee the greatest challenges and get some idea of how to deal with them.

Future Threats

Living organisms are also powered by fuels or sunlight, and also make more of themselves from ordinary materials. But unlike assembler-based systems, they cannot make "almost anything". Genetic evolution has limited life to a system based on DNA, RNA, and ribosomes, but memetic evolution will bring life-like machines based on nanocomputers and assemblers: Assemblers will be able to build all that ribosomes can, and more; assembler-based replicators will therefore be able to do all that life can, and more. From an evolutionary point of view, this poses an obvious threat to otters, people, cacti, and ferns - to the rich fabric of the biosphere and all that we prize. The early transistorised computers soon beat the most advanced vacuum-tube computers because they were based on superior devices.

For the same reason, early assembler-based replicators could beat the most advanced modern organisms. "Plants" with "leaves" no more efficient than today's solar cells could out-compete real plants, crowding the biosphere with an inedible foliage. Tough, omnivorous "bacteria" could out-compete real bacteria: they could spread like blowing pollen, replicate swiftly, and reduce the biosphere to dust in a matter of days. Dangerous replicators could easily be too tough, small, and rapidly spreading to stop - at least if we made no preparation. We have trouble enough controlling viruses and fruit flies. Among the cognoscenti of nanotechnology, this threat has become known as the "gray goo problem." Though masses of uncontrolled replicators need not be gray or gooey, the term "gray goo" emphasises that replicators able to obliterate life might be less inspiring than a single species of crabgrass. They might be "superior" in an evolutionary sense, but this need not make them valuable.

We have evolved to love a world rich in living things, ideas, and diversity, so there is no reason to value gray goo merely because it could spread. Indeed, if we prevent it we will thereby prove our evolutionary superiority. The gray goo threat makes one thing perfectly clear: we cannot afford certain kinds of accidents with replicating assemblers. AI systems that work together as people do will be able to outthink not just individuals, but whole societies.

Again, the evolution of genes has left life stuck. Again, the evolution of memes by human beings - and eventually by machines - will advance our hardware far beyond the limits of life. And again, from an evolutionary point of view this poses an obvious threat. Knowledge can bring power, and power can bring knowledge. Depending on their natures and their goals, advanced AI systems might accumulate enough knowledge and power to displace us, if we don't prepare properly.

And as with replicators, mere evolutionary "superiority" need not make the victors better than the vanquished by any standard but brute competitive ability. This threat makes one thing perfectly clear: we need to find ways to live with thinking machines, to make them law-abiding citizens. Certain kinds of replicators and AI systems may confront us with forms of hardware capable of swift, effective, independent action. But the novelty of this threat—coming from the machines themselves—must not blind us to a more traditional danger.

Replicators and AI systems can also serve as great engines of power, if wielded freely by sovereign states. Throughout history, states have developed technologies to extend their military power, and states will no doubt play a dominant role in developing replicators and AI systems. States could use replicating assemblers to build arsenals of advanced weapons, swiftly, easily, and in vast quantity. States could use special replicators directly to wage a sort of germ warfare - one made vastly more practical by programmable, computer-controlled "germs."

Depending on their skills, AI systems could serve as weapon designers, strategists, or fighters. Military funds already support research in both molecular technology and artificial intelligence. States could use assemblers or advanced AI systems to achieve sudden, destabilising breakthroughs. The advent of replicating assemblers will bring relatively sudden changes: Able to replicate swiftly, they could become abundant in a matter of days. Able to make almost anything, they could be programmed to duplicate existing weapons, but made from superior materials.

Able to work with standard, well-understood components (atoms) they could suddenly build things designed in anticipation of the assembler breakthrough. These results of design-ahead could include programmable germs and other nasty novelties. For all these reasons, a state that makes the assembler breakthrough could rapidly create a decisive military force—if not literally overnight, then at least with unprecedented speed. States could use advanced AI systems to similar ends.

Automated engineering systems will facilitate designahead and speed assembler development. Al systems able to build better AI systems will allow an explosion of capability with effects hard to anticipate. Both AI systems and replicating assemblers will enable states to expand their military capabilities by orders of magnitude in a brief time.

Replicators can be more potent than nuclear weapons: to devastate Earth with bombs would require masses of exotic hardware and rare isotopes, but to destroy all life with replicators would require only a single speck made of ordinary elements. Replicators give nuclear war some company as a potential cause of extinction, giving a broader context to extinction as a moral concern.

Despite their potential as engines of destruction, nanotechnology and AI systems will lend themselves to more subtle uses than do nuclear weapons. A bomb can only blast things, but nanomachines and AI systems could be used to infiltrate, seize, change, and govern a territory or a world. Even the most ruthless police have no use for nuclear weapons, but they do have use for bugs, drugs, assassins, and other flexible engines of power. With advanced technology, states will be able to consolidate their power over people. Like genes, memes, organisms, and hardware, states have evolved. Their institutions have spread (with variations) through growth, fission, imitation, and conquest. States at war fight like beasts, but using citizens as their bones, brains, and muscle.

The coming breakthroughs will confront states with new pressures and opportunities, encouraging sharp changes in how states behave. This naturally gives cause for concern. States have, historically, excelled at slaughter and oppression. In a sense, a state is simply the sum of the people making up its organisational apparatus: their actions add up to make its actions. But the same might be said of a dog and its cells, though a dog is clearly more than just a clump of cells. Both dogs and states are evolved systems, with structures that affect how their parts behave.

For thousands of years, dogs have evolved largely to please people, because they have survived and reproduced at human whim. For thousands of years, states have evolved under other selective pressures. Individuals have far more power over their dogs than they do over "their" states. Though states, too, can benefit from pleasing people, their very existence has depended on their capability for using people, whether as leaders, police, or soldiers. It may seem paradoxical to say that people have limited power over states: After all, aren't people behind a state's every action? But in democracies, heads of state bemoan their lack of power, representatives bow to interest groups, bureaucrats are bound by rules, and voters, allegedly in charge, curse the whole mess.

The state acts and people affect it, yet no one can claim to control it. In totalitarian states, the apparatus of power has a tradition, structure, and inner logic that leaves no one free, neither the rulers nor the ruled. Even kings had to act in ways limited by the traditions of monarchy and the practicalities of power, if they were to remain kings.

States are not human, though they are made of humans. Despite this, history shows that change is possible, even change for the better. But changes always move from one semi-autonomous, inhuman system to another - equally inhuman but perhaps more humane. In our hope for improvements, we must not confuse states that wear a human face with states that have humane institutions. Describing states as quasi-organisms captures only one aspect of a complex reality, yet it suggests how they may evolve in response to the coming breakthroughs.

The growth of government power, most spectacular in totalitarian countries, suggests one direction. States could become more like organisms by dominating their parts more completely. Using replicating assemblers, states could fill the human environment with miniature surveillance devices. Using an abundance of speech-understanding AI systems, they could listen to everyone without employing half the population as listeners. Using nanotechnology like that proposed for cell repair machines, they could cheaply tranquilise, lobotomise, or otherwise modify entire populations. This would simply extend an all too familiar pattern. The world already holds governments that spy, torture, and drug; advanced technology will merely extend the possibilities. But with advanced technology, states need not control people - they could instead simply discard people. Most people in most states, after all, function either as workers, larval workers, or worker-rearers, and most of these workers make, move, or grow things.

A state with replicating assemblers would not need such work. What is more, advanced AI systems could replace engineers, scientists, administrators, and even leaders. The combination of nanotechnology and advanced AI will make possible intelligent, effective robots; with such robots, a state could prosper while discarding anyone, or even (in principle) everyone.

The implications of this possibility depend on whether the state exists to serve the people, or the people exist to serve the state. In the first case, we have a state shaped by human beings to serve general human purposes; democracies tend to be at least rough approximations to this ideal. If a democratically controlled government loses its need for people, this will basically mean that it no longer needs to use people as bureaucrats or taxpayers. This will open new possibilities, some of which may prove desirable.

In the second case, we have a state evolved to exploit human beings, perhaps along totalitarian lines. States have needed people as workers because human labor has been the necessary foundation of power. What is more, genocide has been expensive and troublesome to organise and execute. Yet, in this century totalitarian states have slaughtered their citizens by the millions. Advanced technology will make workers unnecessary and genocide easy. History suggests that totalitarian states may then eliminate people wholesale. There is some consolation in this. It seems likely that a state willing and able to enslave us biologically would instead simply kill us.

The threat of advanced technology in the hands of governments makes one thing perfectly clear: we cannot afford to have an oppressive state take the lead in the coming breakthroughs. The basic problems in the future, as in the past, new technologies will lend themselves to accidents and abuse. Since replicators and thinking machines will bring great new powers, the potential for accidents and abuse will likewise be great.

These possibilities pose genuine threats to our lives. Most people would like a chance to live and be free to choose how to live. This goal may not sound too utopian, at least in some parts of the world. It doesn't mean forcing everyone's life to fit some grand scheme; it chiefly means avoiding enslavement and death. Yet, like the achievement of a utopian dream, it will bring a future of wonders. Given these life-and-death problems and this general goal, we can consider what measures might help us succeed. Our strategy must involve people, principles, and institutions, but it must also rest on tactics which inevitably will involve technology.

Active Shields

It seems that we can build nanomachines that act somewhat like the white blood cells of the human immune system: devices that can fight not just bacteria and viruses, but dangerous replicators of all sorts. Call an automated defence of this sort an active shield, to distinguish it from a fixed wall. Unlike ordinary engineering systems, reliable active shields must do more than just cope with nature or clumsy users. They must also cope with a far greater challenge - with the entire range of threats that intelligent forces can design and build under prevailing circumstances. Building and improving prototype shields will be akin to running both sides of an arms race on a laboratory scale. But the goal here will be to seek the minimum requirements for a defence that reliably prevails. We can test promising shield systems in Earthlike environments in space. Success will make possible a system able to protect human life and Earth's biosphere from the worst that a fistful of loose replicators can do. With our present uncertainties, we cannot yet describe either threats or shields with any accuracy. Does this mean we can't have any confidence that effective shields are possible? Apparently we can; there is a difference, after all, between knowing that something is possible and knowing how to do it.

And in this case, the world holds examples of analogous successes. There is nothing fundamentally novel about defending against invading replicators; life has been doing it for ages. Replicating assemblers, though unusually potent, will be physical systems not unlike those we already know. Experience suggests that they can be controlled. Viruses are molecular machines that invade cells; cells use molecular machines to defend against them.

Bacteria are cells that invade organisms; organisms use cells to defend against them. Similarly, societies use police to defend against criminals and armies to defend against invaders. On a less physical level, minds use meme systems such as the scientific method to defend against nonsense, and societies use institutions such as courts to defend against the power of other institutions. The biological examples in the last paragraph show that even after a billion-year arms race, molecular machines have maintained successful defences against molecular replicators. Failures have been common too, but the successes do indicate that defence is possible. These successes suggest that we can indeed use nanomachines to defend against nanomachines.

Though assemblers will bring many advances, there seems no reason why they should permanently tip the balance against defence. The examples given above—some involving viruses, some involving institutions - are diverse enough to suggest that successful defence rests on general principles. One might ask, Why do all these defences succeed? But turn the question around: Why should they fail? Each conflict pits similar systems against each other, giving the attacker no obvious advantage. In each conflict, moreover, the attacker faces a defence that is well established. The defenders fight on home ground, giving them advantages such as prepared positions, detailed local knowledge, stockpiled resources, and abundant allies - when the immune system recognises a germ, it can mobilise the resources of an entire body.

All these advantages are general and basic, having little to do with the details of a technology. We can give our active shields the same advantages over dangerous replicators. And they need not sit idle while dangerous weapons are amassed, any more than the immune system sits idle while bacteria multiply. It would be hard to predict the outcome of an open-ended arms race between powers equipped with replicating assemblers. But before this situation can arise, the leading force seems likely to acquire a temporary but overwhelming military advantage.

If the outcome of an arms race is in doubt, then the leading force will likely use its strength to ensure that no opponents are allowed to catch up. If it does so, then active shields will not have to withstand attacks backed by the resources of half a continent or half a solar system; they will instead be like a police force or an immune system, facing attacks backed only by whatever resources can be gathered in secret within the protected territory. The immune system, shaped by genetic evolution, meets threats also shaped by genetic evolution. Armies, shaped by human minds, also meet similar threats.

Likewise, both active shields and dangerous replicators will be shaped by memetic evolution. But if the leading force can develop automated engineering systems that work a millionfold faster than human engineers, and if it can use them for a single year, then it can build active shields based on a million years' worth of engineering advance. With such systems we may be able to explore the limits of the possible well enough to build a reliable shield against all physically possible threats. Even without our knowing the details of the threats and the shields, there seems reason to believe that shields are possible. And the examples of memes controlling memes and of institutions controlling institutions also suggest that AI systems can control AI systems.

In building active shields, we will be able to use the power of replicators and AI systems to multiply the traditional advantages of the defending force: we can give it overwhelming strength through abundant, replicator-built hardware with designs based on the equivalent of a million-year lead in technology. We can build active shields having strength and reliability that will put past systems to shame. Nanotechnology and artificial intelligence could bring the ultimate tools of destruction, but they are not inherently destructive. With care, we can use them to build the ultimate tools of peace.

2

Nanotechnology Applications

The overall properties of materials as diverse as paints and silicon chips are determined by their structure at the micro- and nanoscales. As our understanding of materials at the nanoscale and our ability to control their structure improves, there will be great potential to create a range of materials with novel characteristics, functions and applications. We categorise nanomaterials as those which have structured components with at least one dimension less than 100nm. Materials that have one dimension in the nanoscale are layers, such as a thin films or surface coatings. Some of the features on computer chips come in this category. Materials that are nanoscale in two dimensions include nanowires and nanotubes.

Materials that are nanoscale in three dimensions are particles, for example precipitates, colloids and quantum dots. Nanocrystalline materials, made up of nanometre-sized grains, also fall into this category. Some of these materials have been available for some time; others are genuinely new. Two principal factors cause the properties of nanomaterials to differ significantly from other materials: increased relative surface area, and quantum effects. These factors can change or enhance properties such as reactivity, strength and electrical characteristics.

As a particle decreases in size, a greater proportion of atoms are found at the surface compared to those inside.

For example, a particle of size 30 nm has 5% of its atoms on its surface, at 10 nm 20% of its atoms, and at 3 nm 50% of its atoms. Thus nanoparticles have a much greater surface area per unit mass compared with larger particles.

As growth and catalytic chemical reactions occur at surfaces, this means that a given mass of material in nanoparticulate form will be much more reactive than the same mass of material made up of larger particles. In tandem with surface-area effects, quantum effects can begin to dominate the properties of matter as size is reduced to the nanoscale. These can affect the optical, electrical and magnetic behaviour of materials, particularly as the structure or particle size approaches the smaller end of the nanoscale.

Materials that exploit these effects include quantum dots, and quantum well lasers for optoelectronics. For other materials such as crystalline solids, as the size of their structural components decreases, there is much greater interface area within the material; this can greatly affect both mechanical and electrical properties. Most metals are made up of small crystalline grains; the boundaries between the grain slow down or arrest the propagation of defects when the material is stressed, thus giving it strength. If these grains can be made very small, or even nanoscale in size, the interface area within the material greatly increases, which enhances its strength.

Nanocrystalline nickel is as strong as hardened steel. Understanding surfaces and interfaces is a key challenge for those working on nanomaterials, and one where new imaging and analysis instruments are vital. Nanomaterials are not simply another step in the miniaturisation of materials. They often require very different production approaches. Although many nanomaterials are currently at the laboratory stage of manufacture, a few of them are being commercialised. Following are some examples of nanomaterials and the range of nanoscience that is aimed at understanding their properties.

One-dimensionsional Nanoscale

Thin films, layers and surfaces

One-dimensional nanomaterials, such as thin films and engineered surfaces, have been developed and used for decades in fields such as electronic device manufacture, chemistry and engineering. In the silicon integrated-circuit industry, for example, many devices rely on thin films for their operation, and control of film thicknesses approaching the atomic level is routine. Monolayers (layers that are one atom or molecule deep) are also routinely made and used in chemistry. The formation and properties of these layers are reasonably well understood from the atomic level upwards, even in quite complex layers (such as lubricants). Advances are being made in the control of the composition and smoothness of surfaces, and the growth of films.

Engineered surfaces with tailored properties such as large surface area or specific reactivity are used routinely in a range of applications such as in fuel cells and catalysts. The large surface area provided by nanoparticles, together with their ability to self assemble on a support surface, could be of use in all of these applications. Although they represent incremental developments, surfaces with enhanced properties should find applications throughout the chemicals and energy sectors. The benefits could surpass the obvious economic and resource savings achieved by higher activity and greater selectivity in reactors and separation processes, to enabling small-scale distributed processing (making chemicals as close as possible to the point of use). There is already a move in the chemical industry towards this. Another use could be the small-scale, on-site production of high value chemicals such as pharmaceuticals.

Two Dimensional Nanoscale

Two dimensional nanomaterials such as tubes and wires

have generated considerable interest among the scientific community in recent years. In particular, their novel electrical and mechanical properties are the subject of intense research.

Carbon nanotubes

Carbon nanotubes (CNTs) were first observed by Sumio Iijima in 1991. CNTs are extended tubes of rolled graphene sheets. There are two types of CNT: single-walled (one tube) or multi-walled (several concentric tubes) (Figure 1).

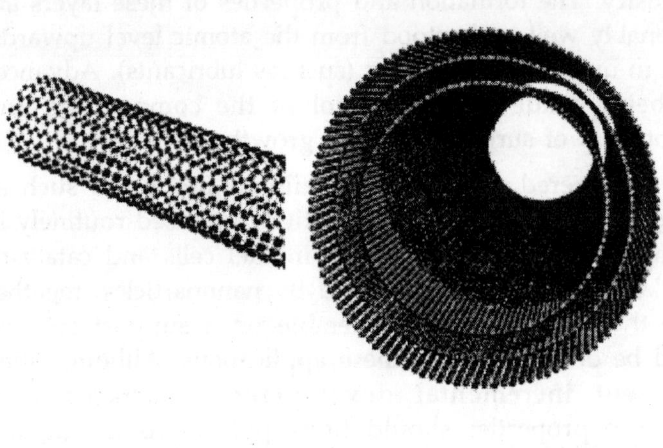

(a) (b)

Figure 1. (a) Schematic of a single-walled carbon nanotube (SWNT) (b) Schematic of a multi-walled carbon nanotube (MWNT)

Both of these are typically a few nanometres in diameter and several micrometres (10^{-6}m) to centimetres long. CNTs have assumed an important role in the context of nanomaterials, because of their novel chemical and physical properties. They are mechanically very strong (their Young's modulus is over 1 terapascal, making CNTs as stiff as diamond), flexible (about their axis), and can conduct electricity extremely well (the helicity of the graphene sheet determines whether the CNT is a semiconductor or metallic). All of these remarkable properties give CNTs a range of potential applications: for example, in reinforced composites, sensors, nanoelectronics and display devices. CNTs are now available commercially in limited quantities. However, the selective and uniform production of CNTs with specific dimensions and physical properties is yet to be achieved.

Inorganic nanotubes

Inorganic nanotubes and inorganic fullerene-like materials based on layered compounds such as molybdenum disulphide were discovered shortly after CNTs. They have excellent tribological (lubricating) properties, resistance to shockwave impact, catalytic reactivity, and high capacity for hydrogen and lithium storage, which suggest a range of promising applications. Oxide-based nanotubes (such as titanium dioxide) are being explored for their applications in catalysis, photo-catalysis and energy storage.

Biopolymers

The variability and site recognition of biopolymers, such as DNA molecules, offer a wide range of opportunities for the self-organisation of wire nanostructures into much more complex patterns. The DNA backbones may then, for example, be coated in metal. They also offer opportunities to link nano- and biotechnology in, for example, biocompatible sensors and small, simple motors. Such self-assembly of organic backbone nanostructures is often controlled by weak interactions, such as hydrogen bonds, hydrophobic, or van der Waals interactions (generally in aqueous environments) and hence requires quite different synthesis strategies to CNTs, for example. The combination of one-dimensional nanostructures consisting of biopolymers and inorganic compounds opens up a number of scientific and technological opportunities.

Three Dimensions Nanoscale

Nanoparticles

Nanoparticles are often defined as particles of less than 100nm in diameter. Nanoparticles exist widely in the natural world: for example as the products of photochemical and volcanic activity, and created by plants and algae. They have also been created for thousands of years as products of combustion and food cooking, and more recently from vehicle exhausts. Deliberately manufactured nanoparticles, such as metal oxides, are by comparison in the minority.

Nanoparticles are of interest because of the new properties (such as chemical reactivity and optical behaviour) that they exhibit compared with larger particles of the same materials. Titanium dioxide and zinc oxide become transparent at the nanoscale, however are able to absorb and reflect UV light, and have found application in sunscreens. Nanoparticles have a range of potential applications: in the short-term in new cosmetics, textiles and paints; in the longer term, in methods of targeted drug delivery where they could be to used deliver drugs to a specific site in the body.

Nanoparticles can also be arranged into layers on surfaces, providing a large surface area and hence enhanced activity, relevant to a range of potential applications such as catalysts. Manufactured nanoparticles are typically not products in their own right, but generally serve as raw materials, ingredients or additives in existing products.

Dendrimers

Dendrimers are spherical polymeric molecules, formed through a nanoscale hierarchical self-assembly process. There are many types of dendrimer; the smallest is several nanometres in size. Dendrimers are used in conventional applications such as coatings and inks, but they also have a range of interesting properties which could lead to useful applications. For example, dendrimers can act as nanoscale carrier molecules and as such could be used in drug delivery. Environmental clean-up could be assisted by dendrimers as they can trap metal ions, which could then be filtered out of water with ultra-filtration techniques.

Quantum dots

Nanoparticles of semiconductors (quantum dots) were theorised in the 1970s and initially created in the early 1980s. If semiconductor particles are made small enough, quantum effects come into play, which limit the energies at which electrons and holes (the absence of an electron) can exist in the particles. As energy is related to wavelength, this means that the optical properties of the particle can be finely tuned depending on its size. Thus, particles can be made to emit or absorb specific wavelengths of light, merely by controlling their size. Recently, quantum dots have found applications in composites, solar cells (Gratzel cells) and fluorescent biological labels (for example to trace a biological molecule) which use both the small particle size and tuneable energy levels. Recent advances in chemistry have resulted in the preparation of monolayer-protected, high-quality, monodispersed, crystalline quantum dots as small as 2nm in diameter, which can be conveniently treated and processed as a typical chemical reagent.

Applications of Nanomaterials

Following are some current and potential short and long-term applications of nanomaterials. Most current applications represent evolutionary developments of existing technologies: for example, the reduction in size of electronics devices.

Current applications

Sunscreens and cosmetics

Nanosized titanium dioxide and zinc oxide are currently used in some sunscreens, as they absorb and reflect ultraviolet (UV) rays and yet are transparent to visible light and so are more appealing to the consumer. Nanosized iron oxide is present in some lipsticks as a pigment but it is our understanding that it is not used by the European cosmetics sector.

Composites

An important use of nanoparticles and nanotubes is in composites, materials that combine one or more separate components and which are designed to exhibit overall the best properties of each component. This multi-functionality applies not only to mechanical properties, but extends to optical, electrical and magnetic ones. Currently, carbon fibres and bundles of multi-walled CNTs are used in polymers to control or enhance conductivity, with applications such as antistatic packaging. The use of individual CNTs in composites is a potential long-term application. A particular type of nanocomposite is where nanoparticles act as fillers in a matrix; for example, carbon black used as a filler to reinforce car tyres. However, particles of carbon black can range from tens to hundreds of nanometres in size.

Clays

Clays containing naturally occurring nanoparticles have long been important as construction materials and are undergoing continuous improvement. Clay particle based composites—containing plastics and nano-sized flakes of clay—are also finding applications such as use in car bumpers.

Coatings and surfaces

Coatings with thickness controlled at the nano- or atomic scale have been in routine production for some time, for example in MBE or metal oxide CVD for optoelectonic devices, or in catalytically active and chemically functionalised surfaces. Recently developed applications include the self-cleaning window, which is coated in highly activated titanium dioxide, engineered to be highly hydrophobic (water repellent) and antibacterial, and coatings based on nanoparticulate oxides that catalytically destroy chemical agents. Wear and scratch-resistant hard coatings are significantly improved by nanoscale intermediate layers (or multilayers) between the hard outer layer and the substrate material. The intermediate layers give good bonding and graded matching of elastic and thermal properties, thus improving adhesion. A range of enhanced textiles, such as breathable, waterproof and stainresistant fabrics, have been enabled by the improved control of porosity at the nanoscale and surface roughness in a variety of polymers and inorganics.

Tougher and harder cutting tools

Cutting tools made of nanocrystalline materials, such as tungsten carbide, tantalum carbide and titanium carbide, are more wear and erosion-resistant, and last longer than their conventional (large-grained) counterparts. They are finding applications in the drills used to bore holes in circuit boards.

Short-term Applications

Paints

Incorporating nanoparticles in paints could improve their performance, for example by making them lighter and giving them different properties. Thinner paint coatings ('lightweighting'), used for example on aircraft, would reduce their weight, which could be beneficial to the environment. However, the whole life cycle of the aircraft needs to be considered before overall benefits can be claimed. It may also be possible to substantially reduce solvent content of paints, with resulting environmental benefits.

New types of fouling resistant marine paint could be developed and are urgently needed as alternatives to tributyl tin (TBT), now that the ecological impacts of TBT have been recognised. Anti-fouling surface treatment is also valuable in process applications such as heat exchange, where it could lead to energy savings. If they can be produced at sufficiently low cost, fouling-resistant coatings could be used in routine duties such as piping for domestic and industrial water systems.

It remains speculation whether very effective anti-fouling coatings could reduce the use of biocides, including chlorine. Other novel, and more long-term, applications for nanoparticles might lie in paints that change colour in response to change in temperature or chemical environment, or paints that have reduced infra-red absorptivity and so reduce heat loss. Concerns about the health and environmental impacts of nanoparticles may require the need for the durability and abrasion behaviour of nano-engineered paints and coatings to be addressed, so that abrasion products take the form of coarse or microscopic agglomerates rather than individual nanoparticles.

The potential of nanoparticles to react with pollutants in soil and groundwater and transform them into harmless compounds is being researched. In one pilot study the large surface area and high surface reactivity of iron nanoparticles were exploited to transform chlorinated hydrocarbons into less harmful end products in groundwater. It is also hoped that they could be used to transform heavy metals such as lead and mercury from bioavailable forms into insoluble forms.

Fuel cells

Engineered surfaces are essential in fuel cells, where the external surface properties and the pore structure affect performance. The hydrogen used as the immediate fuel in fuel cells may be generated from hydrocarbons by catalytic reforming, usually in a reactor module associated directly with the fuel cell. The potential use of nano-engineered membranes to intensify catalytic processes could enable higher-efficiency, small-scale fuel cells. These could act as distributed sources of electrical power. It may eventually be possible to produce hydrogen locally from sources other than hydrocarbons, which are the feedstocks of current attention.

Displays

The huge market for large area, high brightness, flat-panel displays, as used in television screens and computer monitors, is driving the development of some nanomaterials. Nanocrystalline zinc selenide, zinc sulphide, cadmium sulphide and lead telluride synthesised by sol-gel techniques (a process for making ceramic and glass materials, involving the transition from a liquid 'sol' phase to a solid 'gel' phase) are candidates for the next generation of light-emitting phosphors. CNTs are being investigated for low voltage field-emission displays; their strength, sharpness, conductivity and inertness make them potentially very efficient and long-lasting emitters.

Batteries

With the growth in portable electronic equipment (mobile phones, navigation devices, laptop computers, remote sensors), there is great demand for lightweight, high-energy density batteries. Nanocrystalline materials synthesised by sol-gel techniques are candidates for separator plates in batteries because of their foam-like (aerogel) structure, which can hold considerably more energy than conventional ones. Nickel-metal hydride batteries made of nanocrystalline nickel and metal hydrides are envisioned to require less frequent recharging and to last longer because of their large grain boundary (surface) area.

Fuel additives

Research is underway into the addition of nanoparticulate ceria (cerium oxide) to diesel fuel to improve fuel economy by reducing the degradation of fuel consumption over time.

Catalysts

In general, nanoparticles have a high surface area, and hence provide higher catalytic activity. Nanotechnologies are enabling changes in the degree of control in the production of nanoparticles, and the support structure on which they reside. It is possible to synthesise metal nanoparticles in solution in the presence of a surfactant to form highly ordered monodisperse films of the catalyst nanoparticles on a surface. This allows more uniformity in the size and chemical structure of the catalyst, which in turn leads to greater catalytic activity and the production of fewer byproducts. It may also be possible to engineer specific or selective activity. These more active and durable catalysts could find early application in cleaning up waste streams. This will be particularly beneficial if it reduces the demand for platinum-group metals, whose use in standard catalytic units is starting to emerge as a problem, given the limited availability of these metals.

Longer-term Applications

Carbon nanotube composites

CNTs have exceptional mechanical properties, particularly high tensile strength and light weight. An obvious area of application would be in nanotubereinforced composites, with performance beyond current carbon-fibre composites. One current limit to the introduction of CNTs in composites is the problem of structuring the tangle of nanotubes in a well-ordered manner so that use can be made of their strength. Another challenge is generating strong bonding between CNTs and the matrix, to give good overall composite performance and retention during wear or erosion of composites. The surfaces of CNTs are smooth and relatively unreactive, and so tend to slip through the matrix when it is stressed.

One approach that is being explored to prevent this slippage is the attachment of chemical side-groups to CNTs, effectively to form 'anchors'. Another limiting factor is the cost of production of CNTs. However, the potential benefits of such light, high strength material in numerous applications for transportation are such that significant further research is likely.

Lubricants

Nanospheres of inorganic materials could be used as lubricants, in essence by acting as nanosized 'ball bearings'. The controlled shape is claimed to make them more durable than conventional solid lubricants and wear additives. Whether the increased financial and resource cost of producing them is offset by the longer service life of lubricants and parts remains to be investigated. It is also claimed that these nanoparticles reduce friction between metal surfaces, particularly at high normal loads. If so, they should find their first applications in high-performance engines and drivers; this could include the energy sector as well as transport.

There is a further claim that this type of lubricant is effective even if the metal surfaces are not highly smooth. Again, the benefits of reduced cost and resource input for machining must be compared against production of nanolubricants. In all these applications, the particles would be dispersed in a conventional liquid lubricant; design of the lubricant system must therefore include measures to contain and manage waste.

Magnetic materials

It has been shown that magnets made of nanocrystalline yttrium-samarium-cobalt grains possess unusual magnetic properties due to their extremely large grain interface area (high coercivity can be obtained because magnetisation flips cannot easily propagate past the grain boundaries). This could lead to applications in motors, analytical instruments like magnetic resonance imaging (MRI), used widely in hospitals, and microsensors.

Overall magnetisation, however, is currently limited by the ability to align the grains' direction of magnetisation. Nanoscale-fabricated magnetic materials also have applications in data storage. Devices such as computer hard disks depend on the ability to magnetise small areas of a spinning disk to record information. If the area required to record one piece of information can be shrunk in the nanoscale (and can be written and read reliably), the storage capacity of the disk can be improved dramatically. In the future, the devices on computer chips which currently operate using flows of electrons could use the magnetic properties of these electrons, called spin, with numerous advantages. Recent advances in novel magnetic materials and their nanofabrication are encouraging in this respect.

Medical implants

Current medical implants, such as orthopaedic implants and heart valves, are made of titanium and stainless steel alloys, primarily because they are biocompatible. Unfortunately, in some cases these metal alloys may wear out within the lifetime of the patient. Nanocrystalline zirconium oxide (zirconia) is hard, wear resistant, bio-corrosion resistant and bio-compatible. It therefore presents an attractive alternative material for implants. It and other nanoceramics can also be made as strong, light aerogels by sol-gel techniques. Nanocrystalline silicon carbide is a candidate material for artificial heart valves primarily because of its low weight, high strength and inertness.

Machinable ceramics

Ceramics are hard, brittle and difficult to machine. However, with a reduction in grain size to the nanoscale, ceramic ductility can be increased. Zirconia, normally a hard, brittle ceramic, has even been rendered superplastic (for example, able to be deformed up to 300% of its original length). Nanocrystalline ceramics, such as silicon nitride and silicon carbide, have been used in such automotive applications as high-strength springs, ball bearings and valve lifters, because they can be easily formed and machined, as well as exhibiting excellent chemical and high-temperature properties. They are also used as components in high-temperature furnaces. Nanocrystalline ceramics can be pressed into complex net shapes and sintered at significantly lower temperatures than conventional ceramics.

Water purification

Nano-engineered membranes could potentially lead to more energy-efficient water purification processes, notably in desalination by reverse osmosis. Again, these applications would represent incremental improvements in technologies that are already available. They would use fixed nanoparticles, and are therefore distinct from applications that propose to use free nanoparticles.

Applications of metrology

Metrology forms the basis of the semiconductor industry and as such is enormously advanced. The International Technology Roadmap for Semiconductors (ITRS) roadmap highlights a series of challenges for nanometrology if it is to keep pace with the reduction in feature size of semiconductor devices. Shrinking feature sizes, tighter control of device electrical parameters and new interconnect materials will provide the main challenges for physical metrology methods. To achieve desired device scaling, metrology tools must be capable of measurement of properties at atomic distances.

Compounding these is the uncertain nature of the development of device design, making it difficult to predict metrology needs in the long term and in particular the necessary metrology for manufacturing to ensure reliability. A major need is to integrate metrology data into the manufacturing process.

The developing capabilities of semiconductor processing, particularly the ever-reducing dimensions that can be defined using lithographic tools, are being combined with the techniques developed for MEMS device fabrication to enable the manufacture of electro-mechanical components with sub-100nm dimensions. The exploitation of these structures in nano-electromechanical systems (NEMS) devices has produced some interesting and exciting developments in the field of nanometrology.

Applications

Computer chips

The dominant role of miniaturisation in the evolution of the computer chip is reflected in the fact that the ITRS roadmap defines a manufacturing process standard—a technology node—in terms of a length. The current 130 nm technology node that produces the Intel Xeon processor defines the size of the DRAM (dynamic random access memory) half-pitch (half the distance between two adjacent metal wires in a memory cell). This is turn places a requirement on the lithography, process technology and metrology required to manufacture a working device to this tolerance. As a comparison, the 1971 Intel 4004 chip used 10,000 nm technology; the chips of 2007 and 2013 will require 65nm and 32nm technology, respectively.

In the broadest sense, computer chips in current manufacture are therefore already using nanotechnologies and have been so doing for over 20 years. Furthermore, it is not simply the DRAM half-pitch that is on the nanometre scale. All the technology that goes into the research, metrology and production of chips has been working, in some cases, at the sub-nanometre atomic level. The variety of tools that support the IT industry includes computer modelling of advanced devices and materials atom by atom, microscopies that can image single atoms, metrologies that can define the absolute position of a single atomic defect over a 30cm diameter wafer, thin-film growth processes that can produce layers of material with atomic precision, and lithographies that can 'write' features, such as the DRAM cell, with an accuracy of sub-10nm.

Optoelectronics

The other crucial element of the IT revolution, optoelectronics, relates to devices that rely on converting electrical signals to and from light for data transmission, for displays for optical-based sensing and, in the future, for optical-based computing. Technology in this sector is strongly associated with those described above, and relies substantially on the tools developed there. Although some optoelectronic devices do not depend so critically on miniaturisation as computer chips do, there is nevertheless a similar trend towards miniaturisation, with some existing components, such as quantum-well lasers and liquid crystal displays, requiring nanometre precision in their fabrication.

Future Developments

The future development of hardware for the IT industry can

be conveniently separated into two paths: a path that is following the well-established ITRS roadmap; and a path that explores alternative technologies and materials that may supersede the roadmap.

For the roadmap, miniaturisation remains a key driving force, so that a 22nm technology node is envisaged for manufacture in 2016. Having set this technology target, it is possible to anticipate all the challenges associated with realising it. Such challenges are detailed extensively in the roadmap but include enhancing performance by introducing new materials such as low dielectrics and higher-conductivity interconnects (wiring), developing lithographies capable of fabricating structures in the sub-50nm range, and integrating advanced metrology tools into the manufacturing process capable of detecting and sizing defects down to the nanometre size.

As such, nanoscience and nanotechnologies will continue to have a pivotal role in developing new generations of chips. Related technology such as flash memory will evolve in a similar fashion, with the aim of maximising memory capacity in the smallest possible device. Hard disk technologies, although not explicitly part of the ITRS roadmap, will continue to increase in memory density. However, there are prospects for some step changes in technology that may significantly change the data storage industry.

One obvious potential trend is for solid-state memory to replace disk-based memory. This is already obvious in, for example, personal music players where, as solid-state memory increases in density, hard-disk-based storage is competing with the jog-proof solid-state players. It is likely that the hard disk, whether magnetic or optical, will still be the choice for large volume data storage for the foreseeable future, especially as the bit size shrinks even further. This is an active area of nanoscience research.

Optoelectronics, although not as dependent upon length-scale tolerances as computer chips and data storage, will nevertheless have challenges of its own. Integration of optical components into silicon devices has started and can be expected to evolve further. Some of the challenges where nanotechnologies will have an impact will be in the area of photonic band-gap materials, where the propagation of light through a device can be controlled with the aim of computing with light.

Photonic crystals, fabricated either through a lithographic process or through a self-assembly technique, confine light into precisely controlled pathways in a device structure so that both transmission and functionality can be combined into a single structure. A typical photonic crystal would consist of an array of holes in a dielectric material, fabricated with sub-10nm accuracy, so that the periodicity of the holes determines the ability of the material to transmit the light at any given wavelength.

The development of photonic crystals could mean that optical integrated circuits are shrunk further, making a significant impact in areas such as communications and optical computing. Quantum computing and quantum cryptography will also benefit from advances in optoelectronics. Both technologies rely on the fact that discrete energy (quantum) levels increasingly dominate as electromagnetic energy is confined into smaller and smaller structures.

Assuming that the considerable technological challenges of making nanostructures from complex materials can be solved, in some cases by designing at the level of the single atom, then on a 10 year time-scale quantum cryptography (a much more secure encryption technology) will replace current encryption methods. On a similar time-scale, quantum computing will start to provide solutions to complex problems that are difficult or impossible to solve by conventional computing.

Once controlling where, how and when light interacts is possible by the advances in technology alluded to above, there is the potential for developing new types of optical spectroscopy at the level of the single molecule, assembling nanostructures by arrays of optical tweezers placing objects into patterns on surfaces, new optical lithographic methods for fabricating computer chips, and optical devices that act as biosensors with detection of single molecules. The last type of sensor, able to detect the presence of a single molecule in, say, a drop of blood, represents one of the greatest challenges for nanotechnologies.

Not only does it require precision in manufacture, but it also requires a unique mixture of electronics, optics, chemistry, biochemistry and medicine to make devices that can be used routinely, cheaply and reliably to monitor the state of human health. An example of this is in point-of-care health screening where a single drop of blood placed on a sensor chip would be almost instantaneously analysed to provide data to aid a diagnosis. This will require the processing power of a silicon chip with biochemical sensitivity to identify many blood components.

This type of monitoring could also begin to be incorporated within the body to provide constant monitoring of health, such as in the control of diabetes or in critical care. There are many other potential applications of such devices in medicine, making this an area of increasing investment. Alternative, 'off-roadmap' technology will have a similar reliance on nanoscience and nanotechnologies as that of the IT sector described above, but with far greater freedom to explore materials and architectures that may have little resemblance to existing technology.

Plasticbased electronics is an example of an alternative technology. It does not directly compete with siliconbased devices but, because of its vastly cheaper fabrication, offers a far cheaper alternative. For inexpensive electronic and optoelectronic applications where speed and high memory density are less important, such as smart cards, plastic offers a new approach to building electronics. Plastic-based electronics is already moving into the commercial sector with potential for considerable growth.

Similarly, the use of single molecules as functional elements in future circuits will continue to be an important element of nanoscience where the size of the molecule, typically less than 1nm, offers the ultimate in miniaturisation. In fact, the goal of shrinking function down to single molecules and atoms, foreseen by Richard Feynman in 1959, is the only way to go beyond the currently foreseen evolutionary limit of the ITRS roadmap; conventional silicon transistors have a size limit of the order of tens of nanometres.

Nanoscience is still pursuing the concept of storing and processing information at the atomic scale with the hope of, for example, quantum computing and atomic memory where each bit of data is stored on a single atom.

Sensors

Nanotechnologies play several important roles in developing sensor technology. First, the ideal sensor will be minimally invasive and therefore as small as possible. This includes the power supply, the sensing action, whereby the detected property is converted into an electrical signal, and the transmission of the sensing signal to a remote detector. Combining these actions into a device that is smaller than 1mm^2 will certainly require nanofabrication techniques, similar to those employed by the IT industry.

The second role for nanotechnologies will be in designing the sensing element to be as specific and accurate as possible; as the sensor dimension decreases the area of the sensor available to effect detection will also decrease, making increasing demands on sensitivity. In the limit of, say, chemical detection this may require detection at the single molecule level; close to the bottom end of the nanotechnology length scale and a significant technical challenge. Nanotechnologies are therefore expected to enable the production of smaller, cheaper sensors with increasing selectivity, which can be used in a wide range of applications.

These include monitoring the quality of drinking water, measuring mechanical stresses in buildings or vehicles to monitor for structural damage, detecting and tracking pollutants in the environment, checking food for edibility, or continuously monitoring health. Developments could also be used to achieve greater safety, security, and individualised healthcare, and could offer advantages to business. Other potential applications vary from monitoring the state and performance of products and materials to give early warning of the need for repair or replacement to enhancing human capabilities by extending physical performance.

Bio-nanotechnology and Nanomedicine

Without doubt the most complex and highly functional nanoscale machines we know are the naturally occurring molecular assemblies that regulate and control biological systems. Proteins, for example, are molecular structures that possess highly specific functions and participate in virtually all biological sensory, metabolic, information and molecular transport processes.

In this respect the biological world contains many of the nanoscale devices and machines that nanotechnologists might wish to emulate. Bio-nanotechnology is concerned with molecularscale properties and applications of biological nanostructures and as such it sits at the interface between the chemical, biological and the physical sciences. It does not concern the large-scale production of biological material such as proteins or the specific genetic modification of plants, organisms or animals to give enhanced properties.

By using nanofabrication techniques and processes of molecular self-assembly, bio-nanotechnology allows the production of materials and devices including tissue and cellular engineering scaffolds, molecular motors, and biomolecules for sensor, drug delivery and mechanical applications.

Bionanotechnology can be used in medicine to provide a systematic, as well as a screening, approach to drug discovery, to enhance both diagnostic and therapeutic techniques and to image at the cellular and sub-cellular levels, at a much higher resolution than that of magnetic resonance imaging (MRI).

The primary aim of much current research is to obtain a detailed understanding of basic biochemical and biophysical mechanisms at the level of individual molecules. This knowledge will allow the design rules of naturally occurring molecular machines to be determined, which may lead to new technological applications. Examples range from the relatively large (45nm) rotary molecular motors that power bacterial flagella 'propellers' to the tiny enzymes such as ATP-synthase (9nm) that catalyse energy conversion in biological processes.

The intricate sequence of changes in molecular structure that forms the basis of such biomolecular machines can now be measured directly by using AFM and 'optical tweezers'. The recent development of highspeed AFM has enabled real-time molecular movement within a molecular motor to be observed directly.

Future bio-nanotechnology and nanomedicine devices may exploit many classes of functional biological materials. One particular group of proteins that is attracting attention are the membrane proteins; these are another class of protein-based machine that regulate many physiological processes. They include ion channels that enable rapid yet selective flux of ions across the cell membrane, hormone receptors that behave as molecular triggers, and photoreceptors that switch between different conformational states by the absorption of a single photon of light, the process that is the basis of vision and photosynthesis.

That approximately onequarter of all genes code for membrane proteins provides evidence of their immense biological importance; it is estimated that they will be the target of up to 80% of all new drugs. Single molecule techniques for both observation and manipulation are now being used routinely to study the selectivity and gating mechanisms of ion channels, and their response to drugs.

Applications

Bio-nanotechnology is regarded by many experts as a longer-term prospect: much fundamental science must first be investigated and many applications, especially in the medical field, will by necessity have to undergo strict testing and validation procedures. The time-scale for such applications is 10 years and beyond. In the shorter term it may be possible to use proteins, DNA and other bio-polymers directly in nanoelectronics and biosensor applications, but factors such as biocompatibility and robustness may prove to be serious obstacles.

Alternatively, bio-mimetic structures may be devised that are based on naturally occurring machines: examples include catenanes and rotaxanes, compounds that behave as rotary or linear molecular motors, respectively. Applications in the field of medicine are especially promising. Areas such as disease diagnosis, drug delivery and molecular imaging are being intensively researched.

Medical-related products containing nanoparticles are currently on the market in the USA. Examples that exploit the known antimicrobial properties of silver include wound dressings containing nanocrystalline silver, which release ionic silver over a sustained period of time to provide a claimed extensive antimicrobial spectrum of 150 different pathogens. One of the objectives of bio-nanotechnology research is to use the highly specialised functionality of proteins in devices such as molecular sensors. One of the greatest challenges is to understand the fundamental electronic properties of such molecules and the mechanisms by which electronic charge is transferred between them and metals, semiconductors and novel nanoelectronic components such as CNTs.

Progress in this area could allow these 'smart' molecules to be integrated into devices and networks for specific or indeed ICT applications: the realisation of a proteinbased transistor is a major scientific challenge. DNA itself may turn out to be a useful electronic material, although the weight of experimental evidence indicates that it is not a good electrical conductor; however, used as a template, gold or silver 'coated' DNA nanowires can be produced, and integrated circuits using DNA interconnects have already been realised which use the information coded in the DNA.

Thin films and crystals of the membrane protein bacteriorhodopsin have already been demonstrated to have potential photonics applications such as optically addressable spatial light modulators, holographic memories and sensors. The photosynthetic reaction centre in this protein, which is only 5 nm in size, behaves as a nanometre diode and so it may be useful in single molecule optoelectronic devices.

The top-down approach to nanofabrication has the advantage that almost any pre-determined structure can be produced. However, much attention is now being focused on processes that involve some degree of molecular self-assembly, and in this respect biological materials have remarkable advantages over inorganic materials in the diversity of self-assembled structures that they can produce.

Evolution in the natural world has produced an astonishing variety of biomolecular devices, and compared with conventional technologies, many natural molecular devices display enormous functionality.

Among the most outstanding examples of synthetic structures now being fabricated are DNAbased geometrical structures (including artificial crystals) and functioning DNA-based nanomachines. Hybrid nanomachines, composed of biological material with inorganic components, have been suggested as posing a threat if they are able to replicate.

There are ongoing investigations into the application of biological machines that involve incorporation or transport of non-biological components or material, but these are basic molecular constructions compared with even a simple cell. Although they have the ability to move when chemical fuel is added, the working group found no convincing evidence that self-replication, a characteristic of a living organism, is possible. There is enormous potential for nanotechnology to be applied to gene and drug delivery.

The vehicle might be a functionalised nanoparticle capable of targeting specific diseased cells, which contains both therapeutic agents that are released into the cell and an on-board sensor that regulates the release. Different stages of this approach have already been demonstrated, but the combined targeting and controlled release have yet to be accomplished. In this event the way will be opened up for initial trials, and the eventual approval of such techniques will be fully regulated as for any new pharmaceutical.

Gene therapy, where the DNA has been packaged into a nanometre-scale particle, holds much promise for the treatment of genetic defects such as cystic fibrosis and immune deficiencies. Gene therapy using viral vectors has been successfully used to treat ten children with severe combined immunodeficiencies. These are life threatening diseases for which there is no alternative treatment. Unfortunately two of the children subsequently developed leukaemia leading to a temporary moratorium on all gene therapy trials in 2003. After intensive risk assessments most trials have now resumed. Alternative non-viral approaches bionano-technology approaches are being actively researched although none has reached clinical trials.

Advantages of these approaches include the versatility of synthetic chemistry, which allows tailoring of molecular weight, addition of biomimetic features to the manmade construct and even the possibility to include bioresponsive elements.

Nanotechnology techniques offer the possibility of studying drug-receptor interactions at the single molecule level, for example by using optical tweezers and AFM, so that a more direct approach to drug discovery becomes feasible. This approach might also allow, for example, the discovery of disease at the single cell level, long before physical symptoms are manifested. This has been achieved by monitoring changes in atomic forces or ion conductance of a single receptor or ion channel when a drug molecule attaches. However, the industrial process will require the development of large arrays of such instruments working in parallel to create a high-throughput screening capability.

In the USA the National Nanotechnology Initiative has claimed that nanotechnology has potential in the treatment of cancer. It has been stated that 'It is conceivable that by 2015, our ability to detect and treat tumors in their first year of occurrence might totally eliminate suffering and death from cancer'. We have, however, seen no evidence to support the notion that nanotechnologies will eliminate cancer in the short- to medium term, and feel that such a claim demonstrates an over-simplistic view of the detection and treatment of cancer.

Although it is reasonable to hope that some measures based on nanotechnologies may make contributions to detection and treatment of some forms of cancer, other factors such as a greater understanding of environmental causes of cancer, public health measures, and advances in surgical, pharmacological and radiological management are important in the reduction of incidence of and death from cancer.

3

Environmental Applications

Unusual physicochemical properties of semiconductor nanoparticles gave rise to various speculations concerning their practical implementations. Sensors and systems of light energy storage, electronics and photodetoxication of waste waters, non-linear optics and catalysis, and lithography and lasers are considered as possible fields of uses of semiconductor nanoparticles. However, in most cases it is premature to discuss practical application of semiconductor nanoparticles. Only investigations in the field of photocatalysis carried out so far make it possible to consider the possibilities of practical use of nanoparticles.

A decrease in the size of semiconductor nanoparticles results in a shift of the conduction and valence bands towards more negative and more positive potentials, respectively. It seems to be tempting to use the possibility of controlling the redox properties of nanoparticles by changing their size in photocatalytic systems of water decomposition and the synthesis and destruction of organic compounds.

Additionally, the fact that nanoparticles have a large specific surface area is of importance for carrying out photocatalytic processes on the surface of semiconductors. The small size of semiconductor nanoparticles can provide high efficiency of surface trapping of light-generated electrons and holes, thus increasing the probability of a photocatalytic process on the surface of the semiconductor. Indeed, typical recombination time of electrons and holes in semiconductors, τ, is about 10^{-10}s. For typical diffusion coefficient of electrons and holes $D \approx 0.1$ cm^2/s, we have that during the lifetime electrons could diffuse over $R \approx \sqrt{\tau D} \approx 300$ nm. Thus, most electrons and holes generated inside crystal could reach its surface only if the size of the crystal is less than 300 nm. And finally, the absorption coefficient of semiconductors is about 10^5 cm^{-1}. That means that light intensity drops substantially inside the crystal in a thin 10^{-5} cm layer.

Thus only 100 nm thin layers semiconductors or nanonocrystals with an average size of 100 nm provide efficient participation of semiconductor molecules in light absorption. However, it should be noted that the semiconductor nanoparticles used in photocatalytic studies are, as a rule, rather large ($\geq 10^2$ nm) and no pronounced quantum size effects are observed for them.

A correlation between the photocatalytic activity of TiO_2 nanoparticles and their size was found only in one study. High quantum efficiencies of photocatalytic processes with the participation of nanoparticles, are achieved by designing specifically ordered structures based on these particles. The idea of using nanoparticles for photocatalytic water decomposition was first proposed by A. Henglein about twenty years ago who has demonstrated the possibility of photoreduction of methyl viologen in colloidal solutions of semiconductors (TiO_2, and metal chalcogenides). Various dyes could also be photoreduced by nanoparticles. For dyes, photoexcitation of nanoparticles results in one electron reduction of dye molecules followed by the formation of a leuco-product.

The possibility of using nanoparticles in photocatalytic synthesis of organic compounds has also been demonstrated. Photocatalytic synthesis of an amino acid and the Kolbe reaction were carried out by the interband excitation of TiO_2 nanoparticles coated with platinum. Photocatalytic processes of oxidation of a number of alkanes, arenes, amines, and alcohols on the surface of nanoparticles are also known. Light-generated holes can be used in photooxidation of various substrates on the surface of nanoparticles until their complete destruction.

The use of semiconductor nanoparticles for photochemical purification of water from various contaminants seems to be rather tempting and attracts particular interest of researchers in recent years. Systems based on TiO_2 seem to be the most promising for photocatalytic mineralisation of organic compounds in waste waters. Of the three major structural modifications of TiO_2 (rutile, anatase, and brookite), anatase is the most photocatalytically active. The difference in the photocatalytic activity of different TiO_2 modifications is most likely due to their different crystal structures.

Anatase has a bandgap of 3.2 eV and UV radiation needs to be applied for the electronic excitation of this compound; hence, only a small portion of the sunlight can be used for the photocatalytic processes involving anatase to occur. Nevertheless, among a wide variety of semiconductor materials, TiO_2 is most often used as a photocatalyst due to the high oxidation ability of its photogenerated holes (E° = 2.9 V vs. NHE at pH 0), its stability in aqueous solutions, safety for living organisms, and low price. Titanium dioxide has long been used in paint industry as the photocatalyst in the oxidation of organic substances. This property of TiO_2 has determined its wide use as the white pigment. Later, attempts were made aimed at using TiO_2 for photodecomposition of water.

However, its efficiency appeared to be low because of a low quantum yield of charge photoseparation. Recently, the problems of the environment protection forced many researchers to direct their attention again to the systems based on TiO_2 and to make efforts to use TiO_2 for photocatalytic mineralisation of ecologically hazardous organic compounds both in aqueous media and gases. The scheme of the photocatalytic process involving semiconductor nanoparticles is shown in Figure 1. The absorption of a light quantum with an energy of *hν*, that exceeds the bandgap of the semiconductor, results in the primary charge separation.

In this case, the nanoparticle can be considered as a short-circuit electrode initiating the processes of oxidation and reduction of the substrate molecules adsorbed on the surface. The oxidation and reduction of non-adsorbed substrate molecules is possible if the primary electrons and holes are transformed into stable intermediates on the surface of nanoparticles. Good results have been obtained for the detoxication of wastewaters containing hydrocarbons, phenols, chloroaromatic compounds, surfactants, and nitro compounds.

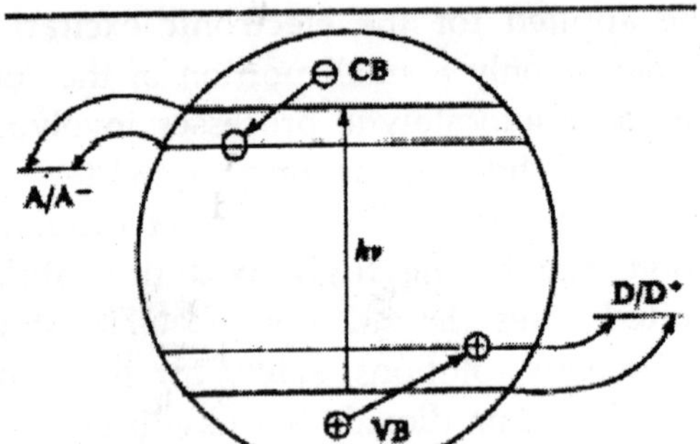

Figure 1. Schematic view of charge separation processes in a semiconductor nanoparticle.

A typical example of photocatalytic mineralisation is the oxidation of the dichloroacetate ion by oxygen in water:

$$CHCl_2COO^- + O_2 \xrightarrow{hv,\, TiO_2} 2CO_2 + H^+ + Cl^-_2$$

The detailed mechanism of the processes of the photoreduction of acceptors and photooxidation of donors with the participation of TiO_2 nanoparticles includes a large number of events occurring both in the bulk and on the surface of nanoparticles. Photostimulated generation of electrons and holes in the conduction and valence band, respectively

$$TiO_2 \xrightarrow{hv} TiO_2(e^- + h^+);$$

charge carrier migration to the surface of the nanoparticle

$$e^- \rightarrow e_s^-,$$

$$h^+ \rightarrow h_s^+,$$

$$(e_s^-, h_s^-) \rightarrow \text{surface-migration};$$

charge carrier trapping by acceptor centers and into shallow traps (ST)

$$e^- + (ST)_e \rightarrow e_t^-,$$

$$h^+ + (ST)_h \rightarrow h_t^+,$$

$$e_s^- + A_s \rightarrow A_s^-,$$

$$h_s^+ + D_s \rightarrow D_s^-$$

$$e^- + Ti^{IV} \rightarrow Ti^{3+},$$

$$h^+ + Ti^{IV} - OH^- \rightarrow Ti^{IV} - OH\bullet,$$

$$e^- + O_2\,(\text{surface}) \rightarrow O_2^-\bullet\,(\text{surface});$$

charge carrier recombination (radiative and nonradiative)

$$e^-, e_t^- + h^+, h_t^+ \rightarrow hv,$$

$$Ti^{IV} - OH\bullet + Ti^{3+} \rightarrow hv + 2Ti^{IV},$$

$$Ti^{IV} - OH\bullet + Ti^{3+} + O_2{-}\bullet\,(\text{surface}) \rightarrow hv + 2Ti^{IV}.$$

It is usually assumed that the photooxidation of organic substrates in aqueous suspensions of TiO_2 can occur by both the direct interaction of the holes with the substrate molecules and the formation of the OH• radicals in the reaction of the holes with H_2O or OH^-.

Colloidal solutions of nanoparticles are suitable objects for the demonstration of the possibility of their utilisation in photocatalysis. However, the practical use of colloidal solutions is difficult because of the need to separate nanoparticles from the solution after the completion of the photocatalytic process. Thin layers of nanoparticles adsorbed on a carrier seem to be much more promising, especially the films composed of hetero-nanoparticles. These films have many advantages over films composed of nanoparticles of the same nature, namely, the expanded spectral sensitivity region of the large-bandgap semiconductor nanoparticles, increased quantum efficiency of charge photoseparation and high efficiency of spectral sensitisation of films by dyes.

An idealised illustration of photocatalytic processes occurring on the surface of a conducting electrode with the participation of films composed of heteronanoparticles is exemplified with TiO_2/SnO_2 films. The position of the bottom of the SnO_2 conduction band is lower than that of the TiO_2 conduction band (0 and -0.5 V vs. NHE at pH 7, respectively). This causes the light-generated electrons to transfer from TiO_2 to SnO_2.

The holes move in the opposite direction and are accumulated on the TiO_2 nanoparticles. As a result, an increase in the quantum efficiency of charge photoseparation and, hence, in the efficiency of the oxidation of donor molecules in solution can be observed in the structure under consideration. High efficiency of the TiO_2/SnO_2 film was demonstrated experimentally in the example of photocatalytic degradation of dyes. The overall processes occurring at the anode and cathode can be described by the following scheme:

— at the **photoanode**

$SnO_2/TiO_2 + h\upsilon \rightarrow [SnO_2(e^-...h^+)]/[\ TiO_2\ (e^-...h^+)] \rightarrow SnO_2(e^-) + TiO_2\ (h^+)$,

$TiO_2(h^+) + OH^- \rightarrow TiO_2 + OH\bullet$,

$TiO_2(h^+)$ or $OH\bullet$ + dye $\rightarrow$ products;

at the cathode

$$Pt(2e^-) + O_2 + 2H^+ \rightarrow H_2O_2.$$

Porous nanostructured films possess high adsorption capacity to organic dyes and organometallic compounds. Large specific surface area of such films allows adsorption of a considerable amount of a dye. The use of these properties of the nanostructured films makes it possible to increase substantially their photocatalytic efficiency due to sensitisation into the visible region.

Nanomaterials in Analytical Chemistry

The use of synthetic microparticles in bioanalysis originated in the mid-1950s, with the invention of latex agglutination tests. These simple, ingenious tests use suspended latex microparticles (diameter ~1 m) that are chemically derivatised with a desired antibody. The analyte is an antigen for this antibody, and this analyte-antigen binds to more than one antibody molecule. In early versions of this test, a drop of homogeneous milky-white antibody-labeled suspension was applied to a glass slide and mixed with a drop of the analyte solution.

The analyte chemically links adjacent latex particles by binding to antibody sites on these particles, resulting in agglutination (or clumping together) of the particles into what looks like curdled milk. Particles with truly nanoscopic dimensions have also been used in tests of this type, such as the Carter-Wallace home pregnancy test "First Response", which uses conventional micrometer-sized latex particles in conjunction with gold nanoparticles (less than 50-nm diameter). Gold nanoparticles show a characteristic visible absorption band called the plasmon resonance absorption, which makes them pink. The micro- and nanoparticles are derivatised with antibodies to human chorionic gonadotrophin, a hormone released by pregnant women. When mixed with a urine sample containing this hormone, the micro- and nanoparticles are coagglutinated and the resulting clumps are colored pink.

This example uses the gold nanoparticle as the indicator in a conventional microparticle-based agglutination test. In addition, nanoparticles have been used as replacements for micrometer-sized particles in an immunoturbidimetric assay for urine albumin, an indicator of kidney problems.

Poly(vinylnaphthalene) particles (40 nm diameter) were coated with an outer layer of a chloromethylstyrene polymer, which was used to immobilise an antibody raised against human albumin. Agglutination in the presence of urine albumin was detected by measuring the change in absorbance caused by light scattering. Using nanoparticles in such assays offers several potential advantages. Suspensions of nanoparticles do not appreciably scatter visible light, which means that the background signal in a turbidimetric assay is lower than in tests that use milky-white suspensions of the microparticles. This results in lower detection limits. In addition, nanoparticles form more stable suspensions and are therefore less susceptible to self-agglomeration.

DNA detection

The plasmon resonance absorption of colloidal gold particles has recently been exploited in a proposed DNA-detection method. Mirkin and co-workers attached 13-nmdiameter gold nanoparticles to single-stranded oligonucleotides. The plasmon resonance absorbance for these particles has a maximum at 520 nm, and the particles appear red. When a linking oligonucleotide was added, the gold nanoparticles agglutinated, and the color changed from red to purple. To attach the single-stranded oligonucleotides to the gold nanoparticles, a gold sol was stirred with a solution of terminally thiolated, 28 base-pair DNA.

The first 13 nucleotides served as a spacer from the nanoparticle surface; the last 15 were the recognition element for the target. Two different recognition-element sequences were used. It is important to note that many oligomers were attached to each gold particle. The target DNA was a 30 base-pair strand, the first 15 bases of which are complementary to the first recognition element, and the remaining 15 complementary to the second recognition element. When the target DNA was added to the modified colloidal suspension, the target linked the individual colloid particles into a polymeric network.

Because the nanoparticles were now much closer together, the plasmon resonance band shifted, and the color changed. Although this detection method had not yet been optimised, the detection limit was 10 fmol for the target oligonucleotide. An additional benefit of this particular method is that it allows visual detection, especially if the sample is developed on a solid support such as a reversed-phase silica TLC plate.

Superparamagnetic Nanoparticles

The basic concept in magnetic bioseparations is to selectively bind the biomaterial of interest (e.g., a specific cell, protein, or DNA sequence) to a magnetic particle and then separate it from its surrounding matrix using a magnetic field. Nanoparticles of $Fe3O_4$ with diameters in the 5-100 nm range are typically used for such separations. These particles are "superparamagnetic", meaning that they are attracted to a magnetic field but retain no residual magnetism after the field is removed. Therefore, suspended superparamagnetic particles tagged to the biomaterial of interest can be removed from a matrix using a magnetic field, but they do not agglomerate (i.e., they stay suspended) after removal of the field. A common use of superparamagnetic nanoparticles is for immunospecific cell separations. Typically, the nanoparticles are dispersed within the pores of larger microparticles.

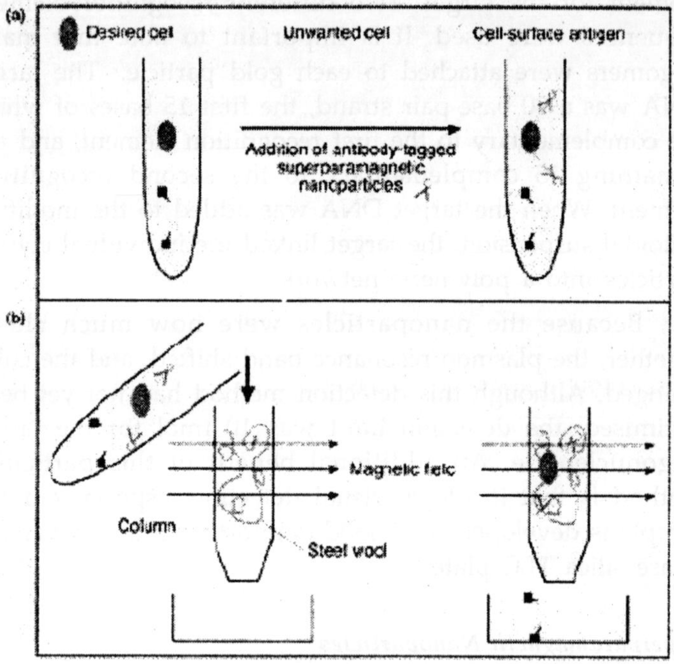

Figure 2. Cell separation using antibody-bound superparamagnetic nanoparticles.

In the simplest (direct) method, the microparticles are coated with a monoclonal antibody for a cell-surface antigen. The antibody-tagged, superparamagnetic microparticles are then incubated with a solution containing the cells of interest. The microparticles bind to the surfaces of the desired cells, and these cells can then be collected in a magnetic field. Methods of this type have been used to isolate or remove numerous cell types, including lymphocytes (cells that control immune response) and tumor cells. In addition to loading microparticles with superparamagnetic nanoparticles, other examples of tagging the desired biomaterial with individual nanoparticles have been reported (Figure 2).

This approach has numerous advantages. Whereas bound microparticles can affect the viability of the selected cells, nanoparticles supposedly do not affect cell viability. In addition, as previously indicated, nanoparticles do not affect the extent of light scattering by the cell solution. The disadvantage of this approach is small magnetic moments of individual nanoparticles; however, this problem can be overcome by using a high-gradient magnetic field.

Contrast agents

Superparamagnetic Fe_3O_4 nanoparticles are also useful as magnetic resonance imaging (MRI) contrast agents. MRI is essentially proton NMR done on tissue. Protons are excited with short pulses of radio frequency radiation; the free induction decay as they relax is measured and deconvoluted by means of a Fourier transform, which provides an image of the tissue that corresponds to proton density. Areas of high proton density, usually in the form of water or lipid molecules, have a strong signal and appear bright.

Areas of bone or tendon, which have a low proton density because of the lack of water and lipids, have a weak signal and appear dark. Traditionally, a major limitation of MRI has been its inability to distinguish differences in soft tissue types (e.g., healthy parts of the liver from diseased lesions), as the relative proton densities can be very similar. Other regions, such as the bowel, are hard to image because air pockets and fecal matter make the proton density inconsistent.

Various contrast agents have been developed to circumvent these imaging problems. Contrast agents work by changing the strength of the MRI signal at a desired location. For example, superparamagnetic contrast agents change the rate at which protons decay from their excited state to the ground state, allowing more effective decay through energy transfer to a neighboring nucleus.

As a result, regions containing the superparamagnetic contrast agent appear darker in an MRI than regions without the agent. For instance, when superparamagnetic nanoparticles are delivered to the liver, healthy liver cells can uptake the particles; diseased cells cannot. Consequently, the healthy regions are darkened, although the diseased regions remain bright.

Superparamagnetic particles have many advantages over other contrast agents. Unlike agents such as perfluorochemicals, oils, and fats, superparamagnetic particles are miscible with aqueous systems, which means they can mix with material in the bowel and be used in small volumes. Immiscible agents must be used in sufficient quantity to displace intestinal matter. This miscibility also allows them to be used intravenously.

Compared with other magnetic contrast agents (e.g., gadolinium chelates), they are much more potent (as much as 50 times more effective per mole). Another advantage is that the particles do not pass the blood-brain barrier; thus, they are well suited for tracking blood flow in the brain. A novel use of these nanoparticles is tracking cells in vivo.

Nanogold particles have been used extensively as specific staining agents in biological electron microscopy. The small sizes of these particles (diameters as small as 1.4 nm) allow them to be physically close to the structures they stain; thus, such particles provide high resolution. Because the nanoparticles are gold, which has a high backscatter coefficient, they appear bright in a scanning electron microscope image. In contrast, the high density of gold makes them appear dark in a transmission electron microscope image. Site-specific staining is obtained by labeling the nanogold particles with antibodies directed against a protein in the region of interest.

Antibody-labeled gold nanoparticles are commercially available, and unlabeled gold nanoparticles can also be purchased and labeled with a specific antibody by the investigator. Direct adsorption of proteins, such as enzymes, onto bulk metal surfaces frequently results in denaturation of the protein and loss of bioactivity. In contrast, when such proteins are adsorbed to metal nanoparticles, bioactivity is often retained, such as when antibody-labeled nanoparticles are used as electron microscopy stains. In another example, it was found that redox enzymes could adsorb to colloidal gold with no loss of enzymatic activity.

The enzyme-covered nanoparticles were then electrodeposited onto platinum gauze or glassy carbon to make enzyme electrodes. In addition, it was found that cytochrome c retained reversible cyclic voltammetry when deposited onto 12-nm-diameter gold particles attached to a conductive substrate. In contrast, if the cytochrome c was deposited on larger surface features (aggregates of the gold nanoparticles), the cyclic voltammetry became quasireversible or irreversible, indicating denaturation of the protein.

These results demonstrate another unique feature of metal nanoparticles-biocompatibility. The repulsive electrostatic forces that keep colloidal particles from aggregating also cause them to form crystalline colloidal arrays (CCAs) when concentrated in a very low ionic strength liquid. The periodicity of such CCAs is in the 100-1000 nm range, so that the arrays refract light in the visible region and thus appear colored. It was found that the periodicity of polystyrene CCAs can be varied after incorporating them into a swellable polymer gel. As the gel swells, the intercolloid distance increases, causing a red shift in the refraction maxima or color of the CCA. For example, a temperatureinduced color change could be obtained by using a temperature-sensitive hydrogel as the CCA matrix. Recently, the same swellable CCA design have applied to chemical sensors. One such sensor used crown ethers in the hydrogel, which bound lead ions.

The localised charge created by the bound lead ions increased osmotic pressure and caused the gel to swell and the CCA to change color. A glucose-responsive gel was also prepared. In this case, glucose oxidase was attached to the gel and the anionic reduced flavin that resulted from oxidation of glucose caused the swelling and color change. This sensor could detect concentrations of glucose as low as 10^{-12} M.

Surfaced-enhanced Raman spectroscopy (SERS) uses roughened metal surfaces to enhance the Raman scattering of surface-adsorbed molecules, which can be as much as 10^6 over the molecule's native Raman scattering in solution. An impediment to using SERS as an analytical technique is the difficulty in reproducibly and uniformly controlling surface roughness. To overcome this difficulty, self-assembled monolayers of metal could be used as substrates for SERS. SERS surfaces have been studied prepared by self-assembling gold and silver nanoparticles on glass and other substrates. The degree of roughness of these surfaces is tunable by varying the diameter of the nanoparticles. Such surfaces have shown a high degree of reproducibility, both for different locations on a single surface and for different-but identically prepared- surfaces.

For the last several years a new method for preparing nanomaterials was invented called "template synthesis". This method entails synthesising the desired material within the pores of a membrane or other solid. The membranes used have cylindrical pores of uniform diameter. In essence, we view each of these pores as a beaker in which a particle of the desired material is synthesised. Because of the cylindrical shape of these pores, a nanocylinder of the desired material is obtained within each pore. Depending on the material and the chemistry of the pore wall, this nanocylinder may be solid (a fibril or nanowire) or hollow (a tubule). This is an extremely general method for preparing nanomaterials. Nanofibers and nanotubules composed of metals, polymers, semiconductors, carbons, and Li^+-intercalation materials have been prepared.

Nearly any chemical synthetic method used to prepare bulk material can be adapted so that the synthesis occurs within the pores of such membranes. One application entails preparing nanoscopic electrodes. We have shown that an electroless plating method can be used to prepare ensembles of gold nanodisk electrodes with a disk diameter as small as 10 nm. Such nanoelectrode ensembles (NEEs) have potential applications in electroanalytical chemistry because the signal-to-background ratio (S/B) observed at the NEE can be orders of magnitude higher than at a conventional gold macroscopic electrode disk, resulting in a detection limit that can be orders of magnitude lower. To understand this dramatic improvement in detection limits, it is important to consider the nature of the background and analytical signals at the NEE.

The predominant background signal in an electroanalytical experiment is the double-layer charging current. Double-layer charging occurs only at the gold surfaces. Because only a small fraction (e.g., 0.1%) of the NEE surface is gold, the double-layer charging currents can be orders of magnitude lower than at a conventional gold macrodisk electrode of the same geometric area. The analytical signal is the faradic current associated with electrolysis of the analyte molecule at the surface of the electrode. For the considered NEEs, this signal can be identical to the current obtained at a macrodisk electrode of the same geometric area, where the entire surface is gold. Hence, the faradic current (analytical signal) at the NEE can be the same as at the conventional gold macrodisk electrode, but the background current is up to 3 orders of magnitude lower. The S/B is dramatically higher, thus providing lower detection limits at the NEE.

The NEEs is a useful tool for studying the fundamentals of electrochemistry and electron-transfer processes at nanoscopic electrodes and nanometal particles. Other analytical applications of nanometer-sized electrodes include high-resolution electrochemical imaging and single-molecule detection.

The NEEs discussed above were obtained by electrolyses plating of gold within the pores of the template membrane for sufficiently long times so that solid nanowires were produced. If plating is done for shorter times, ensembles of nanotubules that span the complete thickness of the template membrane can be obtained. Gas flux data suggest that these tubules can have inside diameters of molecular dimensions (< 1 nm). It was recently shown that these gold nanotubule membranes can be cation permselective, anion permselective, or nonpermselective, depending on the potential applied to them.

This is unique to these membranes because the nanotubules are metal. Because of this switchability, these membranes can be viewed as universal ion exchangers. Nanotubule membranes also have applications in chemical and bioseparations. For example, it was shown that the inside tubule diameter can be decreased until the tubule is just large enough to accommodate a small molecule but too small to accommodate a big molecule. Hence, these nanotubule membranes allow for "molecular filtration", where molecules are separated in a simple filtration-type experiment on the basis of molecular size.

Template-synthesised nanotubules can be prepared as high-density ensembles, in which the tubes protrude from a substrate surface like the bristles of a brush. Such brushlike ensembles can have high surface area, which could be useful in enzyme immobilisation. To explore this point, brush-like ensembles was synthesised of enzymeloaded polypyrrole tubules. Using glucose oxidase as the enzyme, it was found that the glucose-oxidation rate to be seven times faster for the template-synthesised bioreactor than for a more conventional thin-film design using the same components. Nanomaterials have unique chemical and physical properties that offer important possibilities for analytical chemistry.

Nanotechnology and Environment

New technologies are needed to speed the discovery process that are rapid, highly parallel, and cost-effective. Reductions in the scale of analysis tools and automation are proving critical to enabling the discovery of the fundamental changes associated with the development of cancers, and insight into the molecular processes of the cell. The identification of molecular signatures of cancers will enhance our ability to identify and accurately diagnose disease.

Realisation of this goal will only be possible if technologies exist that allow us to scan the living body for the earliest signatures of emerging disease and support immediate, specific intervention. The ability to scan the body for early signatures requires these technologies to be minimally invasive. The ability to scan the body for molecular signatures will also allow us to monitor the progress of disease and effects of interventions. Nanotechnologies are emerging as enabling components to these goals. Ongoing efforts highlight that full systems will require the integration of new discoveries from a variety of fields including nanoscience, chemistry, photonics, computational sciences, and information science and technology.

With the help of nanotechnology we will able to gain the means not only to heal ourselves, but to heal Earth of the wounds we have inflicted. Since saving lives will increase the number of the living, life extension raises questions about the effect of more people. Our ability to heal the Earth will lessen one cause for controversy.

Still, cell repair machines themselves will surely stir controversy. They disturb traditional assumptions about our bodies and our futures: this makes doubt soothing. They will require several major breakthroughs: this makes doubt easy. Since the possibility or impossibility of cell repair machines raises important issues, it makes sense to consider what objections might be raised. What sort of argument could suggest that cell repair machines are impossible?

A successful argument must manage some strange contortions. It must somehow hold that molecular machines cannot build and repair cells, while granting that the molecular machines in our bodies actually do build and repair cells every day. A cruel problem for the committed skeptic! True, artificial machines must do what natural machines fail to do, but they need not do anything qualitatively novel. Both natural and artificial repair devices must reach, identify, and rebuild molecular structures. We will be able to improve on existing DNA repair enzymes simply by comparing several DNA strands at once, so nature obviously hasn't found all the tricks. Since this example explodes any general argument that repair machines cannot improve on nature, a good case against cell repair machines seems difficult to make.

For centuries, people have longed to escape their short life spans. Every so often, a Ponce de Leon or a quack doctor has promised a potion, but it has never worked. These statistics of failure have persuaded some people that, since all attempts have failed, all always will fail. They say "Aging is natural," and to them that seems reason enough. Medical advances may have shaken their views, but advances have chiefly reduced early death, not extended maximum life-span. But now biochemists have gone to work examining the machines that build, repair, and control cells. They have learned to assemble viruses and reprogramme bacteria.

For the first time in history, people are examining their molecules and unravelling the molecular secrets of life. It seems that molecular engineers will eventually combine improved biochemical knowledge with improved molecular machines, learning to repair damaged tissue structures and so rejuvenate them. This is nothing strange - it would be strange, rather, if such powerful knowledge and abilities did not bring dramatic results.

The massive statistics of past failure are simply irrelevant, because we have never before tried to build cell repair machines. Nature has beer building cell repair machines. Evolution has tinkered with multicelled animals for hundreds of millions of years, yet advanced animals all age and die, because nature's nanomachines repair cells imperfectly. Why should improvements be possible? Rats mature in months, and then age and die in about two years - yet human beings have evolved to live over thirty times longer. If longer lives were the chief goal of evolution, then rats would live longer too.

But durability has costs: to repair cells requires an investment in energy, materials, and repair machines. Rat genes direct rat bodies to invest in swift growth and reproduction, not in meticulous self-repair. A rat that dallied in reaching breeding size would run a greater risk of becoming a cat snack first. Rat genes have prospered by treating rat bodies as cheap throwaways. Human genes likewise discard human beings, though after a life a few dozen times longer than a rat's. But shoddy repairs are not the only cause of aging. Genes turn egg cells into adults through a pattern of development which rolls forward at fairly steady speed. This pattern is fairly consistent because evolution seldom changes a basic design. Just as the basic pattern of the DNA-RNA-protein system froze several billions of years ago, so the basic pattern of chemical signals and tissue responses that guides mammalian development jelled many millions of years ago. That process apparently has a clock, set to run at different speeds in different species, and a programme that runs out. Whatever the causes of aging, evolution has had little reason to eliminate them. If genes built individuals able to stay healthy for millennia, they would gain little advantage in their "effort" to replicate. Most individuals would still die young from starvation, predation, accident, or disease.

As Sir Peter Medawar points out, a gene that helps the young (who are many) but harms the old (who are few) will replicate well and so spread through the population. If enough such genes accumulate, animals become programmed to die. Experiments by Dr. Leonard Hayflick suggest that cells contain "clocks" that count cell divisions and stop the division process when the count gets too high.

A mechanism of this sort can help young animals: if cancerlike changes make a cell divide too rapidly, but fail to destroy its clock, then it will grow to a tumour of limited size. The clock would thus prevent the unlimited growth of a true cancer. Such clocks could harm older animals by stopping the division of normal cells, ending tissue renewal, The animal thus would benefit from reduced cancer rates when young, yet have cause to complain if it lives to grow old. But its genes won't listen - they will have jumped ship earlier, as copies passed to the next generation. With cell repair machines we will be able to reset such clocks.

Nothing suggests that evolution has perfected our bodies even by the brute standard of survival and reproduction. Engineers don't wire computers with slow, nerve-like fibres or build machines out of soft protein, and for good reason.

Genetic evolution has been unable to leap to new materials or new systems, but has instead refined and extended the old ones. The cell's repair machines fall fa short of the limits of the possible—they don't even have computers to direct them. The lack of nano-computers in cells, of course, shows only that computers couldn't evolve gradually from other molecular machines. Nature has failed to build the best possible cell repair machines, but there have been ample reasons.

Potential for Nanotechnology

For computer services, only about 4% is due to the sector itself, with 96% due to suppliers. Thus, if both sectors could use less electricity and steel and aluminum, their environmental footprint would be appropriately smaller. In particular, if nanotechnology enabled electricity to be generated with less fuel and less environmental discharges, that would make a huge contribution to decreasing the environmental footprint of this sector. Similarly, if computers could be made with less energy and raw materials, it and computer services would be enormously benefited. These lifecycle calculations demonstrate the potential benefits for improving environmental quality and sustainability. Nanotechnology could make a large contribution to lower resource use and environmental discharges. The general public has become increasingly concerned about the safety and environmental implications of new technologies, from nuclear power to chemicals to biotechnology.

Statutes such as the Toxic Substances Control Act and Food, Drug, and Cosmetic Act require government review of new chemicals and other technologies before they can be sold. Although proponents of nanotechnology view it as benign, there are likely to be some unforeseen, undesirable effects. Even at the basic research stage, nanotechnology advocates need to inform the public about the prospects and risks. They need to engage and involve the public and the groups that represent them. While this will delay the introduction of new technologies, in the end it is likely to save time.

Protecting the Earth

The failure of Earth's biological systems to adapt to the industrial revolution is also easy to understand. From deforestation to dioxin, we have caused damage faster than evolution can respond. As we have sought more food, goods, and services, our use of bulk technology has forced us to continue such damage. With future technology, though, we will be able to do more good for ourselves, yet do less harm to the Earth. In addition, we will be able to build planet-mending machines to correct damage already done. Consider the toxic waste problem Whether in our air, soil, or water, wastes concern us because they can harm living systems. But any materials that come in contact with the molecular machinery of life can themselves be reached by other forms of molecular machinery. This means that we will be able to design cleaning machines to remove these poisons wherever they could harm life. Some wastes, such as dioxin, consist of dangerous molecules made of innocuous atoms.

Cleaning machines will render them harmless by rearranging their atoms. Other wastes, such as lead and radioactive isotopes, contain dangerous atoms. Cleaning machines will collect these for disposal in any one of several ways. Lead comes from Earth's rocks; assemblers could build it into rocks in the mines from which it came. Radioactive isotopes could also be isolated from living things, either by building them into stable rock or by more drastic means.

Using cheap, reliable space transportation systems, we could bury them in the dead, dry rock of the Moon. Using nanomachines, we could seal them in self-repairing, selfsealing containers the size of hills and powered by desert sunlight. These would be more secure than any passive rock or cask. With replicating assemblers, we will even be able to remove the billions of tons of carbon dioxide that our fuel-burning civilisation has dumped into the atmosphere.

Climatologists project that climbing carbon dioxide levels, by trapping solar energy, will partially melt the polar caps, raising sea levels and flooding coasts sometime in the middle of the next century. Replicating assemblers, though, will make solar power cheap enough to eliminate the need for fossil fuels. Like trees, solarpowered nanomachines will be able to extract carbon dioxide from the air and split off the oxygen. Unlike trees, they will be able to grow deep storage roots and place carbon back in the coal seams and oil fields from which it came. Future planet-healing machines will also help us mend torn landscapes and restore damaged ecosystems.

Mining has scraped and pitted the Earth; carelessness has littered it. Fighting forest fires has let undergrowth thrive, replacing the cathedral-like openness of ancient forests with scrub growth that feeds more dangerous fires. We will use inexpensive, sophisticated robots to reverse these effects and others.

Able to move rock and soil, they will recontour torn lands. Able to weed and digest, they will simulate the clearing effects of natural forest fires without danger or devastation. Able to lift and move trees, they will thin thick stands and reforest bare hills. We will make squirrel-sized devices with a taste for old trash. We will make treelike devices with roots that spread deep and cleanse the soil of pesticides and excess acid. We will make insect-sized lichen cleaners and spray paint nibblers. We will make whatever devices we need to clean up the mess left by twentieth-century civilisation.

After the cleanup, we will recycle most of these machines, keeping only those we still need to protect the environment from a cleaner civilisation based on molecular technology. These more lasting devices will supplement natural ecosystems wherever needed, to balance and heal the effects of humanity. To make them effective, harmless, and hidden will be a craft requiring not just automated engineering, but knowledge of nature and a sense of art. With cell repair technology, we will even be able to return some species from apparent extinction.

Machines that compare several damaged copies of a DNA molecule will be able to reconstruct an undamaged original - and the billions of cells in a dried skin contain billions of copies. From these, we will be able to reconstruct undamaged DNA, and around the DNA we will be able to construct undamaged cells of whatever type we desire. Some insect species pass through winter as egg cells, to be revived by the warmth of spring. These "extinct" species will pass through the twentieth century as skin and muscle cells, to be converted into fertile eggs and revived by cell repair machines.

Dr. Barbara Durrant, a reproductive physiologist at the San Diego Zoo, is preserving tissue samples from endangered species in a cryogenic freezer. The payoff may be greater than most people now expect. Preserving just tissue samples doesn't preserve the life of an animal or an ecosystem, but it does preserve the genetic heritage of the sampled species. We would be reckless if we failed to take out this insurance policy against the permanent loss of species. The prospect of cell repair machines thus affects our choices today. About 65 million years ago, most then-existing species vanished, including all species of dinosaur. In Earth's book of stone, the story of the dinosaurs ends on a page consisting of a thin layer of clay.

The clay is rich in iridium, an element common in asteroids and comets. The best current theory indicates that a blast from the sky smashed Earth's biosphere. With the energy of a hundred million megatons of TNT, it spread dust and an "asteroidal winter" planetwide. In the eons since living cells first banded together to form worms, Earth has suffered five great extinctions. Only 34 million years ago - some 30 million years after the dinosaurs died - a layer of glassy beads settled to the sea floor. Above that layer the fossils of many species vanish. These beads froze from the molten splash of an impact.

As people have long suspected, the dinosaurs died because they were stupid. Not that they were too stupid to feed, walk, or guard their eggs - they did survive for 140 million years - they were merely too stupid to build telescopes able to detect asteroids and spacecraft able to deflect them from collision with Earth. Space has more rocks to throw at us, but we are showing signs of adequate intelligence to deal with them. When nanotechnology and automated engineering give us a more capable space technology, we will find it easy to track and deflect asteroids; in fact, we could do it with technology available today. We can both heal Earth and protect it.

People commonly seek long, healthy lives, yet the prospect of a dramatic success is unsettling. Though most effects cannot be foreseen, some can. For example, as cell repair machines extend life, they will increase population. If all else were equal, more people would mean greater crowding, pollution, and scarcity - but all else will not be equal: the very advances in automated engineering and nanotechnology that will bring cell repair machines will also help us heal the Earth, protect it, and live more lightly upon it. We will be able to produce our necessities and luxuries without polluting our air, land, or water. We will be able to get resources and make things without scarring the landscape with mines or cluttering it with factories. With efficient assemblers making durable products, we will produce things of greater value with less waste.

More people will be able to live on Earth, yet do less harm to it - or to one another, if we somehow manage to use our new abilities for good ends. If one were to see the night sky as a black wall and expect the technology race to screech to a polite halt, then it would be natural to fear that long-lived people would be a burden on the "poor, crowded world of our children." This fear stems from the illusion that life is a zero-sum game, that having more people always means slicing a small pie thinner. But when we become able to repair cells, we will also be able to build replicating assemblers and excellent spacecraft. Our "poor" descendants will share a world the size of the solar system, with matter, energy, and potential living space dwarfing our entire planet.

This will open room enough for an era of growth and prosperity far beyond any precedent. Yet the solar system itself is finite, and the stars are distant. On Earth, even the cleanest assembler-based industries will produce waste heat. Concern about population and resources will remain important because the exponential growth of replicators can eventually overrun any finite resource base. But does this mean that we should sacrifice lives to delay the crunch?

A few people may volunteer themselves, but they will do little good. In truth, life extension will have little effect on the basic problem: exponential growth will remain exponential whether people die young or live indefinitely. A martyr, by dying early, could delay the crisis by a fraction of a second - but a halfway dedicated person could help more by joining a movement of long-lived people working to solve this longrange problem.

After all, many people have ignored the limits to growth on Earth. Who but the long-lived will prepare for the firmer but more distant limits to growth in the world beyond Earth? Those concerned with long-term limits will serve humanity best by staying alive, to keep their concern alive. Long life also raises the threat of cultural stagnation.

If this were an inevitable problem of long life, it is unclear what one could do about it - machine-gun the old for holding firm opinions, perhaps? Fortunately, two factors will reduce the problem somewhat. First, in a world with an open frontier the young will be able to move out, build new worlds, test new ideas, and then either persuade their elders to change or leave them behind.

Second, people old in years will be young in body and brain. Aging slows both learning and thought, as it slows other physical processes; rejuvenation will speed them again. Since youthful muscles and sinews make young bodies more flexible, perhaps youthful brain tissues will keep minds somewhat more flexible, even when steeped in long years of wisdom.

People such as Ehrlich have been deeply concerned about over-population and the ability of the Earth to feed increasingly large populations. The Earth currently supports 6 billion people. As noted above, aside from political problems, wars, and occasional natural disasters, the 6 billion people have enough to eat and many are far above subsistence level. This is not saying that the quality of life is high for all 6 billion people, since there would be less crowding with fewer people. It seems self-evident that the Earth could not support 6 billion people if they were all foragers. There are not enough roots and berries and game to support so many people. If foraging were the technology for feeding people, most would starve.

Similarly, if the technology were early agriculture with its primitive grains, lack of pesticides, fertilisers, and irrigation, most people would starve. There simply is not enough good farmland to support so many people without the improvements that have come from plant breeding, pesticides, fertiliser, and irrigation. The standard of living in the United States is far above subsistence because only about 2% of the workforce is required to produce the food. Particularly in the last century, the combination of technological change and clever use of resources has outpaced population growth, especially in the developed nations.

However, current agriculture, and the economy more generally is built on a foundation of fossil fuels, underground aquifers, and other resources that are very finite. If current technology were used to provide all 6 billion people with American lifestyles, we would quickly exhaust petroleum resources, ores, water supplies, and pollute the environment. Can technological change and clever resource use continue to outpace population growth? Will world population growth slow and then be transformed into decreasing world population? Burning fossil fuels is the primary source of pollution, including polluted air and greenhouse gas emissions in the USA.

Nanotechnology offers the promise of being the foundation for the next wave of technological change. The energy from fossil fuels is used extremely inefficiently. Nanotechnology could provide improved services for a small fraction of current energy in lighting, computing, printing, water filtration, and many other areas.

Sustainable Implications

Two centuries ago, Thomas Malthus explored the same notions, concluding that humans would continue to breed until starvation, pestilence, and war limited the population size. Income in England is far greater than in Malthus' time. While there is starvation, this seems to have more to do with conflict than any inherent shortage of food. Life expectancy has increased in all the developed nations and in almost every part of the world.

Thus, aside from human conflict and a relatively small burden of disease and natural disasters, people live much better than Malthus predicted. Malthus and Meadows et al. erred by not accounting for the effects of technological change, with its inherent ability to substitute abundant materials for scarce ones. They also erred by not accounting for the feedback in a market economy. Scarcity causes increasing prices, which signal inventors to find substitutes, prospectors to find other supplies, and consumers to use less or find substitutes.

Humans are different from other animals in explicitly and implicitly accounting for the systems wide impacts of their actions, including having more children. Even when consumers don't think about the economy-wide effects of increased population, a market will react to increasing population by increasing the price of scarce food and other materials and by lowering family income. Both effects lower the standard of living and cause people, eventually, to think about the desirability of having so many children.

The feedback effect can take decades and the signals often are misinterpreted, but the market signals get stronger as population outpaces the ability to support the population. Thus, humans are fundamentally different from bacteria, plants, and other animals. We have institutional feedback systems that prompt people to reassess their decisions to have more children before there is a disaster.

The importance of technological change cannot be overstated. Humans started out as foragers, dependent on the bounty of nature. To support a growing population and to ensure a steady food supply, humans developed agriculture. Agricultural techniques developed over time, including breeding more productive plants and animals, irrigation, mechanisation, and the use of fertilisers and pesticides. Wood was a primary energy source for cooking and smelting metals.

As the forests of Europe were depleted, people hunted for, and eventually found a substitute in coal, and later in petroleum and natural gas. Mining coal, transporting it, using it to reduce iron ore, and learning to burn it without excessive pollution required vast improvements in technology. Finding and producing petroleum and natural gas posed still greater challenges to technology. Rich deposits of ores for tin, copper, lead, and iron were gradually exhausted in Europe.

Technology developed to produce the metals from less rich ores and to find substitutes. Iron ore is more plentiful than ores for tin, lead, and copper (used to make bronze). Tin cans for storing food compete with glass jars. The competition among materials led to recycling as well as thinning the layer of tin in order to lower cost. Technology was called upon to use expensive resources more productively and to find substitutes.

4

Industrial Applications

The characterisation of materials—the determination of their shape, size, distribution, mechanical and chemical properties—is an important part of the industrial process. It serves two broad purposes: as quality control, and as part of the research and development of new processes, materials and products. Evidence taken during our industry workshop suggested that many areas of industry did not consider nanotechnologies to be new (for example, nanoscale structures have been important to the catalyst industry for over 100years). However, the industrialists believed that a nanotechnology 'breakthrough' had occurred in the tools used to observe and measure properties and processes at the nanoscale level.

Sophisticated tools, such as the STM, AFM and TEM, enable surface and interfacial characterisation of materials at the nanoscale, allowing individual atoms to be observed and analysed. This is leading to greater understanding of the relationship between form and material properties, and enabling the control of processes at the nanoscale and the design materials with specific properties. However, the commercialisation of such advanced functional materials requires that they can be made in a predictable, reliable way, and in sufficient quantities. Until that is achieved production will be limited to academia and R&D departments within industry.

Techniques for Fabrication

There are a wide variety of techniques that are capable of creating nanostructures with various degrees of quality, speed and cost. These manufacturing approaches fall under two categories: 'bottom-up', and 'top-down'. In recent years the limits of each approach, in terms of feature size and quality that can be achieved, have started to converge.

Bottom-up manufacturing involves the building of structures, atom-by-atom or molecule-by-molecule. The wide variety of approaches towards achieving this goal can be split into three categories: chemical synthesis, self-assembly, and positional assembly. As discussed below, positional assembly (with its many practical drawbacks as a manufacturing tool) is the only technique in which single atoms or molecules can be placed deliberately one-by-one. More typically, large numbe.'s of atoms, molecules or particles are used or created by chemical synthesis, and then arranged through naturally occurring processes into a desired structure.

In other words, the phase change itself could bring about nanoparticle formation (rare but possible) although generally the circumstances are created whereby nanoparticles can be made, for example vaporisation of a precursor mixture. Once in a state where nanoparticles can be made, usually a chemical reaction of some description is performed to generate the desired material. A further phase transformation or even solid-state reaction may be necessary to produce the final product.

Potential exposure of the workforce to nanoparticles is likely to be greatest when these materials are processed in a gaseous environment; in such cases worker exposure will need to be monitored closely. However, nanoparticles have a tendency to agglomerate, and are therefore often manufactured from a liquid phase as this enables surface energies to be better controlled, reducing agglomeration.

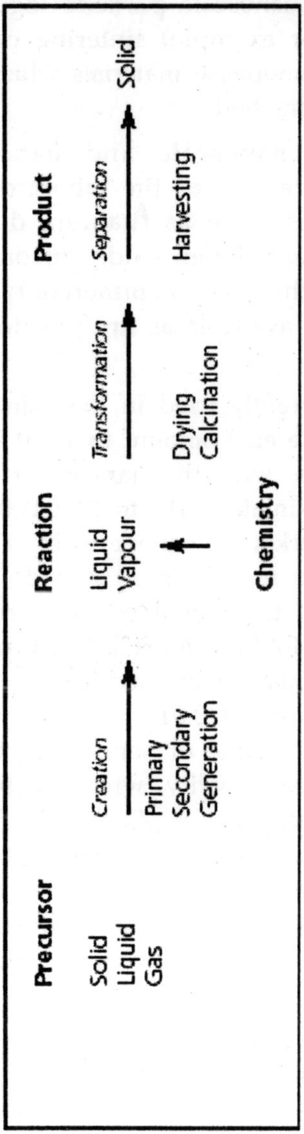

Figure 1. The generic processes that are involved in the production of nanoparticles

This also reduces the potential exposure level of workers. Processing and handling ability is very important for nanomaterials: mixing nanoscale particles together before agglomerating and (for example) sintering can generate wholly new complex nanophase materials which could not be made by any other method.

Most genuinely nanoscale and nanostructured materials, however, are still at the laboratory scale of synthesis. Metal oxides, such as titanium dioxide, zinc oxide, silicon dioxide, aluminium oxide, zirconia and iron oxide, are currently the most commercially important nanoparticles. They are available as dry powders or liquid suspensions.

The quantities currently used in the skincare market sectors (titanium dioxide etc.) amount to 1,000-2,000 tonnes per annum worldwide with the nanoscalar component materials worth approximately $10 to $100,000 per tonne. Although the world market for nanoparticles is expected to increase during the next few years, to provide perspective, it is worth noting that the global production rate of all chemicals is around 400M tonnes per annum, and so chemicals in nanoparticulate form account for only a tiny fraction of the total (around 0.01%) currently produced. Nanoscalar inorganic, metallic or semiconductor material often will have multifunctionality, which enables it to be used across many industry sectors. Zinc oxide, for example, will have more commercial use as an optoelectronic material (for displays or advanced solar and photovoltaic cells) where it will be fixed in the final product, than as an ingredient for skincare products, where particles will be free.

Self assembly is a bottom-up production technique in which atoms or molecules arrange themselves into ordered nanoscale structures by physical or chemical interactions between the units. The formation of salt crystals and snowflakes, with their intricate structure, are examples of self-assembly processes.

Although self assembly has occurred in nature for thousands of years, the use of self assembly in industry is relatively new. There is an economic and environmental interest in processes through which materials or product components essentially form themselves, creating less waste and using less energy. However, current understanding extends only to the creation of fairly rudimentary systems. Improved understanding of thermodynamic and kinetic processes at the nanoscale, enabled through advances in the characterisation techniques and improved computer modelling, are expected to aid the development of more complex systems.

One potential processing technique involves the use of an external force or field (for example, electric or magnetic) to accelerate the often slow selfassembly process, which is attractive in an industrial context. This is known as directed self assembly. CNTs are generating interest within industry because of their remarkable properties. Potential applications include composites, conductive plastics, sensors, batteries and fuel cells.

CNTs can be grown by several techniques, such as the laser ablation of metal-doped graphite targets, carbon arc discharge, and the pyrolysis of hydrocarbons over metal catalysts. However, because of a lack of understanding of the growth mechanism, the selective and uniform production of CNTs with specific dimensions and physical properties has yet to be achieved.

Current production capacity for CNTs is estimated to be around 100 tonnes per annum; the actual production output remains commercially confidential, but is expected to be lower. Most of the capacity is estimated to be multi-walled tubes, with single-wall tubes accounting for about 9 tonnes of capacity.

The final bottom-up technique is positional assembly, whereby atoms, molecules or clusters are deliberately manipulated and positioned one-by-one. Techniques such as

SPM for work on surfaces, or optical tweezers in free space, are used for this. Positional assembly is extremely laborious and is currently not suitable as an atomic-scale industrial process. The fact that (albeit very rudimentary) structures can be fabricated atom-by-atom has lead to speculation that tiny nanoscale machines could be made which could be used in parallel to manufacture materials atom-by-atom. The idea is to fabricate one or a few machines (or assemblers) that would first make copies of themselves, and then go on to make materials in parallel, in principle solving the problem of slow production speed.

Top-down manufacturing

Top-down manufacturing involves starting with a larger piece of material and etching, milling or machining a nanostructure from it by removing material. This can be done by using techniques such as precision engineering and lithography, and has been developed and refined by the semiconductor industry over the past 30 years. Top-down methods offer reliability and device complexity, although they are generally higher in energy usage, and produce more waste than bottom-up methods. The production of computer chips, for example, is not yet possible through bottom-up methods; however, techniques using bottom-up methods are under exploration.

In general, ultra-precision engineering and manufacture underpin much of the micro-electronics industry in everything from the production of the flat low-damage semiconductor wafers used as substrates for computer chips, to the mechanical stages used to position the wafers, to the manufacture of the precision optics used to print the patterns on the wafers. In addition, the techniques of ultra-precision engineering are used in a variety of consumer products such as computer hard disks, CD and DVD players. Ultra-precision machine tools can now achieve very high performance in terms of both the accuracy with which form can be defined (up to 1 part in 107, or better than 100nm over distances of tens of centimetres) and the surface finishes that can be achieved (0.5-1nm root mean square surface roughness), although these are currently on simple shape surfaces and with low output levels.

This capability, which is bringing benefits in several areas, has been achieved through a combination of advances. These include: the use of advanced materials for cutting tools, based on diamond or cubic boron nitride; very stiff, precise machine tool structures; new linear and rotary bearing designs employing fluid films; and sensors for size control combined with numerical control and advanced servo-drive technologies. Very precise process and temperature control is needed to achieve this performance (the latter being of the order of ±0.01°C).

Manufacturing in the ICT sector predominantly involves lithographic processes that pattern a semiconductor wafer in a sequence of fabrication steps. Lithography involves the patterning of a surface through exposure to light, ions or electrons, and then subsequent etching and/or deposition of material on to that surface to produce the desired device. The ability to pattern features in the nanometre range is fundamental to the success of the IT industry and the ITRS roadmap. The main lithographic tools can be conveniently separated into methods that use a focused beam of electrons or ions to write patterns, and those that rely on the projection of light through a mask to define a pattern over a complete semiconductor wafer. Electron-and ion-based methods are both capable of making sub-10nm structures (with electron beam lithography having the greatest routine resolution), but they are too slow to be used directly in production.

Optical lithography is used for production of semiconductor devices. Although it does not have the resolution of the beam-based techniques, it provides rapid throughput and cost-effective manufacture. Electron beam lithography is primarily used to fabricate the masks used for optical lithography, and ion beam techniques are mostly used to repair masks and for specialist device applications. The requirement for ever-shrinking device structures has placed enormous technical demands on optical lithographic process, as the nanostructures have length scales similar to or less than the wavelength of the illuminating light (ultraviolet).

Despite these difficulties, the ITRS roadmap implicitly expects optical lithography to keep track of future device dimensions until 2016 when the target critical device dimension reaches 22nm. Techniques developed in the microelectronics industry have also enabled the miniaturisation of small mechanical moving devices (MEMS), which in turn have lead to research into NEMS. MEMS technology seeks to exploit and extend the capabilities that have been provided by silicon integrated circuit manufacturing from one of making chips for electronic signal processing to the provision of on-chip sensing and/or actuation through the use of moving mechanical parts. Some MEMS technologies are starting to attain maturity in manufacture (for example, MEMS accelerometers are used widely in air-bag sensors). However, there are currently difficulties in the reproducible large-scale manufacture of more complex MEMS systems. Although not strictly a 'nanotechnology' as defined in this report, MEMS, NEMS and the technologies used to make them are used extensively in techniques that can access and exploit the nanoscale (such as SPMs or lab-on-a-chip and biosensing).

The reducing dimensional tolerances (less than 100nm) being provided by modern lithographic patterning techniques are now enabling the production of structures of such small dimensions that they are becoming a legitimate part of nanotechnologies in their own right.

Top-down and Bottom-up Techniques

The relationship between top-down and bottom-up manufacturing is illustrated in Figure 2.

Future Development

There are strong drivers to reduce tolerances in engineering, including miniaturisation, improved wear and reliability characteristics, automated assembly and greater interchangeability, reduced waste and requirement for re-work. As the trend towards miniaturisation continues, research and the industrial application of energy beam processing methods will increase, driven in particular by the electronics and computer industries. Techniques such as electron beam lithography (EBL), focused ion beam (FIB), reactive ion etching (RIE) and femtosecond pulsed laser ablation are becoming more accurate and cheaper to apply in a production context. Some examples of future applications of high-precision engineering are given below.

ICT: the machines used to fabricate chips depend fundamentally upon the use of ultra-high precision techniques for their manufacture and nanometrology techniques for their operation. The manufacture of larger-diameter semiconductor wafers with improved flatness and reduced sub-surface damage should lead to improved device yields and reduced costs.

— *Optics*: innovative ductile-mode grinding processes, together with electrolytic in-process dressing (ELID), should result in the elimination of polishing in the production of high-quality optical devices. This is likely to be of particular importance in the production of the optics for extra-large astronomical telescopes such as the proposed 50m and 100m systems (Euro50 and OWL), which will consist of many individually figured segments.

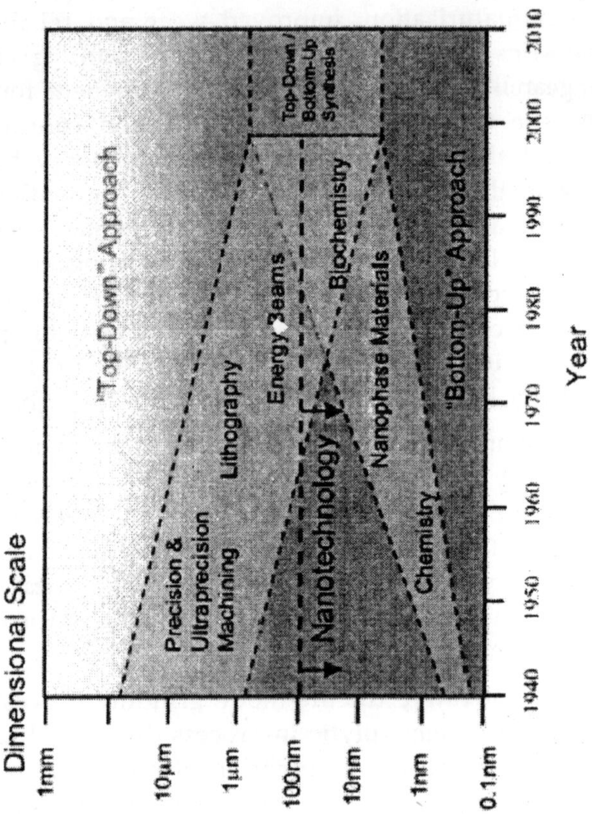

Figure 2. The convergence of top-down and bottom-up production techniques

— *Transport*: precision-machined parts should be more reliable, because of reduced wear, requiring fewer replacement parts and less energy consumption. For example, the ability to produce surfaces with controlled textures through finishing to 10nm average roughness followed by laser surface treatment is expected to lead to improved power transmission trains with losses through slip reduced by up to 50%. Precision manufacturing is predicted to lead to weight reductions in airframe wings and to improve the performance of internal combustion chambers.

— *Medical*: it is hoped that the use of ultra-precision machining techniques to produce improved surface finishes on prosthetic implants should lead to lower wear and better reliability.

It is hoped that advances in precision engineering will enable the reduction of environmental impacts by, for example, reducing the use of lubricants. However, for any particular product, the whole life cycle needs to be taken into account before it can be established whether there is a net environmental benefit.

The long-term goal within the chemicals industry is to use nanoscale 'building blocks' to assemble organised nanostructures, that can in turn be manufactured into commercially useful products. From an understanding of the chemistry and physics of nanoscale materials, and top-down/bottom-up modelling and measurement, industry will concentrate on processes that use manufacturing at the nanoscale in a way that preserves the desired effect and function as nanoscale components are combined into macroscale materials and products.

This will involve the development of technologies based on self-assembling materials, or more probably on directed-assembly methods, which allow for some form of massively parallel production, along with modelling and measuring tools. The vision is the manufacture of reproducible, accurate and designable nanomaterials.

The time-scale for the commercial exploitation of these types of highly organised structures or quantum materials is approximately 2020 and beyond, for use in the biotechnology and IT sectors. These materials will be extremely valuable, in excess of $1,000,000 per tonne, with the production rates of the order of 10-10,000 tonnes a year. The price is expected to remain relatively high because, though the effect of the nanomaterial will be to add value to consumer products, it will only form a tiny fraction of the final product as sold. The desired functionality is created through exploiting structure—property relationships. Measurement, modelling and simulation are essential for the characterisation and subsequent control of property and functional performance and therefore the production of desirable materials.

The development of measurement tools for use at the nanoscale will move from laboratory-based characterisation to in-line and on-line methods of monitoring and controlling accuracy at the 6-sigma level (99.9997% accurate) in terms of reproducible structure, texture and surface properties. The use of computer simulation based on advanced structure - property - process predictor codes will become the key technology for manufacture-by-design, where the characteristics of the material are effectively 'dialled up' through morphology, texture, structure and reactivity based on the interaction of materials across molecular- and nano-length scales.

The structure or form of the material then dictates the processing options for economic, reliable and reproducible operation. The combination of measurement, modelling and manufacturing technologies will be the basis for intelligent material systems. It is also hoped that it will be possible to produce materials with less waste. The synthesis and control of micro- and nano-scale structures may yield unprecedented control of meso and macro-scale properties in functional materials for use in applications of direct relevance to industry. It has been predicted that over the course of the century, many of the needs of commerce and society may be satisfied through a materials revolution involving synthesis and smart fabrication.

There are other techniques that are increasingly being applied both to on-roadmap developments and to alternative approaches to device materials. Soft lithography techniques where a flexible master is used to stamp out patterns on a range of surfaces have been available for several years. The accuracy demands imposed by the silicon-based industry have, until now, prohibited the use of soft lithographies as the elastic nature of the stamp can cause small, but still unacceptable, physical distortions across a wafer surface.

However, for small-area device fabrication and for applications where spatial tolerances are less restrictive, they offer a real alternative to conventional methods, although the fabrication of the master still requires optical or electron beam methods. Soft lithographies can be used for plastic electronics, as can alternative ink-jet based methods which use essentially the same technology as desktop printers. Although plastic electronics are not truly in the nano-range in terms of critical dimensions, a relatively simple manufacturing technique that can deal with wet chemistries will enable cheap electronic and photonic devices. Such developments, combined with advances in directed self-assembly, may bring the semiconductor, materials and chemical industries closer together, in order to create novel alternative methods for chip production as the end of the roadmap approaches.

Resource Management

It has been claimed that several nanotechnologybased applications and processes will bring environmental benefits, for example through fewer resources required in manufacture or improved energy efficiency in use. It is important to substantiate such claims by checking that there are indeed net benefits over the life of the material or product. The potential benefits of nanotechnologies should be assessed in terms of life cycle assessment (LCA) (sometimes referred to as 'cradle-to-grave' analysis). LCA is the systematic analysis of the resource usages (for example, energy, water, raw materials) and emissions over the complete supply chain from the 'cradle' of primary resources to the 'grave' of recycling or disposal.

One of the areas of application foreseen for nanomaterials is in photovoltaic (PV) energy converters in order to increase efficiency. An LCA would investigate the extent to which the additional energy yield over the service life of a PV device would be offset by any additional energy used in manufacturing the device and in recovering or disposing of its material content at the end of its life.

To illustrate the importance and associated complexity of such analyses, an example can be taken from the possible use of nanotechnologies in the transport sector. The first assumption has therefore been that technological developments towards 'lightweighting' are always beneficial. This assumption would need to be tested for nano-engineered materials where end-of-life disposal may have an adverse environmental impact.

Also, the basis on which reducing aircraft weight is assessed needs to be defined carefully to avoid reaching simplistically optimistic conclusions. In practice, it is likely that reductions in aircraft weight will be exploited by increasing payload, i.e. carrying more passengers, which if the market were fixed would bring environmental benefits due to fewer flights. However, if this is used to decrease ticket costs, it could stimulate additional passenger movements, albeit using less fuel per passenger-kilometre flown.

The true trade-off to be considered is between the benefits of additional passenger movements rather than the environmental performance of the aircraft and the impacts of producing nano-engineered materials. Thus the superficially simple environmental assessment ends up involving social and ethical issues. There are several factors that will influence whether nanotechnologies will be used routinely within industrial processes. Some of these are economic or social, others are technical.

The technical barriers should not be underestimated: as well as the difficulty in scaling a process up from the laboratory to an industrial operation, more fundamental barriers stem from a lack of understanding of nanoscale properties and the techniques to characterise and engineer them to form useful materials and products.

Alongside purely technical barriers to progress are those relating to regulation such as classification and standardisation of nanomaterials and processes, and the management of any health, safety and environmental risks that may emerge. Until these regulatory measures are in place, industry will be vulnerable to reduced consumer confidence, uncertainty over appropriate insurance cover and litigation should some nanomaterials prove to be harmful.

Industrial Application

In July 2001, the Ministry of Science and Technology issued a policy plan for a national nanotechnology development strategy for the period 2001 to 2010. This draft plan confirmed the general strategy and objective of nanotechnology development in China.

Objective of Nanotechnology Development

According to the policy plan, the Chinese government is committed to continuously improve innovative capability, develop advanced technology, and finally attain industrial applications relevant to China's present status with a focus on national long-term development. With this plan the Chinese government also made clear that it will insist on its set principle that it will support what is beneficial to China, i.e. catching up with international development in general, while finding breakthroughs that can solve key problems in China. The development of bio-nanotechnology and nanomedical technology is a main objective for the medium term, whereas the development of nanoelectronics and nanochips is a long-term objective.

5

Nanotechnology for Poverty Reduction

Nanotechnology manipulates atoms and molecules to make or build things (or living beings). One may imagine a laboratory which, combining suitable molecules in quality and quantity could create electric drills. Although this is theoretically possible, it would take some time, at least until there were nanobots that could do the job by themselves. But this will be at a later stage, if ever. At the moment, what can be made are nanoprcducts, in which scientists manipulate matter at the nanoscale to give them special or more efficient uses.

According to the Nanotech Report, among the first products commercialised in 2004 with nano-technological content were the following: thermal shoes (Aspem Aeogels); dust and sweat-repelling mattresses (Simmons Bedding Co.); more flexible and resistant golf clubs; personalised cosmetics for different ages, races, genders, types of skin and physical activities (Bionova); dressing for cuts and burns that prevent infections; disinfectants and cleaning products for planes, boats, submarines, etc. (EnviroSystems); spray that repels water and dirt that is used in the building industry (BASF); treatment for glass to repel water, snow, insects etc. (Nanofilm); cream that combats muscular pain (CNBC); and dental adhesives that set the tooth crown better (3M ESPE). Nanotechnology builds from the smallest number of atoms and molecules to make the biggest final product-the bottom-up process.

Nanotechnology can also reverse the process-instead of starting with physical matter as it is found in nature, according to its own structures, and reducing it to the size of the objects to use as has been done until now-the top-down process.. Despite this road being familiar in chemical processes, the novelty is that, now, atoms and molecules can be directly manipulated to manufacture products. This constitutes a novelty in the history of humanity and a new way of thinking in the world. Its consequences are unlimited. It is even conceivable to think that a process of production that manufactures by summing up molecules will, in theory, generate no waste. Second, at this nanoscale level, there are few differences between biotic matter and abiotic matter in that it is potentially possible to apply biological procedures to material processes or interfere with materials in living bodies, adapting the latter to certain purposes or offering certain advantages, or also creating artificial life to perform specific tasks.

One example would be a way of allowing the body to rest without sleep, which would be very useful in war and other activities that are very physically or mentally demanding. Third, nanoparticles may have physical and chemical properties (conductive, electric, mechanical, optical, etc.) which differ from the same elements on a macroscopic scale. Many nanomaterials that are on sale offer great advantages in this way.

Carbon nanotubes, for instance, are harder than diamonds and can be up to fifty to a hundred times stronger than steel. Finally, nanotechnology combines several kinds of technologies and sciences such as information technology, biotechnology and materials technology. The latter is not a lesser element if we consider that the true development of nanotechnology will require a totally new professional education which will require rethinking schooling, maybe from the primary level. The potential benefits of nanotechnology are impossible to calculate. In the field of health, it could increase the quality and length of life.

Nanosensors, incorporated into the organism, could travel through the bloodstream similar to the way a virus does and detect illnesses before they spread to the rest of the body and combat them efficiently. In the future, drugs may no longer be generic for all people, but may be specifically designed according to the genetic make-up of the individual and his/her gender, age, diet, etc.

Ageing mechanisms could be retarded and even reversed, with the human lifespan being lengthened significantly. With these artificial sensors, a person could become a bionic being, improving her biological capacities and developing others. Some even envision nanotechnology applications that will improve human perception and ability at fundamental levels.

The field of prostheses is also among the most promising. In the materials field, one novelty will be intelligent nanoparticles. Your wardrobe, for example, could be reduced to one single article. The item of clothing you have will react to changes in temperature, rainfall, snow, sun, etc., keeping the body always at the programmed temperature.

Furthermore, it will repel sweat and dust, which will mean that it will not require washing. As if this were not enough, it would stop bacteria or viruses from penetrating it, protecting it even from possible bioterrorist attacks. In the case of an accident, your clothes would have healing effects, offering first aid. The same that applies to clothing could be adapted to certain dwellings and modes of transport. Another novelty is that carbon nanotubes are stronger than steel and only 1/6 of its weight. This will have a special impact on the aerospace, construction, automobile industries and many others. The field of computer science will be one of the earliest industries and will enjoy the most revolutionary change.

Computers can be a hundred times faster and much smaller and lighter, and can be custom build according to the tastes of the buyer in terms of design, size, shape, colour, smell, resistance, etc. Prototypes with built-in sensors will speed up designs, adapting to flexible production processes in different parts of the world, overcoming many of the barriers that distance now imposes.

The old "justin-time" production mode will become obsolete and may very well become the "as-you-need" mode of production. The possibilities for monopolistic concentration of production (global business enterprises) will multiply. The combination of computerised systems, chemical laboratories, miniature sensors and living beings adapted to specific functions will revolutionise medicine (e.g., lab-on-a-chip) and also provide rapid solutions to the historical problems of contamination.

Small bacteria with sensors may be able to consume bodies of water that have been contaminated by heavy metals, or decontaminate the atmosphere in record time. Nanocapsules with combined systems of sensors and additives will revolutionise the industries of lubricants, pharmaceuticals, filters, etc. Nanotechnology may become a disruptive technology that will make obsolete the current competitive technologies, once established and entrenched in economies around the world.

The social and economic effects on the international and national levels are difficult to foresee, but an effort must be made at this critical juncture in order to reduce the possible negative or unwanted consequences that have historically accompanied such dramatic transformations.

Despite the voices that warn of the possible negative consequences or risks of nanotechnology, there are others that suppose that the new technology will be beneficial to everyone, including the poor. In this light, the recent U.N. Millennium Project Report, Task Force on Science, Technology and Innovation, puts forward the idea that nanotechnology will be important to the developing world because it harbours the potential to transform minimal work, land and maintenance inputs into highly productive and cheap outputs; and it requires only modest quantities of material and energy to do so.

However, these same qualities could be seen as harmful because poor countries have abundant labour, and, in many cases, land and natural resources. In this way, nanotechnology may cause displacements and disruptions in the economies of poorer nations. Reasoning in a purely technical and linear fashion, any country could theoretically join the nanotechnology wave.

An effort for public funding may create the bases to establish specific nanocomponent industries to meet determined needs; or it is possible that businesses with a scientific tradition might justify a technological leap at a relatively low cost. This seems to be the opinion of the authors of at least one article that has received a great deal of attention from the international scientific press. The technologies range from energy production and conservation systems, with sensors that will increase agricultural productivity and the treatment of water, to the diagnosis of diseases.

Overflowing with good intentions, the proposal reflects the mechanical idea that if a problem can be identified correctly, then all that has to be done is to apply a suitable technology, and it will be solved. Most of the examples used do not take into account the reality that the relationship between science and society is much more complex than identifying a technology and its potential benefits. Salamanca-Buentello and colleagues suggest that quantum dots could detect HIV/AIDs molecules in the early stages, thereby facilitating the treatment of AIDS and reducing the number of new cases. While quantum dots may, in fact, provide a useful solution to the HIV/AIDS crisis in developing countries, Salamanca-Buentello's article does little to place this novel technology into the historical experience of poorer nations with advances in the medical field more generally. In this conflict, the World Trade Organisation ("WTO") and the Commercial representative of the United States have systematically played the role of front-line soldier for these corporations.

The rigours of the patenting system have used monopolist economics to drive medicine pricing for the last twenty years. This makes it impossible for poor people to buy medicine from companies that hold patents. Experience over the last several years has shown that when an epidemic occurs, some countries could not afford to cover the cost of remedies very much needed by people within these poorer countries. One of the most alarming historical cases, illustrating the behaviour of the multinational pharmaceutical corporations that tends to undermine public health, was the action brought in 2001 by thirty-nine of the major pharmaceutical corporations against the government of South Africa.

In that case, several major pharmaceutical corporations prevented the government of South Africa's producing generic medicine for AIDS treatment. A lawsuit over the matter was soon filed. The lawsuit, which the South African government won, showed total insensibility to human rights on the part of the pharmaceutical corporations. The statements of one of the pharmaceutical company's representatives bore out this insensitivity.

According the reasoning of certain pharmaceutical companies, the court's ruling allowing the government of South Africa to produce affordable generic medicine could have a precedential effect allowing other governments to cheaply develop generic medicines: "while South Africa may represent less than 1% of world drug sales, the precedent of allowing a government to step on drug companies' patent rights would have far-reaching effects, beyond the questions of cost and crises." Nanotechnology products are already being patented, typically by the most important and largest corporations in the world.

A patent in the U.S. costs $30,000 in legal bureaucracy, and a worldwide patent may be as much as a quarter of a million dollars. For an underdeveloped country it is very difficult to develop any medicine for which there is an important market (as is the case of AIDS) if we take in account the economic and legal medicine market's international "war," as well as the bureaucratic restrictions which drive up costs and limit reduce availability. Salamanca-Buentello and his colleagues identify nanotechnology as the solution to five of the eight Millennium Development Goals of the United Nations.

Among these supposed solutions are nanosensors and nanocomponents to improve the dosage of water and fertilisation of plants. With this technology, it would be possible to reduce poverty and hunger in the world. Simply identifying a potentially useful application, however, overlooks the clear historical experience of poorer countries. Not so long ago, in the 1980s, genetically modified organisms were hailed as the solution that would put an end to hunger and poverty. However, genetically modified organisms ended up being used mainly in developed countries; and three out of four patents are today in the hands of four large multinational companies.

There has been no improvement for Third World countries; quite the contrary, transgenics turned up where they were not wanted or expected, as was the case of the contamination of corn in Oaxaca, Mexico. In the case of genetically modified organisms, commercial and technological dependence was increased, not reduced. This historical example could well foreshadow the path that nanotechnology takes in worsening existing gaps between the developed and less developed world unless steps are taken now to avert a repeat of history. That agricultural nanotechnology will follow the controversial road taken by genetically modified organisms. However, avoiding such a situation requires a healthy debate concerning the possible social, economic and political implications in real time.

Take the following two statements as an example: nanotechnology products face the paradox that they are (1) elementary particles of known chemical elements; and (2) manipulated in a way that is not natural. As for the first statement, nanoproducts do not always need to go through drug trials and registration. Regulations seem not to accompany the speed of technical improvements. Salamanca-Buentello and his colleagues also presuppose that interviewing thirty-eight scientists from developing countries and twenty-five from developed countries permits them to speak of the interests of the developing countries as if they were, in fact, spokespeople for those within developing countries.

Unfortunately, the opinion of scientists involved in nanotechnology does not necessarily fall within with the most appropriate of pathways for satisfying the needs of the poor. The relationship between scientists and socio-political pressures are replete with examples of doubtful practices. In the biomedical arena, for example, we can find cases of independent determination of standards in biomedical trials compromised or auto-censored by the influence of pharmaceutical corporations; and there are examples of funds given by pharmaceutical corporations to universities in order to have influence on decisions pertaining to research and development ("R&D") and to gain the right for subsequent licenses. Even still, there are examples of pharmaceutical companies' bankrolling academic studies that downplay their interests. Some have made claims of fraudulent or doubtful laboratory trials conducted by some large pharmaceutical companies.

Still others describe the pharmaceutical corporations' inciting physicians to use governmental forms fraudulently in order to obtain reimbursements for medicine obtained for free from pharmaceutical companies. Pharmaceutical corporations have also been accused of putting pressure on researchers to impede the flow of detrimental information into public forums.

And the list can go on and on. Academic opinions, therefore, can hardly be said to represent completely the voices of the poor. Technology is simply a part of a puzzle. Scholars may concur, for example, that infectious diseases constitute one of the main problems that the developing world is facing, but they may differ radically on how a solution to this problem should be attained. Prevention is not the equivalent of a cure. Nanotechnology is not necessary to reduce malaria radically, for example, as is suggested by Salamanca-Buentello and colleagues. There is no doubt that nanosensors could help to clean water, nor that nanocapsules could make drugs more efficient.

Nevertheless, in the Hunan Province of China, malaria was reduced by 99% between 1965 and 1990 as a result of social mobilisation backed up by fumigation, the use mosquito nets and traditional medicine. Vietnam reduced the number of malaria-related deaths by 97% between 1992 and 1997 with similar mechanisms. Organising people-which some refer to as social technology-can be just as important. In this way, identifying potentially useful scientific technologies for the developing world must become part of a much larger and inclusive social technology if gains are to be actualised in poorer countries.

Nanotechnology in Socio-economic Context

The history of science and technology is full of examples of technologies that have not always helped the poor. In order to serve the needs of the poor, technology has to be used in a favourable socioeconomic context. Furthermore, the building characteristics of the technology, and the technological path, usually impede it from being freely used for the benefit of the majorities in developing countries.

Despite the optimistic assessments recently offered, experience suggests that nanotechnology could follow the mainstream economic trends that increase inequality. First, the development of nanotechnology faces many of the same problems faced by prior technological developments because large multinational corporations are patenting the majority of the nanotechnology products. Patents are monopolistic guarantees of earnings for twenty years-something that certainly works against the rapid diffusion of the beneficial potentials of this technology for the poor.

Second, nanotechnology's novel solutions and potentially laudable achievements may never come to fruition in developing countries because the main problem for a developing country is not so much the fixed costs of a laboratory of average sophistication, but the social context that is necessary for really incorporating nanotechnologies into the economy. Without fluid mechanisms of vertical integration between the sectors that produce nanoparticles and the companies that are potential buyers, the nanoparticles will never get out of the laboratory. From many accounts, this seems to be happening, nowadays, in developed countries.

Third, nanotechnology's development in much of the world will do little to help the developing world due to the difficulty in finding qualified workers. A country's ability to foster and support technological careers requires a social context that supplies the necessary equipment and human capital in the long term. It will be difficult for many Third World countries to find the staff necessary to work interdisciplinarily in nanotechnology. Mexico, for instance, the thirteenth largest exporting power in the world, only has eleven research teams in three universities and two research centers in nanotechnology, with a total of ninety researchers and no official support program for field research.

Brazil, which launched a pioneer program for research and development in nanotechnology in Latin America-considering that it was in the same year as the U.S. initiative-had between fifty and one hundred researchers in 2002 and probably around 300 in 2004. Despite these seemingly impressive numbers in Brazil, challenging barriers remain which will continue to plague the ability of nanotechnology scientists in developing countries to produce benefits for the poor. Many nanotechnologists in developing countries may be driven by higher wages out of poorer countries and into richer ones.

The reason that this potentiality must be addressed now is as follows. Some estimate that nanotechnology will mean restructuring all learning to break down the traditional disciplinary frontiers, which, in practice, nanotechnology has already overcome. It is possible that changes in study plans would have to take place starting at primary education.This means that multi-sector efforts are gambled on these changes, and elevated social demands are required. In many instances, poorer nations lack the resources, infrastructure and facilities for such interdisciplinary efforts as nanotechnology-particularly, where transformations must take place at so fundamental a level.

Given the higher stakes and more interdisciplinary nature of nanotechnology, therefore, it is possible that the race for qualified scientists will heat up and increase the brain drain from the Third World into more advanced countries. This polarisation of the labor market will punish poorer countries with less qualified labor. It is unlikely that the vast majority of developing countries will have the wherewithal, infrastructure and labor force to be able to join the nanotechnology wave and capitalise on its potentials to transform society and industry. Finally, even if large developing countries that could join the nanotechnology wave (such as China, India, Brazil, etc.) can produce nanoproducts that could eventually result in clean and cheap energy options, in clean drinking water or in greater agricultural yields, this does not mean that the poor majority will benefit.

For the poor, socio-economic structure is a much more difficult barrier than technological innovation. Nanotechnology, even where fully integrated in developing countries, does nothing to change these socio-economic structures; instead, it could serve to exacerbate existing gaps and further the technological and socio-economic isolation of the poor.

Nanotechnology and Human Society

The term "nanotechnology" may include such products as mono-layered materials, nanocomponents in smarter MEMS, and Fullerene-based computers. Some decades from now, it may also include communicating and/or programmable molecular machines.

In the short-term, incremental improvements in processes and materials can come about by improved knowledge and skills in the nano-realm. The additive effects of these changes can have secondary and tertiary impacts that are transformational. For example, the social, ethical, and legal impacts of the World Wide Web were not originally thought to be considerable. The Web's enormous impacts are still not fully understood. In a similar way, nanotechnology may appear gradually and yet have a revolutionary effect. In the longer-term, the risks and rewards of nanosystems will certainly be exaggerated as our technological capabilities improve. Virtually every "millennium survey" of the future poses some social, ethical, or legal questions about nanotechnology. Just as fear of cloning could slow efforts in biomedicine and fear of genetically modified foods could contribute to hunger, fear of futuristic nanobots running amok could delay the benefits offered by nanotechnology.

When discourse is founded on emotional prejudices, its unreasonableness discredits the legitimate need to identify and assess risks. Nanotechnology could ultimately turn out to be risky, but the prudent way to assess the risks is not the abandonment of the field. Following are some examples of possible social, ethical, and legal implications that bear some thought and consideration.

Short Term (3-5 years)

— The NNI will fund careers for scientists and graduate students; commercial firms will invest in nanotechnology R&D. These efforts will be widely dispersed politically, geographically, and scientifically.

— Nanotechnology research will both require and produce enabling technologies that will have beneficial spin-offs.

— There will be unintended consequences, both good and bad.

— We will have to balance the opportunity costs of studying assembler-based nanotechnology (with its huge potential payoffs) against research in fields where advances might have nearer-term but smaller payoffs.

— Designs for future nanosystems will be created, challenged, modelled, improved.

Medium Term (5-15 years)

— Nanotechnology research may allow an otherwise moribund Moore's Law to continue operating.

— Fullerene-based computer chips may require enormously expensive fabrication facilities that turn out chips by the millions—needed for smart packaging, foods, Bluetooth devices, etc. This could result in a proliferation of inexpensive unit costs but prohibitively (and anti-competitively) expensive initial capital costs.

— We may discover and perfect nano-sized sensors and tools that can diagnose disease much sooner than ever before—perhaps long before we have cures.

— We should expect revolutionary advances in materials, MEMS, etc., resulting in abundant markets but also in an upheaval in global financial and manufacturing systems.

— Public education may be needed to balance the views expressed by anti-technology writers and press.

Long Term (over 20 years)

— Nanosystems may help solve problems of disease and aging, pollution and scarcity, overpopulation and starvation, and could create revolutionary changes unlike any ever seen.

— Nanosystems could help produce alternatives to fossil fuels and their high environmental price and reliance on foreign sources.

— The transition from a pre-nano to a post-nano world could be very traumatic and could exacerbate the problem of haves vs. have-nots. Have-nots do not easily obtain access to new technologies; the difference between the lives of the nano-rich and the nano-poor will likely be striking.

— Potential harmful uses—intentional and unintentional—need to be studied well in advance: nano weapons; intelligence-gathering devices; nanotechnology combined with Artificial Intelligence to form super-intelligent but virtually invisible devices; artificial viruses to which humans have no immunity, etc.

Flavours of Nanotechnology

Accounts of the coming nanotechnology revolution seem to

involve two somewhat separable agendas—each with its own distinctive social implications. The first agenda links nanotechnology to chemical engineering and material science. This variety of nanotechnology focuses on controlling the nano-scale organisation of macro-scale substances.

Examples of such "nanomaterials" or "nanates"—might include wear-resistant nanostructured polymers for tires and drive belts, super-hard nanostructured ceramics for drill bits and cutting surfaces, or ultra-fine nanostructured membranes for filters and seals.

The second (and, in the long run, probably more disruptive) agenda links nanotechnology to mechanical engineering and robotics. This variety focuses on constructing nano-scale devices for operation in macro-scale environments.

Examples of such "nanomechanisms"—or "nanites"—might include ultra-small in-vivo medical devices, miniaturised surveillance systems, or lilliputian mining and manufacturing equipment. For many industries and many aspects of social life, nanostructured materials are likely to represent profoundly important technological developments.

Indeed, if nanates live up to their early billing, the resulting societal transformations could equal the transformations that attended the development of bronze implements at the end of the stone age or the introduction of nuclear weapons in the 20th century. Given this, it may seem odd to predict that the impacts of nano-materials will be "localised and manageable," as asserted above.

Admittedly, particular new materials may engender the development of particular new products that profoundly transform particular areas of social life—and the ripples from such transformations may spread through society in complex and unpredictable ways. But such transformative potential is hardly unique to nanoscience.

Nanotechnology may be more likely to yield these radically new materials, but humanity has developed quite a few other transformative compounds—from glass to gasoline to plastic—without the aid of nano-scale understanding. Thus, although the introduction of new nanates may be revolutionary, it promises to be revolutionary in relatively familiar ways. Recent years have generated a substantial literature on the industrial impact of technological discontinuities.

During this ferment, businesses, public agencies and other "technology champions" jockey for position, attempting to mobilise various economic, cultural and political forces to frame and tame the discontinuity, and to thereby establish a new "dominant design."

Once such a dominant design emerges, however, the affected sectors restabilise—although often in significantly different configurations than before. Presumably, a similar dynamic would attend the introduction of new nano-materials, albeit perhaps at a higher intensity and a broader scale.

Of course, this hardly obviates the need for foresightful policy attention: The changes initiated by even a relatively modest technological discontinuity can be quite farreaching, and the framing and taming process can be intensely political, both within the affected industries themselves and at the level of the larger polity. However, the differences between previous technological discontinuities and the discontinuities resulting from nano-materials seem likely to be matters of degree, rather than of kind. Industries will certainly be transformed, and some of these transformations will be wrenching and risky, but the involvement of nanotechnology will not, in itself, make the transformations any more wrenching and risky than the transformations that we have seen in the past.

It is in this sense that the impact of nano-materials will be "localised and manageable": The policy issues, even if large, will arise from the particular performance characteristics of particular products, not from the inherent nature of nanotechnology per se. If so, case-by-case planning would appear to represent an appropriate and, arguably, sufficient response.

In contrast to the relatively familiar challenges of nano-materials, nano-mechanisms promise (or threaten) to confront society with policy issues that are as unprecedented as they are profound. By allowing humans to manipulate the world at a previously unattainable scale, nano-mechanisms open a genuinely new frontier, beyond the contemplation of traditional legal and governmental regimes. While, as Richard Feynman put it, "there is plenty of room at the bottom," at the moment there are very few sheriffs at the bottom, to keep that room safe and productive. As currently envisioned, nano-mechanisms are likely to possess at least three properties that will generate novel safety and governance challenges: invisibility, micro-locomotion, and self-replication.

1. Invisibility is, of course, an inherent property of nano-scale objects, whether natural or artificial. Artificial nanites, however, would be among the first complex constructions intentionally engineered to accomplish human purposes at a microscopic (or sub-microscopic) level, and their introduction into the technological armamentarium would dramatically increase the potential for orchestrated covert activities.
2. Micro-locomotion is less inherent in nanotechnology than is invisibility, since some nano-mechanisms will undoubtedly work best when anchored to substrates. Nonetheless, free ranging nanites have clear advantages for certain tasks, and as such devices are introduced, they will radically challenge traditional understandings of macro-boundaries and barriers. Fences, walls and even human skin are largely open space, at the nano-scale.

3. Self-replication is clearly not an inherent property of nano-mechanisms, and indeed, creating self-replicating nanites may prove to be one of the most difficult technical hurdles of the nanotechnology revolution. Self-replication, however, is essential for the economical production of complex nano-mechanisms in useful quantities, and thus it seems likely that by the time such nano-mechanisms become socially significant, self-replication will in fact be a fairly common attribute. Unfortunately, self-replication also poses profound challenges to human foresight and control, since a population of carelessly designed self-replicating nanites could grow exponentially, without a ready "off switch."

Even "dumb" nano-mechanisms would require a dramatic rethinking of society's current legal and normative structures. Three governance issues promise to be particularly acute: monitoring, ownership, and control. Moreover, these issues may play out not merely with respect to nanomechanisms themselves, but also with respect to the "nanospace" that such mechanisms render accessible:

Monitoring: Invisible, micro-locomoting, self-replicating nanites will severely test society's established assumptions about what can and should be monitored, and by whom. On the one hand, the lay public may find itself inundated (or even interpenetrated) by complex devices whose presence, provenance and purpose remain undetectable without sophisticated technical assistance. On the other hand, those actors that can produce or purchase nanites will find themselves able to monitor their worlds (including their social worlds) in more profound and surreptitious ways than ever before.

Contrary to traditional assumptions, ordinary people will no longer be able to observe all the socially relevant activities in their own surroundings; yet public authorities will be hard pressed to provide policing assistance without further endangering individual privacy. In the absence of trustworthy institutions to regulate this newly-opened invisible frontier, the potential for rampant abuse will be matched only by the potential for rampant paranoia.

Ownership: Nano-mechanisms will also severely test society's assumptions about what can and should be owned, and by whom. Self-replication raises difficult questions of whether property rights persist from one generation of mechanisms to the next—not to mention difficult practical problems of "branding" proprietary nanites and policing "nanite rustling."

Equally importantly, micro-locomotion raises difficult questions of who owns the nanospace through which nanites pass. Controversies akin to historical debates over airspace and rights-of-way may emerge over the nanospaces within macroscopically "solid" objects.

Finally, and perhaps most significantly, nano-mechanisms will test established assumptions about responsibility and control. Traditionally, legal liability for mechanical devices can outlast ownership, but can be attenuated by unforeseeable circumstances or by the intervention of a third party's will.

The viability of these principles, however, becomes unclear in a world of self-replicating nano-mechanisms that operate invisibly in an only partially understood micro-environment.

One might imagine governing the control of nano-mechanisms by analogy to defective products, or to toxic emissions, or to speeding vehicles, or to straying livestock—but the implications of these analogies are not entirely congruent with one another. Moreover, a parallel set of complexities and contradictions surround the control of nanospace: Who is responsible for policing the boundaries between "open range" and "enclosed territory" at the nanoscale? Can negligently maintained nanospace pose an "attractive nuisance" to passing nanites? Does a state maintain territorial rights to the nanospace within the bodies of citizens travelling abroad?

Security and Nanotechnology

The social issues of nanotechnology will be at least as complex as its consequences for the environment and design. In his book Normal Accidents, the sociologist Charles Perrow has argued that some technologies are both nonlinear and tightly coupled. That is, they can feed on themselves and a single mistake can be readily transmitted through the system.

Nanotechnology may reduce these forms of risk significantly, especially by promoting energy efficiency and making it possible to reduce or eliminate nuclear power production. But it is also possible that some otherwise extremely desirable nanotechnology processes may meet Perrow's definition. They may require the kind of strict controls that we now associate with the nuclear industry—controls not only on operations and physical access but also on the sharing of knowledge.

To von Neumann's generation these appeared the inevitable costs of a national security state. In the early twenty-first century, as the problems of America's national laboratories show, this system of command is harder to sustain. Knowledge has become far less viscous. Laptop computers and Web connections are sabotaging decades of carefully defined security procedures, yet we are warned that stringent new security could wreck the morale of the producers of classified knowledge.

Innovations flow readily across national borders because the sheer volume of world trade and communication overwhelms controls. The programmers in recent headlines have been Finnish, Swedish, and Belgian;

tomorrow's may be from any part of the world. Proliferation of bureaucratic controls, extending in the United States to state and local levels, creates a new set of problems in the selection and supervision of controllers.

Although some forms of research will be clearly unethical, and already banned under treaties against chemical and biological warfare (CBW), the line often is not clear. Haber and Bosch originally developed their method for military purposes, yet until comparatively recently it was acclaimed as a humanitarian miracle.

But what if the order had been reversed? Is it really possible to develop the countermeasures against CBW without gaining knowledge that could be used aggressively? John von Neumann, despite his misjudgements of other issues, argued persuasively that benign and threatening research could not be neatly separated, observing that scientific and technological branches are linked so closely that only the end of technological progress could hold back potentially dangerous knowledge.

Even entirely innocuous applications could lead to surprising social changes. Will nano fabrication be controlled, for example, by a small number of patents? If so, who will hold them and how will they be licensed? Will high fixed costs tend to concentrate production in a few global firms, as in the microchip industry, or will there be opportunity for independents alongside the giants?

These questions may seem remote now, but are likely to have consequences as dramatic as the effects of personal computing and the Internet. The benefits of successful nanotechnology could raise living standards globally while creating local crises, for example by slashing the world prices of minerals, gemstones, and other resources that are the mainstays of national and regional economies. Many resource-rich countries are already unstable. And even the United States could be adversely affected; the worldwide spread of nanotechnology processes and skills may reduce the advantages of our agricultural and mineral wealth. In the West, improvements may have paradoxical consequences.

If nanotechnologybased medical tests follow the pattern of previous advances, they may increase anxiety and medical costs by producing large numbers of false positives and requiring further testing. While many cancers and other diseases can be treated effectively if detected early, information about incipient disease or a nontreatable genetic predisposition could actually be a psychological threat to health: "toxic knowledge," some have called it. Every important new therapy should be reason for rejoicing, but we should not suppose that more effective prevention and treatment will lower medical costs.

To the contrary, as health and longevity improve, society pays more for medical care because large numbers of people live to an advanced age and require even more treatment. In 1997, a research group in the Netherlands even found that if all smokers immediately quit, prolonging their lives, medical expenses to society would increase over time.

We all hope that nanotechnology will improve the quality as well as the length of life, but because medical advances tend to increase rather than reduce the long-term need for the time of skilled professionals, they are unlikely to be cheap. Already parts of the United States face severe a severe shortage of nurses. Alzheimer's disease threatens to be the epidemic of the twenty-first century, according to some commentators, compounding the need for personnel.

Hidden labour costs of technological breakthroughs are not peculiar to medicine. Software for conventional computer processors now requires ever-larger teams of well-paid programmers writing ever-bulkier code. Nanotechnology may accelerate the increase of processor speed and storage capacity, but even with new programming tools, it may require even more programming time.

Certainly the explosion of electronic resources in education has tended to increase rather than reduce costs. In all fields, the success of new high-technology methods also has the unintended effect of eroding older skills that remain needed if only as backups.

Thus many young physicians now are said to be unable to use a stethoscope properly. Many craft and industrial skills are also declining. Yet in the event of major environmental or social disruption in which high technology no longer functions, these abilities would be crucial resources, as paper-based information would be.

In fact some traditional skills remain crucially important even for the most sophisticated technology; experimentation in physics and chemistry still depends on machinists, glassblowers, and other master artisans and technicians. While many paradoxes accompany radical innovation, opposing it can bring equally strange results. If we freeze technology, we perpetuate and amplify the environmental and social costs of the status quo, including the degradation of air and water quality and the acceleration of climate change.

We are on a technological treadmill. We have to find new ways to do things, and nanotechnology can not be excluded. Very possibly, its greatest benefit may be an apparently humble one, like the reduction of rolling friction with a new generation of bearings. Nanotechnology promises new beginnings. Researchers should bring not only a strong ethical sense but awe at the complexity with which the natural and human worlds interact.

6

Development of Nanotechnology

The prospect of a large variety of commercial applications in materials, medicine, informatics, and the energy sector lead to heavy investment of large firms as well as small start-ups in the last years. In contrary, the public awareness of nanotechnology is still comparatively low. However, critical comments and fictional dystopias directed some attention to nanotechnology's potential downsides recently.

Although still limited, a debate on nanotechnology developed. Main contributions to this debate came from non-governmental organisations (NGOs) like ETC-Group, Greenpeace and Genewatch UK and were acknowledged and answered by scientists and their journals. The ability to communicate is a fundamental prerequisite for any kind of interaction between science and others in society. Against the background of the 'New production of knowledge' approach by Gibbons et al., intense and felicitous communication is an indication for a specific interaction between science and others—the contextualisation of knowledge production. In Nowotny et al.'s enhancement of this theoretical framework the concept of contextualisation is focussed on the interaction between science and society. NGOs are here seen as forms of collective behaviour of citizens and therefore a special form of 'representative' or 'spokesperson' of society.

Like the field of nanotechnology itself, science and technology-studies' (STS) interest in nanotechnology is relatively new and still developing. This "formation phase" of STS-research on nanotechnology can be visualised with some examples. Besides several individual researchers working on the topic, Nano-science and technology study group was founded in 2002/2003 as part of the NanoCenter at the University of South Carolina forms a new cluster of 19 STS-researchers accompanying, reflecting and interpreting nanotechnology with different research projects.

In Europe, the European Commission has included the need for work on ethical, social and legal aspects (ELSA) of nanotechnology in its 6th Framework Programme and allocates resources to ELSAstudies on nanotechnology. But also single nation-states fund STS-research projects on nanotechnology, e.g. Brian Wynne's, Robin Groove-White's and Phil Macnaghten's study under way "Nanotechnology, Risk and Sustainability: Moving Public Engagement Upstream" at the IEPPP (Institute for Environment, Philosophy & Public Policy) at Furness College, Lancaster University in collaboration with the London-based think-tank 'demos'. These examples should only give a feeling for the current efforts and the still ongoing process of formation.

On the one hand, this newness simplifies a review of selected research results, but on the other hand it also means that the coverage of the phenomenon is still patchy—different approaches and interpretations are still competing and broader research projects are still in progress. But nevertheless there are a few articles, some working-papers and several conference-abstracts which have already been published and allow to carefully reviewing the state-of-the art in the STS-debate on nanotechnology. In his writings, the philosopher of science Alfred Nordmann attempts to characterise nanotechnology on an abstract and epistemological level.

Nordmann interprets Nanotechnology/Nanoscience as NanoTechnoScience abandoning the distinction between science as a process of understanding nature and technology as transforming nature altogether. He identifies NanoScience and NanoTechnology as 'site-oriented' enterprises in comparison to issue-driven 'classical' investigative enterprises: "(...)nanoscience does not derive its research agenda from the development of extant theoretical traditions but instead it finds itself at a certain site, place, or environment, and is driven by the specific demands of the local size-regime."Furthermore, NanoTechnoScience according to Nordmann's concept does not strive for extensive falsification and quantitative prediction, but for quantitative affirmation and structural similarities. It does not word causal or mechanical laws of nature, but explores beneficial properties. Instead of separation between scientific legality and technical feasibility, Nordmann sees a programmatic equation of both in NanoTechnoScience.

The perspectives Nordmann offers in his papers and presentations are both helpful and deficient. On the one hand they provide in their broadness a very inspiring picture of nanotechnology and -science, which could help put other questions in perspective and could form a point of contact for further thinking. But on the other hand they rest only upon few examples and sources and are therefore not yet sufficiently elaborated and.

In their report "Bringing visibility to the invisible: towards a social understanding of nanotechnology" documenting a series of preparatory studies, Hans Fogelberg and Hans Glimell from the Göteborg University's STS-Section work on cultural, political, and sociological aspects of nanotechnology. This includes dealing with the definition of nanotechnology itself. In Fogelberg's and Glimell's preparatory study on the different approaches, claims, and tensions in the field of nanotechnology, the authors view nanotechnology as a still open field. They see the field as an "epistemological battlefield" where different concepts and definitions in the field "may be understood as vital resources in a 'politics of epistemology' where cognitive authority and political legitimacy are mutually dependent phenomena".

Enlarging this approach, Fogelberg in his exploratory study on the scientific, technological and political construction of nanotechnology on the macro-level concludes after viewing available material on nanotechnology: "There are no stable, precise or generally agreed definitions of nanotechnology..." But by analysing these different definitions, he identifies certain patterns and dichotomies which serve as "demarcations" in the field and thereby characterise the field in its fuzziness.

The identified dichotomies are between top-down vs. bottom-up methods of fabrication, scientific vs. industrial orientation, and inorganic vs. organic materials. As recurrent topics in the different definitions Fogelberg identifies the scale—ranging usually from 0.1 nanometre (nm) up to 100 nm, but sometimes stretching above, the possible technical applications, inherent interdisciplinarity, and particular nanoscale objects. From Fogelberg's point of view, the lack of coherence between the definitions is partly due to the very character of nanotechnology as new and still developing technoscientific collection of different disciplines, and partly due to the use of the term nanotechnology as a mere conceptual abstraction used in conversation between policy-makers and the heterogeneous group of nano-experts.

This strategic use of definitions is the object in Fiedeler's conference-abstract. In his opinion, the strategic opportunities for both policy-makers and researchers offered by the very fuzzy definition based solely on the scale-aspect explain its widespread use. For researchers, the fuzzy definition allows the inclusion of various projects, the formation of a broad and therefore strong coalition of disciplines in funding-negotiations, and the transfer of positive connotations from other disciplines. In Fiedeler's opinion, it allows various researches to benefit from the positive connotation of, e.g., "increasing the life expectancy" as common project of nanotechnology, while in the same time rejecting responsibility for it also referring to the fuzziness of the definition.

The concentration on different definitions, their causes and effects and finally their use indicate some important points. Another strand of research tries to shed light on the inherent constitution of nanotechnology. In a bibliometric study, Joachim Schummer analyses multidisciplinarity, interdisciplinarity and research collaboration in nanoscience and technology. By analysing papers in nano-specific journals and comparing them to a "classical" disciplinary journal regarding their degree of interdisciplinarity measured by co-authorship, he challenges the notion of a singular inter-disciplinarity in Nanoscience and technology. According to Schummer, nanoscale research as the accumulation of different journals in the field consists of the disciplinary categories physics, chemistry, material science and engineering, electrical engineering, chemical engineering, biomedical science, and mechanical engineering.

Even though there are comparatively many links between the comparatively equal-sized disciplines, the links are comparatively week. He concludes that there is no significant higher degree of interdisciplinarity in nanoscale-research compared to the "classical" disciplines. Furthermore, he indicates that even the semblance of a high degree of multidisciplinarity dissolves, when the journals are analysed separately. This results question earlier outcomes based on a different scientometric approach.

Martin Meyer and Olle Persson classify in their study on a similar topic nanoresearch papers on the basis of inter-

and multidisciplinarity of the journal they are published in. Contrary to Schummer they conclude, that nanoscience is more interdisciplinary than other areas of science. In a contribution to a book on new ways of knowledge production, Meyer combines a scientometric analysis of publications and patents with explorative firm cases and interprets the results against the background of Gibbon's "new production of knowledge"-theory in order to test not only the transdisciplinarity but also the science/technology-linkage.

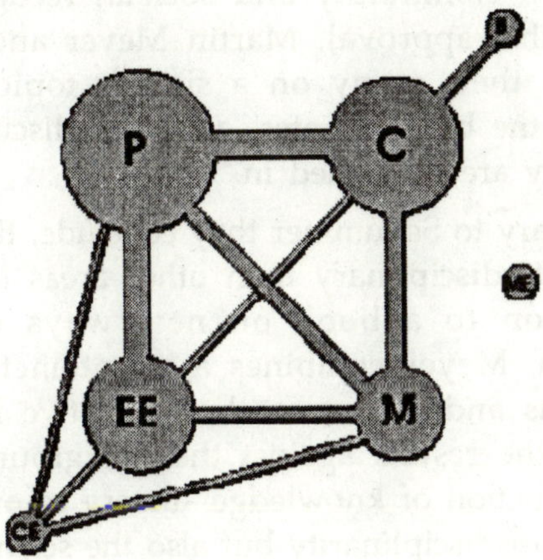

Figure 1. Interdisciplinarity patterns of nanoscale research

In this very conscientious interpretation, he shows a "tendency towards more cross-boundary research as well as a greater orientation of scientific actors towards the application of their research results."

Still another perspective on the inherent constitution of nanoscience takes Glimell in his work on nanotechnology from an ethnographic point of view. He identifies scientists working in nanotechnology as diverse in disciplinary and visionary backgrounds and conceptualises the "nano-site" as boundary-object facilitating communication between different epistemic cultures and visions.

The problematic role of experts in nanoscience and — technology as result of interdisciplinary is Edward Munn's topic in a conference paper. In Munn's opinion, since nanoscience and technology are interdisciplinary and transformative, expertise as relying on the approval by both society and the professional community faces specific problems.

Epistemic and political authority of experts is according to Munn not possible, because interdisciplinarity and newness hamper the approval of experts inside the professional community and societal recognition in turn relies on this approval. Martin Meyer and Olle Persson classify in their study on a similar topic nanoresearch papers on the basis of inter- and multidisciplinarity of the journal they are published in.

Contrary to Schummer they conclude, that nanoscience is more interdisciplinary than other areas of science. In a contribution to a book on new ways of knowledge production, Meyer combines a scientometric analysis of publications and patents with explorative firm cases and interprets the results against the background of Gibbon's "new production of knowledge"-theory in order to test not only the transdisciplinarity but also the science/technology-linkage. Another aspect of nanotechnology some research has been done on is views, images and visions of nanotechnology.

A study for the Dutch Rathenau Instituut carves out 'social points of attention' and their enclosed terrifying and ideal visions appertaining to the manifold fields of application of nanotechnology. Overall issues connected with nanotechnology as a whole are, according to van Est et al., patents, distribution of benefits and risks and orientation of nanotechnology. While the scary visions are a monopolisation of knowledge and profit resulting in a global nanodivide and technological determinism, the bright pictures of the nanotechnological future embody a spread of knowledge, fair distribution of welfare and socially aware aims of nanotechnology. The public perception and view of nanotechnology is explored in two empirical studies — one limited to Great Britain prepared by 'BMRB Social Research' for the "The Royal Society and Royal Academy of Engineering Nanotechnology Working Group" and one limited to the United States interpreted by Bainbridge.

Bainbridge's study is based on supplementary questions in an internet-survey and a qualitative analysis of written comments and concludes the public attitude towards nanotechnology to be highly enthusiastic and little concerned about the risks. Quite differently, BMRB's study concludes that the awareness of nanotechnology is limited and the attitudes are mixed depending on the expected use of nanotechnology. More from the 'governance of technology' point of view another strand of research addresses topics like risk assessment, public participation and regulation.

The already mentioned research project by Brian Wynne, Robin Groove-White and Phil Macnaghten from Lancaster University in collaboration with the London-based thinktank 'demos' aims at enhancing the governance process of nanotechnology by moving public participation 'upstream' within R&D processes.

Many scholars report on the relevance of the recent experience with the governance of biotechnology regarding nanotechnology as the first stages of the research project. Instead of 'instrumental learning' as piling up insights and consecutively adding new forms of engagements, they call for 'reflective learning' leading to critique of one's position in the past and consequent alteration of future options.

According to Grove-White et al. the importance of tacit visions and imaginaries underlying scientific research needs to be acknowledged and should lead to more frankness in future debates on nanotechnology. Frther reflection on the diverse roles and nature of NGOs needs to be incorporated in future discussions about social and political processes for nanotechnology.

Furthermore, the predominant deficit model that is still underlying assessment and regulation procedures needs correction. A similar subject has James Wilsdon's and Rebecca Willis' report "Seethrough science:Why public engagement needs to move upstream". Their assessment of nanotechnology sees a new stage in the science-society relation. They argue that science and policy increasingly embraced the idea of public involvement in the last years and "that we are on the cusp of a new phase, in which public engagement moves upstream". Despite few, mostly technical critiques already mentioned, the research on nanotechnology and nanoscience from STS-perspective seems to suffer from a lack of coherence.

Nordmann's thoughts can provide a larger background and helpful insight in the constitution and aim of NanoTechnoScience and therefore help to understand nanoscience's reactions to NGOs as well as NGOs' attempts to describe and address nanoscience. The studies dealing with the term and definition of nanotechnology can despite their vagueness serve as background for the whole analysis.

The insight, that there is nothing like one common definition indicates a crucial and potentially difficult point in the communication between NGOs and science. Second, the further systematisation of different reoccurring themes and dichotomies in different definitions, and the thoughts about the strategic advantages and disadvantages can contribute to the analysis of different definitions and underlying strategies.

Greenpeace

Greenpeace is one of the largest environmental non-profit NGOs with global scope. In 1971, Greenpeace's Canadian forerunner organisation 'Don't make a wave committee' sparked first public attention with an attempt to stop nuclear testing in Alaska.

Since 1971 named Greenpeace, the organisation campaigns nonviolently, but with direct action for environmental protection in the tradition of 'bearing witness'. While Greenpeace focussed in the early days on nuclear testing and whaling, the scope of action broadened over the years and includes now the areas oceans, ancient forest, toxic chemicals, climate change, sustainable trade, genetic engineering and nuclear power. Currently present in 41 countries across Europe, North and South America, Asia and the Pacific, the organisation has its headquarter "Greenpeace International" in Amsterdam, Netherlands. Despite its origin in the peace-activism and hippy-culture of the 60's, Greenpeace is according to Pearce organised "more in the form of a multinational corporation than the conventional democratic and devolved structure adopted by most green groups that formed during and after the late 1960s."

Although this structure fostered some struggles during the 90s, it allowed Greenpeace to evolve into the biggest environmental NGO with a clear ecocentric "branding". Campaigns are strictly limited to environmental issues, factoring out other in the green ideology connected topics like gender, racism or third-world. During the 80s and under the influence of David McTaggert, Greenpeace underwent a slow conversion to science, but still under the dominance of the ecocentric ethic agenda. Before largely ignoring scientific findings in favour of strong ethical claims, the organisation slowly began to employ natural scientists as staff members, to run own laboratories on its ships and finally to build up an own scientific unit to back up its claims.

Strategy, development and target groups of Greenpeace's engagement in nano Since Greenpeace has only published one report on nanotechnology, there is no development visible from the outside. It is not even clear, if Greenpeace's work on nanotechnology qualifies as separate issue on their agenda. As Charlie Kronick puts it: "Strictly speaking GP doesn't work on nanotech as a specific issue—we do work on the development and deployment of new technologies that have potential impact on the environment. "This assessment of Greenpeace's activity in the nano-field makes it equally difficult to name the way and scope of the work: "We don't have a nanotech campaign, but the technology may have impacts on many areas in which we do work—agriculture, biotech, renewable energy, etc."

Greenpeace's relation to science is insufficiently described when only the group's perception of science is presented. Beyond this uptake of science as category in world order, Greenpeace has a relation to science in its strategic work as NGO -even though these levels are not strictly separate. Although Greenpeace is sometimes accused of being 'anti-science', the group rejects this image roundly. Greenpeace describes its own relation to science as double edged. On the one hand, Greenpeace campaigns against technologies, the group assesses as hasardous for the environment.

On the other hand, the group relies on scientific and technological solutions for environmental problems, uses science to inform its campaigns, works on the science-public interface to spread scientific knowledge, and contributes to the scientific knowledge base with its own analysis. Greenpeace has its own laboratory to do so, but also commissions reports like in the case of nanotechnology. This strategy of 'borrowing expertise' could be interpreted in the same moment as 'borrowing scientific reputation'. This interpretation is supported by Doug Parr's explicit statement in the foreword that the report is "from an organisation with a reputation for technological expertise—Imperial College London." But in the communication with

Charlie Kronick, this interpretation has been rejected in favour of the related goal to commission somebody, who is not perceived as anti-science.

That the 'borrowed expertise' is just the base for one's own position but does not determine the campaign is visible when Greenpeace decides to call for a moratorium on nanoparticles, even though the report is not definite in its results in this point. Scientific expertise is used to monitor the field and gain basic insights, and one's own opinion is formed on its grounds.

Greenpeace has not published extensively on questions regarding nanotechnology. The issue is mentioned first in the briefing "Transforming science: A Matter of public involvement" published in 2002. Starting from the diagnosis of a lack of comprehensive information on nanotechnology, in 2003 the report "Future Technologies, Today's Choices Nanotechnology, Artificial Intelligence and Robotics; A technical, political and institutional map of emerging technologies" commissioned by the Greenpeace Environmental Trust and written by Alexander Huw Arnall from the Imperial College London is published.

Although the report is not exclusively dealing with nanotechnology around 20 pages were committed to nanotechnology and form the reference centre for later statements and positions by Greenpeace. The report consists of a literature review with discussion written by Alexander Huw Arnall and a foreword written by Doug Parr, where Greenpeace's motivation for commissioning the report and positions resulted from the review are clarified. Starting from the report as point of reference, Greenpeace represented by its Chief scientist Doug Parr participated in different conferences and seminars, gave evidence in the Royal Society/Royal Academy of Engineering workshop on nanotechnology and wrote at least two articles in the popular science magazine 'New Scientist' and the online news forum 'Small times'. Unlike ETC-Group's report that combined literature review, own analysis and own positions and claims, Greenpeace commissioned a separate 'scientific' report and grounded its own positions on it. Greenpeace's definition and contextualisation of nanotechnology and nanoparticles In the Report "Future Technologies, Today's Choice" the term nanotechnology is described as ambiguous, but a most common definition, which is again open to different interpretations, is identified: "The most common definition of nanotechnology is that of manipulation, observation and measurement at a scale of less than 100 nanometres."

On its homepage, Greenpeace's perception of nanotechnology is clarified, when the text emphasises that nanotechnology "is not really a single technology—it is about doing things at a very small scale". This definition of nanotechnology as array of different technologies, which are basically about 'doing things', is complemented with the notion of nanotechnology as a multidisciplinary field which arose from the combination of progress in instrumentation, an 'arms race' between governments regarding funding and an interest in nanotechnology from transnational companies and the investment community.

Here, Greenpeace's uptake of nanotechnology as constructed is visible and matches up with Doug Parr's statement, that "Nanotechnology is really a convenient label for a variety of scientific disciplines which serves as a way of getting money from Government budgets." Based on Arnall's report and driven by the desire to distinguish hype from reality, Greenpeace sees the next longer-term applications of nanotechnology in the semiconductor industry and the medical field. But also the mysterious 'grey go'-scenario with its underlying predictions of molecular assembly is discussed.

The current driver for nanotechnology and consequently subject of near-term concerns is in Greenpeace's opinion the 'new materials'-sector with its production of different nanosised particles and devices. Nanoparticles are defined only in a few publications, for example, an the article on the small times homepage as clusters of atoms at the nanoscale with novel properties or on Greenpeace's homepage as "very tiny particles which are so small that their chemical and biochemical properties will be different from the familiar bulk solids". In other respects, the term is used without definition, the broader term nanomaterials is used or it is referred to other scientists or group's definitions. Greenpeace's publications on nanotechnology and nanoparticles are contextualised mainly with environmental and health questions. Deduced from this aspect, Greenpeace contextualises nanotechnology and nanoparticles with the question for ownership.

The argument goes that owners can determine what an inherently neither good nor bad technology is used for. Therefore, ownership is critical for environmental questions too. But beyond these 'traditional' Greenpeace issues, broader questions surround Greenpeace's engagement with nanotechnology. Democratic rights and consequently participation in science and technology as "most powerful transformative forces of society today" are reoccurring in Greenpeace's statements on nanotechnology. Greenpeace's position on nanotechnology with emphasis on nanoparticles In general, Greenpeace sees new technologies as neither good nor bad, but as determined by its owners and users to become good or bad for the environment, health, equity and democracy. This goes for nanotechnology, too. On the one hand, Greenpeace is worried that nanoparticles may cause environmental damage through their novel properties. On the other hand, the group sees a potential for positive effects of nanotechnology in the future, too.

Greenpeace calls for a moratorium on nanoparticles "until the hazards are characterised and understood." This position grounds on the opinion that there is a significant scientific uncertainty concerning property, behaviour and effect of nanoparticles, which are in some cases already used in commercial products. In Greenpeace's opinion, this uncertainty must be answered according to the precautionary principle with a moratorium.

The positions on longer-term applications of nanotechnology are less clear-cut. In the foreword to the report "Future Technologies, Today's Choice" general concerns of patenting, ownership and continuous debate are voiced.

In addition, the often cited "grey goo" scenario is discussed and even though the prospect of molecular assembly is judged as way off, if possible at all, the concern is voiced that a convergence between biotechnology and nanotechnology might perhaps lead to a 'green goo' consisting of self-replicating 'machines' with living material, which has to be carefully monitored in Greenpeace's opinion in order to avoid potential environmental damage.

Based on the evaluation of nanotechnology's 'social constitution' seen as the social and political processes surrounding nanotechnology, Greenpeace foresees difficulties with nanotechnology's acceptance in public. These difficulties are in Greenpeace's perspective mainly connected to globalised, rapid technology transfer and public distrust in the information concerning risk and benefits from government, science and commerce.

Greenpeace has invested some effort in developing a clear position on science in contemporary society and its own relation to science. In 2002, Greenpeace jointly organised a debate on science and society together with the popular science magazine 'New Scientists' to discuss different aspects of the relation between science and society

In the briefing "Transforming society: a matter of public involvement" as well as on the homepage Greenpeace's own position on this topic becomes eventually clear. Science is viewed as most important transformative power in society, which is increasingly interwoven with commerce and politics. This association leads, in Greenpeace's opinion, ultimately to a crisis of public confidence in science, which is otherwise "potentially, a force for so much good for everyone" The current scepticism is not explained single-causal with the experiences in the GMO-debate, but seen as a cumulation of a long line of events, of which the GMO debate is just the latest manifestation. This perception of importance and potential neutrality of science is contrasted with Greenpeace's view of the current governance of science.

In the group's view, public influence on science is nearly not existent, while scientific priorities are set by governments, industry and science itself. Here, science has in Greenpeace's view a superior position, since its competence as experts for decisions both on the own behalf and in other policy-areas is rarely challenged.

But Greenpeace tries to challenge the superiority of science as experts at least rudimentary, when they ask for integration of "Farmers, health workers, patients, naturalists and others can all have important insights into how policy might work, or failings in the empirical knowledge base" and allude to the often confused difference between scientific results and scientists' opinion. But in the same moment, Greenpeace distances oneself from relativistic positions when the group states, "that most science is NOT controversial".

Greenpeace rejects a deterministic view on science's progress and stresses that scientific progress is constructed through numerous decisions on different levels is therefore never inevitable. According to Greenpeace, the outcome of scientific work does not appear on its own, but is determined by political, social and economical forces and decisions. In this view, society and politics are free to choose where science is going.

Vice versa, science is perceived as changeable. But it also contains a view of science as 'open system', which works only with external influences. That science is despite other influences seen as in charge for e.g. communication with the public, is visible in Greenpeace's call for proactivity of the scientific community in the case of nanotechnology.

NGOs, public and Nanotechnology

The three NGOs Greenpeace, ETC-Group and Genewatch UK agree with 'science' represented by articles and interviews with nanoscientists on several aspects of the definition of nanotechnology. They all see nanotechnology as defined by the nanoscale, they all understand nanotechnology as an array of different technologies, and they all agree on at least three disciplines working together in the field.

The perception of the inherent constitution varies, but there is no clear demarcation between 'science' and 'NGOs' as units. While ETC-Group regards nanotechnology as transdisciplinary with a tendency to convergence; Greenpeace sees the field as multidisciplinary. In the articles, different notions ranging from 'disciplines are meeting' up to 'convergence' are visible, while both interviewees agree that nanotechnology is in the same moment inter- and multidisciplinary.

Nanoparticles are seen by ETC-Group, Greenpeace and 'science' congruently as deliberately produced materials with nanoscale dimensions and novel properties. In unison, ETC-Group and 'science' count buckeyballs, nanotubes and nanosised particles as belonging to this category. Although NGOs and 'science' agree on the fuzziness of the term nanotechnology, and in an article the fear is expressed, that NGOs might misuse this fuzziness to count everything as belonging to nanotechnology, the comparison does not show significant differences in the actually used definitions of both nanotechnology and nanoparticles.

Against the background of earlier research on nanotechnology, where a lack of a common definition was stated, at first glance this result is surprising. But at a closer inspection, this seeming contradiction can be dissolved. Denoted "the least common denominator" by Fogelberg, without an additional reference to for instance methods of fabrication or resulting devices the definition solely by size leads in his and Fiedler's opinion to a huge diversity of interpretations. From this point of view, the agreement on a 'common' definition of nanotechnology purely by size does not necessarily mean that the 'nature' of nanotechnology is commonly agreed upon.

In this logic, even the additional 'common' aspects, that nanotechnology consist of different technologies, or in the case of nanoparticles, that they exhibit novel properties do not lead to a common understanding of the 'nature' of the issue, since neither the technologies nor the novel properties are specified sufficiently. On an abstract level, both 'science' and NGOs contextualise nanotechnology congruently with the influence of the public as well as with commercial potential of nanotechnology. But on a concrete level, these issues take shape quite differently.

Although the different NGOs approach the issue of commercial potential from their specific perspectives and priorities, they all monitor ownership and patenting as specific issues. 'Science' on the contrary, concentrates on the commercial potential of applications against the background of regulation and public influence. Consequently, public influence as science's context-issue takes shape as 'public attitude' towards nanotechnology both regarding nanoscientific research and commercialisation.

In NGO's contextualisation of nanotechnology, public influence is concretised as public participation in the larger framework of democratic rights. These context-issues can be seen as implicit messages in Nowotny et al's sense. From this perspective, at utmost a shallow understanding based on an abstract congruence of the issues is reached, while due to the differences on the concrete level a deeper understanding between the two groups cannot be stated.

NGOs and science agree on the identification of certain problems and share some opinions on nanotechnology. In unison, both groups agree on the general assessment of nanotechnology as hyped. Both groups judge this hype as possibly dangerous for the further development of nanotechnology. Both groups agree, that public acceptance of nanotechnology is important and foresee problems on the way to gain this acceptance.

Both groups commonly see nanoparticle toxicity and the possible effects on human health and environment as a problem and agree on a scientific uncertainty surrounding this topic. But there are as well a considerable number of problems they do not agree upon and a noticeable quantity of opinions, they do not share. All NGOs identify the potential intersection of nanotechnology with biotechnology as a problem.

Greenpeace and ETC-group discuss this problem as potential 'green goo', while Genewatch UK does not name it explicitly. The NGOs also discuss the possibility of a 'grey goo' scenario and even if they do not say that it is probable, they still identify the possibility as a problem. Both problemidentifications are not shared by 'science'.

Either the long-term scenarios of 'green-goo' and 'grey-goo' are dismissed explicitly as science-fiction, or long-term scenarios are not discussed at all. In the NGOs opinion, various broader problems surround nanotechnology. Though for different reasons, all NGOs agree that patenting of nanodevices and monopolised ownership of nanotechnology might be a problem.

In addition, each NGO identifies specific broader question according to their agenda. Science does not identify any specific broader question surrounding nanotechnology, but regards 'broader questions' in general as worthy to discuss. Although 'science' and NGOs commonly identify the scientific uncertainty concerning nanoparticle toxicity as problem, they differ about the consequences. While 'science' rejects a moratorium and is not even at one whether regulation of nanotechnology and nanoparticles is necessary, two of the NGOs agree on the need for a moratorium, while Genewatch UK does not express any opinion on this topic.

The relation between science and the public has been changed in the last years. That the distrust in science and technology has increased and public has begun to scrutinise science more thoroughly is the common analysis of this change. 'Science' and NGOs concur, too, that this change is at least partly due to the characteristics of the debates on genetic technologies and genetically modified foods.

Resulting from this experience with the GMO debate and its outcome, both agree on the necessity of an earlier incorporation and participation of 'the public'. Beyond this common analysis, they neither agree on the shape and extent of this earlier participation, nor does the perception of each other match up with the concept of the own role in this process. The NGOs see science congruently as increasingly interwoven with commerce and understand this new constitution of science as an additional reason for the crisis of public confidence in science.

They see science, its results and its technical applications as shaped by different, non-scientific forces and therefore reject technological determinism. Instead, they emphasise on the one hand the possibility and authorisation of society to influence science and on the other hand, the responsibility of science for both its results and the proactive inclusion of social concerns.

This understanding of science comes along with an appreciation as important part of modern societies and an emphasis on collaboration with science for NGOs own work. This understanding of science by NGOs clashes with 'sciences' own perception of its role. Both interview partners agree in complete contrast to NGOs position, that technological progress cannot be stopped and will take place any way.

At least in many articles and both interviews, 'science' perceives itself as a more or less innocent victim of public's sometimes irrational fears and opinions, which can easily manipulated by NGOs. NGOs are on the one hand perceived as important, since they raise awareness, warn and serve as indicators for public fears and moods.

On the other hand, a certain amount of distrust and suspicion is detectable. This takes shape in accusations that NGOs are playing on fears, are scientifically illiterate and misinform the public for their own best or are against new technologies in general. Even though the Greenpeace, ETC-group and Genewatch UK have significantly different agendas, strategies and priorities, they are summarised by 'science' under terms like 'environmental groups' alike-only exception is the Chemist, who makes a difference between ETC-Group as completely untrustworthy and Greenpeace, which work scientifically.

This mutual perceptions and the assessment of the relation between science and 'the public' can be used as approximation to the role of research in problems in nanotechnology. Even though there are several points, which are hard to compare directly, the perception of science seems to be quite different.

Equally, the role and authorisation of the public is, although an agreement on its power is reached, perceived differently. Finally, the perception of NGOs by science seems to lack unambiguous appreciation and is ambivalent. These differences can be interpreted in two ways. Firstly, the lack of agreement on the role of science indicates a lack of common understanding of an issue in the dialogue. Secondly, science's lack of appreciation regarding NGOs can be seen as a fundamental flaw in communication.

7

Application of Nanomaterials

Integration of top-down physical assembly concepts with bottom-up chemical and biological assembly concepts may be required to create fully functional nanostructures that are operational at mesoscopic scales. The combination of new nanoscale building blocks and new paradigms in assembly strategies will provide nanostructured materials and devices with new, unprecedented capabilities limited only by the imagination.

Technological Advancements

Polymeric materials, dendrimers, and block copolymers: The last decade has seen tremendous advances in the preparation of organic building blocks of considerable complexity. The discovery of a new topology for polymers, dendrimers, has led to an exciting new class of nanoscale component, with interesting optical and mechanical properties. Precise nanoscale architectures ranging between 10 and 100 nm have been successfully synthesised. These constructions involve the reaction of an excess of dendrimer shell reagent with a reactive dendrimer core reagent. The new compositions are referred to as tecto (dendrimer) coreshell molecules. These molecules have demonstrated potential as unique nanoscale reactors, intermediates for new coatings/ controlled delivery, compatibilisers, and building blocks for higher order nanoscale constructions. There have also been steady advances in engineering new phases using block copolymers; the recent development of tri-component block copolymer is noteworthy in this regard.

Nanocrystals: There has been significant progress made in the preparation of nanocrystals in recent years. Many common materials, such as metals, semiconductors, and magnets, can be prepared as nanocrystals, using colloidal chemistry techniques. The concepts of ligand exchange and surface derivatisation have been well developed, and these methods permit nanocrystals with narrow size distribution (typically 5-15% variation in diameter) to be isolated and then used further as chemical reagents. This field has been aided greatly by improved understanding of size-dependent scaling laws, which have emerged from fundamental studies in chemical physics and condensed matter physics. The fact that a simple property like light emission depends so strongly upon size in semiconductors has greatly facilitated the development of reliable preparations. The same size dependence has also led to a wide range of applications in unexpected areas, such as in biological tagging.

Nanotubes and rods: The exciting discovery of the fullerenes was followed closely by the discovery of nanotubes of carbon. Nanotubes show tremendous promise as building blocks for new materials. Because of their topology, nanotubes have no dangling bonds, and so despite being very small, they do not exhibit "surface effects." As a consequence, individual nanotubes exhibit nearly ideal electrical, optical, and mechanical properties. Nanorods are also under extensive development and investigation.

Nanoparticle structures: Controlled particle formation is an important synthetic route to nanoscale building blocks relevant to many technologies from ceramics to pharmaceuticals. Some interesting new nanoparticle structures are composed of chainlike arrays of nanoparticles of relatively low coordination number. There are two main types: agglomerates (or aggregates) and aerogels. In particular, these structures can be characterised by their morphology (for example, fractal dimension and coordination number) and the energies of the bonds that hold the primary (individual) particles together.

Nanostructures

Assembly: The development of self-assembly methodology, which is the archetypal bioinspired synthesis route, has greatly expanded the methods of construction of nanostructures. In the design of complex materials such as electrical devices, we currently rely on our ability to create designed patterns lithographically. New ways of bonding, assembly, and linking macromolecules and nano-objects have been developed that are based on interactions that are both more complex and individually weaker (e.g., steric, electrostatic, hydrophobic, and hydrogen bonding) than the classical electronic bond. Multiple bonding interactions are often needed to stabilize complex nanostructures. These interactions are the basis for coding information into nanostructures. In the last decade, nanoscale objects such as nanoparticles or nanocrystals have been assembled into periodic arrays, or supercrystals. Such arrays exhibit novel optical and electrical characteristics. Several proposals have been put forward for how to pattern nanocrystals and nanotubes using biological molecules.

Templated growth of mesoporous materials: In the last decade, tremendous advances have occurred in the preparation of mesoporous inorganic solids. The initial work showed that it is possible to use organic surfactant molecules to prepare a complex pattern. That pattern can serve as the template for the formation of an inorganic phase. This has led to many exciting discoveries in chemical synthesis and to immediate practical advances in catalysis.

Nanoporous media science (the control of void space) has advanced in some very important ways. For example, new scaffolds and matrices for tissue repair and engineering have been realised, and a large range of tailored porous catalysts and membranes, such as Mobil's MCM-41, have achieved commercial success. In another example, Nylon-6 nanocomposite with only two volume percent clay nanoparticles has a heat deformation temperature of 150°C, as opposed to 60°C for traditional Nylon-6.

Direct structuring: The ability to direct the assembly and organisation of materials with nanomanipulation and nanolithography, based, for example, on scanning microprobe techniques, has achieved directed assembly and structuring of materials at the molecular level. New methodologies in this area include 3-D printing and various forms of soft lithography.

Nanoimprint lithography: Nanoimprinting will allow for patterning at scales up to 10 nm on large surfaces and with a relatively low cost.

Technological development

One key to advanced technology emerging over the past decade has been nanomaterials. The aggressive advance of smart materials, solid state devices, and biomimetic technologies and the concurrent push towards miniaturisation are making the understanding and development of materials on the nanometer level critical and are encouraging the design of nanoscale structure and functionality into materials systems. The focus on nanostructuring of materials systems has been further sharpened by the need to develop materials having novel and/or enhanced properties without resorting to new synthetic chemistries with the associated environmental and cost issues. Enhancements in mechanical performance, wear resistance, integrity under thermal stress, flammability, and transport properties have all been linked to nanostructure in materials systems within the past five years, demonstrating that the technology has reached a level of maturity where it is ripe for exploitation in systems demanding both high performance and reliability.

A very important technological advance in recent years has been in the area of largescale, reliable production of uniform, nano-sized particles. This has been particularly important in the high-performance ceramic materials and the pharmaceutical areas, where materials properties, through defect control, drug delivery, and control of uptake, have been favourably influenced by nanoparticle production. Aerogels are normally fabricated by condensed phase (sol-gel) methods, even though the final product is a gas/solid system. Recently, aerogel-like structures have been fabricated directly by gas-phase processes without passing through the sol-gel state. This could lead to less expensive fabrication processes, use of a wider range of materials in aerogel fabrication, and excellent control of multilayer deposition processes, with applications in magnetic (giant magnetoresistance, GMR) and optical devices.

Soft lithography and nanoimprinting have been developed and identified as low-cost patterning approaches, with several new applications on the horizon. Nanostructured zeolite catalysts can be tailored to perform oxidation reactions more efficiently than enzymes. While not strictly speaking a nanotechnology, the tremendous advances in organic electronics, such as organic lightemitting diodes, must be noted, since that field is highly likely to benefit from advances in organic nanoscale synthesis in the future. New nanostructured materials have the potential to significantly reduce production costs and the time of parts assembly, for example, in the automotive, consumer appliance, tooling, and container industries.

The potential of significant reductions in weight due to these new materials as they are applied in the transportation industries will have great impact on energy consumption and the environment. Understanding nanoparticle formation is paying dividends in dealing with environmental issues such as atmospheric particulate formation as well. Many fundamental phenomena in energy science, such as electron transfer and exciton diffusion, occur on the nanometer length scale.

Thus, the ability to arrange matter, i.e., to inexpensively pattern and to develop effective nanostructuring processes, will be a vital asset in designing next-generation electronic devices, photovoltaics, and batteries. Size and cost reduction due to advances in the design and manufacture of healthcarerelated diagnostic systems has the potential to empower individuals to diagnose and treat diseases in their own homes, decentralising the healthcare system. Sensors based on nanotechnology will revolutionise healthcare, climate control, detection of toxic substances, and energy consumption in homes, consumer appliances, and power tools. The ability to assemble and interconnect nanoparticles and molecules at nanometer dimensions will enable the development of new types of nanoelectronic circuitry and nanomechanical machinery.

Scientific Infrastructure

In the area of synthesis, assembly, and processing of nanostructures, several kinds of infrastructure are very important. State-of-the-art characterisation tools underpin all efforts to synthesise and manufacture high-precision, high-purity substances; advanced characterisation methods must be accessible to those doing this type of work. These include, but are not limited to, neutron, X-ray, and light-scattering tools; surface and interface analytical tools; particle characterisation; microscopy of all types; and rheological methods.

Equally important are synthesis tools themselves, such as nano-fabrication facilities. New synthesis facilities, particularly those that might make new materials widely available to a broader range of investigators, could advance the field significantly. Large-scale scientific computation facilities are very important in the design and characterisation of nanostructures.

The guiding principles of R&D investment should be (1) support work that crosses all traditional boundaries, and (2) maintain appropriate balance between centers, teams, and single-investigator grants, and between basic science work and device/applications work. Boundaries to be crossed include those between traditional academic disciplines, between universities and industry, and between countries. Nanoscience and technology requires a spectrum of diversity of talent and approaches that cannot be achieved without crossing boundaries.

Fullerenes and nanotubes

Fullerene nanotubes hold tremendous promise for numerous applications, owing to their remarkable materials properties, including strength, stiffness, toughness, chemical robustness, thermal conductivity, and perhaps most interestingly, electrical conductivity.

Depending on their precise molecular symmetry, some nanotubes are semiconducting, while others exhibit truly metallic conductivity. This behaviour, coupled with their nanoscale geometry, makes them ideal-perhaps unique-candidates for wires, interconnects, and even devices for true molecular electronics. One application of nanotubes-as probe tips in scanning probe microscopy has already been developed.

Many others, such as fieldemission displays; high-strength composites, and various electronic applications, are being pursued vigorously now, largely enabled by the discovery in 1995 of the laser-vaporisation process for producing single-wall nanotubes in high yield. In the three years since this breakthrough, a tremendous amount has been learned about the fundamental physical characteristics of fullerene nanotubes, mostly consistent with early expectations of extraordinary material properties. The gram quantities of nanotubes provided by the laser process, and now by the arc process as well, are enabling a period of research on chemical methods for manipulating and assembling short lengths of nanotubes.

These are expected, in turn, to provide the enabling technologies for the applications exploiting the material properties discussed above. It must be stressed that the full realisation of most applications exploiting these properties will be made possible by the very high degree of structural perfection exhibited by nanotubes. This molecular aspect of fullerene nanotubes permits us to develop chemical strategies for assembling them into useful structures, materials, and perhaps molecular electronic devices.

Nanoimprint lithography (NIL) is a revolutionary approach to low-cost and highthroughput nanolithography. NIL patterns a resist by physically deforming the resist shape with a mold (i.e., embossing), rather than by modifying the resist chemical structures with radiation as in a conventional lithography. This fundamental difference in principles frees NIL from many problems suffered in conventional lithography, such as diffraction limit, scattering, and chemistry.

As a result, NIL can achieve sub-10 nm structures over large areas with low cost and high throughput-a feat currently unachievable using existing lithographies. Successful development of NIL will bring a revolution to nanostructure research, because NIL will remove the key obstacle-cost-to nanostructure commercialisation and will make nanostructures easily accessible to everyone. To a great extent, one can compare the impact of NIL with that of personal computers, which have made computation so widely accessible.

Therefore, NIL will not only impact future integrated circuit development, but will also impact many other disciplines, such as biology, chemistry, medicine, and materials, to name a few.

Lithographically Induced Self-Assembly (LISA)

Lithographically-induced self-assembly (LISA) is a recent discovery that will have a great impact on science and technology. In LISA, a mask is used to induce and control the self-formation of periodic supramolecular pillar arrays in a thin polymer melt that was initially flat on a substrate. The mask was initially placed above the polymer film with a gap.

The pillars, formed by rising against the gravitational force and surface tension, bridge the two plates. The boundary of the pillar array is precisely aligned to the bounding contour of the patterns on the mask. (Fig. 1) The principle for LISA is, although still unclear, fundamentally different from self-assembly by phase-separation and surface chemistry modification. It is believed that LISA is related to electrostatic forces and electrohydrodynamic instabilities.

LISA opens up exciting new areas for fundamental scientific study and practical applications. Scientifically, understanding of the LISA principle requires combining several disciplines. Technologically, LISA offers a solution to the two long-sought goals:

(a) precise control of the orientation and location of a self-assembled polymer structure, and

(b) making the self-assembled features smaller than those of mask patterns.

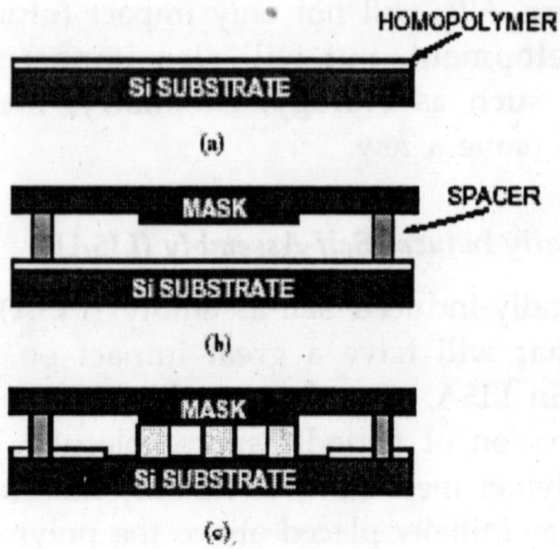

Figure 1. Schematic of lithographicallyinduced self-assembly (LISA)

Furthermore, the LISA process should, in principle, be applicable to other polymers and perhaps even other single-phase materials, such as semiconductors, metals, and biological materials. The periodic arrays formed by LISA have many applications, such as memory devices, photonic materials, and new biological materials, to name a few. Finally, LISA offers a unique way to pattern polymer electronic and optoelectronic devices directly without using the detrimental photolithography process.

DNA chips and microarrays represent a technology which has immediate applications in genetic research and diagnostics. DNA array technology may also play a future role in enabling nano-fabrication. DNA chips or arrays are devices in which different DNA sequences are arrayed in a microscopic format on a solid support (glass, silicon, plastic, etc.). DNA arrays can have anywhere from 100 to 100,000 different DNA sites (pixels) on the chip surface. Depending on the chip, the sites can range in size from 10 microns to over 100 microns. Each DNA site can contain from 10^6 to 10^9 DNA sequences. In a DNA hybridisation assay, the DNA array is contacted with a sample solution that contains the unknown target DNA sequences. If any of the sequences are complementary to those on the array, hybridisation occurs and the unknown sequence is identified by its position on the array.

A number of companies are now involved in the development of DNA chips and arrays, including Affymetrix, PE Applied Biosystems, HySeq, Nanogen, Incyte, Molecular Dynamics, and Genometrix. Present DNA chip devices will have applications in genomic research, pharmacogenetics, drug discovery, gene expression analysis, forensics, cancer detection, and infectious and genetic disease diagnostics. Newer generations of electronically active DNA microarrays that produce controlled electric fields at each site may have potential applications for nanofabrication.

These active microelectronic devices are able to transport charged molecules (DNA, RNA, proteins, enzymes), nanostructures, cells and micron-scale structures to and from any test site on the device surface. When DNA hybridisation reactions are carried out, these devices are actually using electric fields to direct the self-assembly of DNA molecules at specified sites on the chip surface.

These active devices are serving as semiconductor hosts or motherboards for the assembly of DNA molecules into more complex three-dimensional structures. The DNA molecules themselves have programmable and self-assembly properties and can be derivatised with a variety of molecular electronic or photonic moieties.

DNA molecules can also be attached to larger nanostructures, including metallic and organic particles, nanotubes, microstructures, and silicon surfaces. In principle, active microelectronic arrays and DNA-modified components may allow scientists and engineers to direct self-assembly of two- and three- dimensional molecular electronic circuits and devices within the defined perimeters of larger silicon or semiconductor structures. Thus,

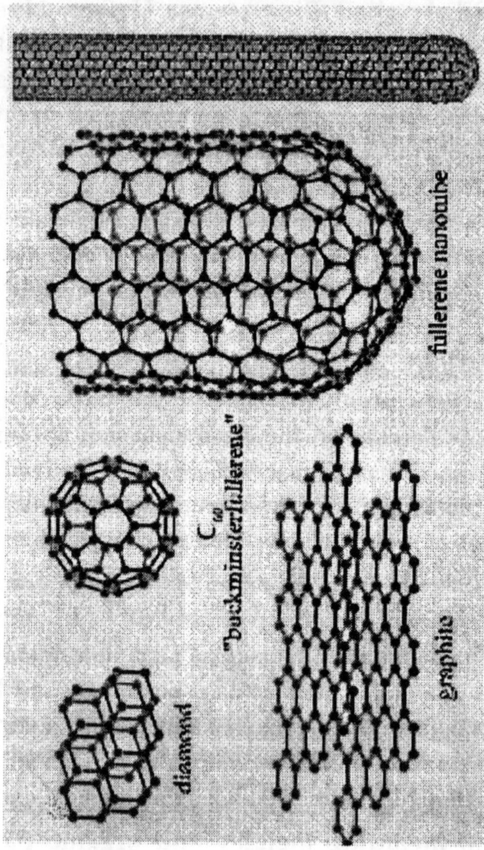

Figure 2. Fullerene nanotubes

electronically directed DNA self-assembly technology could encompass a broad area of potential applications from nearer term heterogeneous integration processes for photonic and microelectronic device fabrication to the longer term nano-fabrication of true molecular electronic circuits and devices.

The integration of top-down physical and bottom-up chemical or biological assembly methods will be crucial for the fabrication and interconnection of wires and switches. The strain-directed assembly of nanoparticle arrays in a solid, where a top-down physical process (lithographically defined surface structure) is integrated with a bottom-up chemical assembly process (strain and compositionally controlled precipitation), represents a step in this direction.

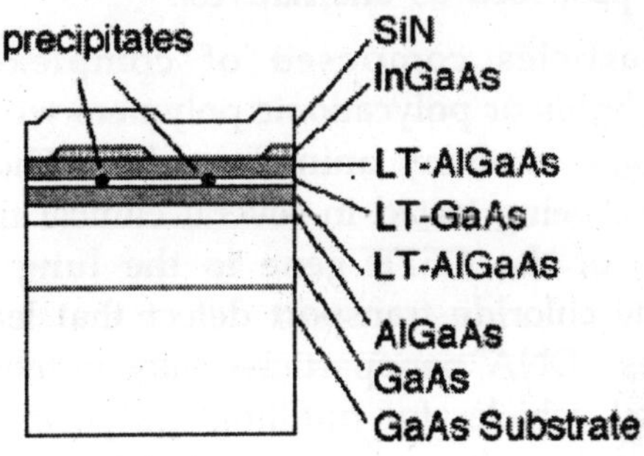

Figure 3. Strain-directed assembly

More generally, the development of such techniques will provide the means for introducing functionality in the substrate that is coupled to functionality on the surface. The horizontal positions of the 20 nm particles are controlled by the 200 nm surface stressors, while the vertical positions are confined to a 10 nm GaAs layer. One-dimensional arrays of closely spaced particles are formed along lines running into the plane.

Nanotechnology synthesis and processing

Almost half of therapeutically useful drugs are

hydrophobic. Administration of these water-insoluble drugs is problematic. The bioavailability of these drugs can be significantly enhanced by reducing the size of the drug particles to the nanoscale. Thus small enough to pass through the capillaries, the drug may even be administered via intravenous injection. The benefit to the pharmaceutical industry of this nanotechnology processing has been enormous. Genetic medicine continues to hold exciting promise in the future of healthcare.

A major challenge for successful gene therapy has been the development of safe and efficient gene vectors. While viruses in some cases can efficiently deliver exogenous genes to cells in vivo, the long-term safety of this approach remains a major concern. Non-viral vectors have been increasingly proposed as alternatives.

Nanoparticles composed of complexes between polycationic lipids or polycationic polymers with DNA have shown efficacy in many animal models. The lipid-DNA complexes are being tested in several clinical trials, notably the delivery of the CFTR gene to the lung airways for correcting the chloride transport defect that leads to cystic fibrosis. These DNA nanoparticles may potentially be the most practical vehicles for fulfilling the promise of genetic medicine.

Nano-sized Polymers

Nano-sized polymers shaped as rounded bricks, cones, mushrooms, and plates have been prepared in laboratories and found to self-assemble into tubular, spherical, layered, and lamellar constructs, respectively. These new types of polymers may eventually be useful in applications ranging from sophisticated sensors to de-icing agents.

A key element in the utilisation of nanostructures for as many applications as possible is the ability to inexpensively mass-produce them. The technique of polymer molding, long used for replication of micron-sized structures in such devices as diffraction gratings, compact disks, and microtools, has now been shown to work on the nanoscale as well. Beginning with a master nanostructure, a mold is made using an elastomer such as polydimethylsiloxane (PDMS).

The demonstration that this replication process works on the nanoscale was carried out using a master pattern fabricated via a unique new process known as laser-focused atomic deposition. In this process, a laser standing wave forms an array of atomic "microlenses."

These concentrate chromium atoms as they deposit onto a surface, building nanoscale objects "from the bottom up" in a single step without the use of any resist. Replication of the laser-focused chromium structure is only one example of the use of polymer molding on the nanoscale. For example, nanostructures with ~30 nm lateral dimensions have been produced based on gold patterns made using conventional lithography. Given these demonstrations, it is now clear that a new tool is available for nanoscale fabrication, with a direct avenue to mass production. As applications for nanostructured materials continue to expand, this technology stands ready for implementation in a manufacturing setting, enabling the type of inexpensive production techniques that new technologies critically depend on.

Robotic assembly

Nanoparticles may be positioned accurately and reliably on a surface by using the tip of an atomic force microscope (AFM) as a robot. The AFM images the original, random distribution of particles in dynamic (non-contact) mode, and then pushes each particle along a desired trajectory by moving against the particle with the feedback turned off.

Potential application of nanomanipulation to NanoCDs by using ASCII language has been illustrated. The new type of digital storage could have with densities several orders of magnitude larger than those of current compact disks. Nanomanipulation of nanoparticles with AFMs has been demonstrated at room temperature, in ambient air and in liquids.

The resulting structures can be linked chemically, e.g., by using di-thiols or DNA as glue, to produce nano-components that can themselves be manipulated as sub-assemblies. Robotic operations with standard, single-tip AFMs have low throughput, and are useful primarily for prototyping. Largescale production requires massively parallel tip arrays, which are under development at several laboratories.

Testing of Nanomaterials

The most common context for nanotechnology is within manufacturing engineering, where nanotechnology has evolved gradually from microtechnology. Here any physical phenomenon, functional behaviour of a technical process or product, to be subsumed under the term nanotechnology depends on at least one-dimensional quantity (critical quantity) that is expressed in the length unit nanometer (1 nm is 10^{-9}m and one μm is 10^{-6} m).

This characterisation includes the investigation and manufacture of any mechanical, electronic, chemical, and biological system by molecular assembly, the so-called bottom-up approach, as well as the so-called top-down approach by miniaturisation of processes and products, like machining and multi step processes of bulk materials, e.g. optical components of form precision and surface integrity with nanometer and even subnanometer accuracy for ultra violet (UV) and extended ultraviolet (EUV) lithography. The critical dimension is to be read as that interesting dimension of a specimen that is important for its function, and not necessarily restricted to very small-sized samples. Examples of critical dimensions are:

— Roughness of a sheet metal for car body production where paintability is the required function

— The edge in an optical filter for telecommunication, where the edge itself may be several mm

— Porosity of polymer molecular membranes for advanced drug delivery

— Distances in molecules, where the function is associated with a particular configuration.

The continuous miniaturisation in manufacturing technologies now allows fabrication of nano-sized samples as well as nanoscale precision and nanoscale features. This progress is achieved by a variety of techniques such as ultra precision grinding and honing of automotive parts, plasma and ion beam finish of UV and EUV for a new generation of optics lithography, beam sputtering, and photolithography as well as molecular manipulation.

Nano-technology products are now found in pharmaceutical industry, microelectronics, and in precision engineering. Nano-technology is not only a simple continuation of micro technology. It marks the ultimate end of materials science (where properties of individual atoms disappear for the benefit of the continuum of many atoms), namely the dimensions where materials properties stop and molecular properties start. One can also say that nano-technology is where molecular features (including atoms) and materials meet. However, the relevance of molecular features is often implicit. Whereas the study of DNA is obviously related to nano-technology, the "nano"-aspects of sheet metal for its paintability, and the "nano"-aspects of a honed car-engine cylinder easily escaped the uninitiated eye. Nevertheless the two latter examples have been projects within measurement and testing under previous framework programmes.

To support nano technology in the above sense with measurement and testing means to provide "rulers" that allow measurements of very small dimensions. These rulers must measure "correctly" meaning that they must be traceable to the definition of the meter in the SI. Also the angle must be measured to characterise dimensions correctly.

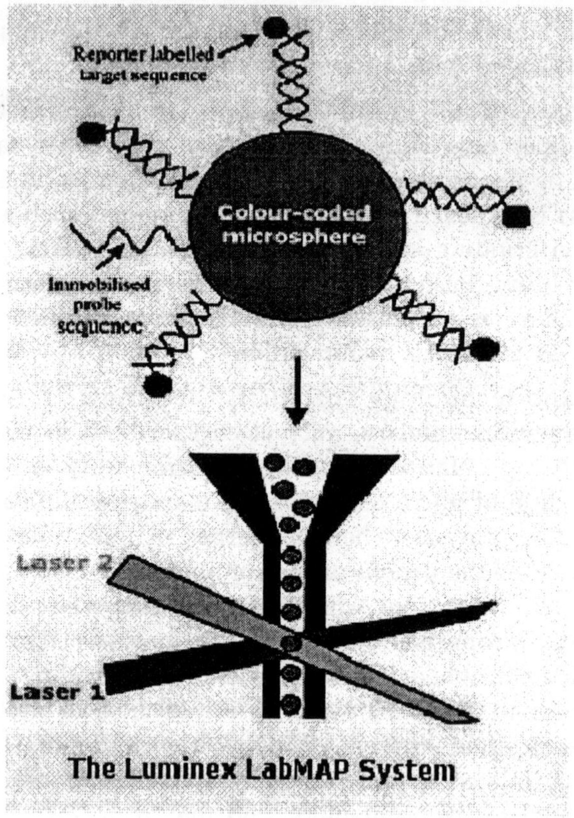

Figure 4. Conceptual device to detect DNA sequence changes at the single base-pair level

Measurement and Testing

To demonstrate that any product or manufacturing process meets a specified functional demand requires quantitative measurements traceable to an agreed metrology scale.

Hence, to bring nanotechnology into a successful business, calls for access to the relevant metrology tools that give ability to measure in three dimensions with atomic resolution over large areas.

Measurements are required of all important physical, chemical and biological quantities at various stages in the development of nanosystems, from design, prototype evaluation, and implementation. Therefore, nanometrology should be seen as an indispensable part of nanotechnology. It should develop hand in hand with the development of nano-science and -technology, respectively.

In order to apply practical metrology the field of nano technology i.e. to make measurement in the nanometer range traceable to the SI units (of length, angle, quantity of matter, and force) practical measurement standards must be constructed. So far the following areas have been identified:

— Written standards
— Scientific instrumentation.
— Validated measurement methods
— Measurement standards
— Chemical analysis
— Biology

It is also important to notice that nano technology will be a global enterprise. Therefore, standards—both written and measurement standards - should be developed in global consensus. In particular, efforts in the US and EU should be coordinated. It goes without saying that nano-metrology without nano-technology is not meaningful. Without a measurement-demanding technology there is no need for metrology; but further, practical nanometrology relies to a large degree upon the technology to manufacture practical standards.

Hence written standards are necessary and must be from the very beginning international—at least European—

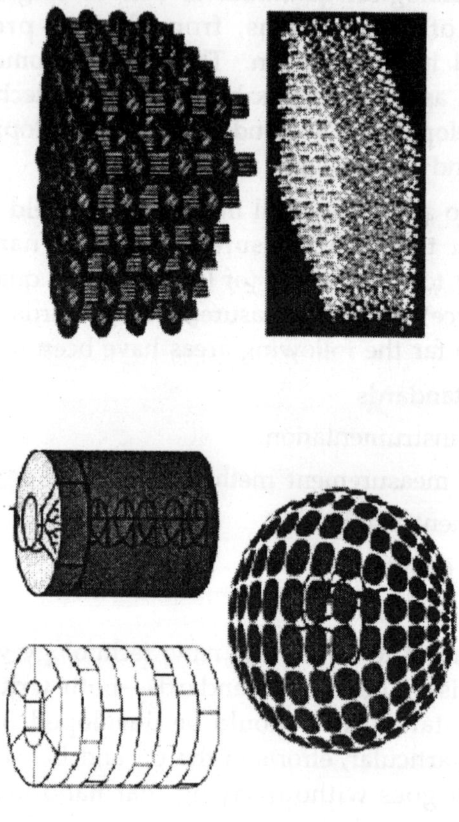

Figure 5. Nano-sized polymers self-assembling into functional structures.

standards. As far as possible, those standards should be included in the format of existing standards, e. g. for dimensional specifications it should be implemented into the format of the GPS (Geometric Product Specifications). In general it seems to us necessary to generate or support pre-normative research, which should have unequivocally a European dimension.

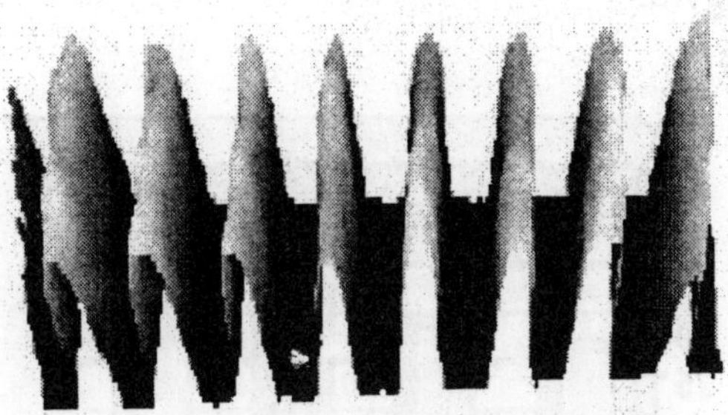

Figure 6. Ridges of photoresist on silicon wafer approximately 80nm high, approximately 100 nm wide and spaced with approximately 250nm

Reliability of and confidence in measuring results depend strongly on the experience, gained from collaboration and knowledge about what partners are doing. Measurement standards and standard instruments have turned out to being very important measures for establishing reliability and confidence. This seems to be a particular challenge and is combined with manifold difficulties, because the nanometer range (0.1 nm till 100 nm) is that area where the atomic world starts and continuum mechanics ends. This transient area is the so-called mesoscopic area, where it is extremely difficult to describe the interaction of sensors with the measurand precisely. But this is a necessary precondition to derive from this interaction correct and reliable measurement results. Physical standards for surface roughness, subsurface properties, form (flatness, sphericity, asphericity) glass, ceramics and metals are urgently needed. Besides those standards, made of anorganic materials, equivalent standards are very desired for nanotechnology in all kind of processes (manufacture, monitoring, measurement) of organic materials including living cells in special cases. Several member states and applicant countries have set up programmes and networks for nano technology and are actively funding dedicated project, including nano metrologyxi

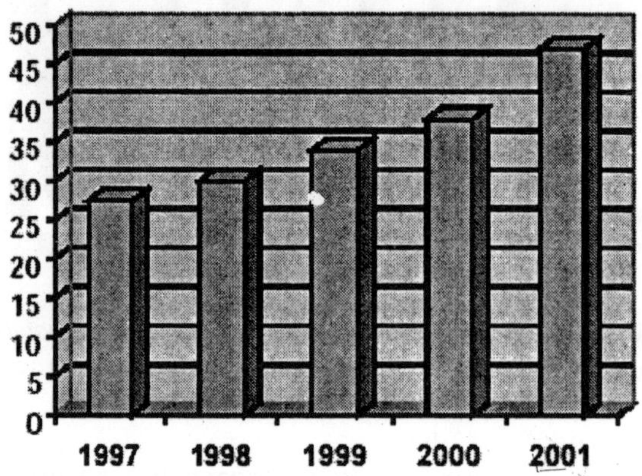

Figure 7. German support for nanotechnology

As an example figure 7 shows the annual funding of the German Government supporting RTD-projects of nano technology for the period 1997 to 2001 However, a coherent European approach is missing and urgently needed for a Europe-wide coordinated development, although the M&T generic activity of the 5th framework programme and its predecessors in the 3rd and 4th framework programmes has funded several projects within nano technology. In few special cases a traceability chain for dimensional measurements in the nm range have been established, so that examples of all five areas have been addressed.

European organisations such as EUROMET (European collaboration on measurement standards), Eurachem, Eurolab (European Federation of National Association of Measurement, Testing, and Analytical; aboratories), and euspen (European Society for Precision engineering and nanotechnology) are addressing various aspects of nano-measurement and testing. EUROMET is investigating in detail the available measurement capabilities and forecasting the needs, and a global workshop is being planned, and a EUROMET project is being formulated to get things started, but these activities are not funded as yet.

Bulk Nanostructured Materials

Bulk nanostructured materials has historical roots going back many decades but has a relatively recent focus due to new discoveries of unique properties of some nanoscale materials. Early in the century, when "microstructures" were revealed primarily with the optical microscope, it was recognised that refined microstructures, for example, small grain sizes, often provided attractive properties such as increased strength and toughness in structural materials. A classic example of property enhancement due to a refined microstructure-with features too small to resolve with the optical microscope-was age hardening of aluminum alloys. The phenomenon, discovered by Alfred Wilm in 1906, was essentially explained by Merica, Waltenberg, and Scott in 1919, and the microstructural features responsible were first inferred by the X-ray studies of Guinier and Preston in 1938.

With the advent of transmission electron microscopy (TEM) and sophisticated X-ray diffraction methods it is now known that the fine precipitates responsible for age hardening, in Al-4% Cu alloys, for example, are clusters of Cu atoms-Guinier-Preston (GP) zones-and the metastable partially coherent θ' precipitate. Maximum hardness is observed with a mixture of GPII (or θ") (coarsened GP zones) and θ' with the dimensions of the θ' plates, typically about 10 nm in thickness by 100 nm in diameter.

Therefore, the important microstructural feature of age-hardened aluminum alloys is nanoscale. There are a number of other examples of nanoscale microstructures providing optimised properties. The critical current density JC of commercial superconducting Nb_3Sn is controlled by grain size and is inversely proportional to grain size, with grain sizes of 50-80 nm providing high values of JC.

The field of nanocrystalline (or nanostructured, or nanophase) materials as a major identifiable activity in modern materials science results to a large degree from the work in the 1980s of Gleiter and coworkers, who synthesised ultrafine-grained materials by the in situ consolidation of nanoscale atomic clusters. The ultrasmall size (< 100 nm) of the grains in these nanocrystalline materials can result in dramatically improved-or different-properties from conventional grain-size (> 1 μm) polycrystalline or single crystal materials of the same chemical composition.

This is the stimulus for the tremendous appeal of these materials. While there are a number of bulk properties that may be dramatically changed when the microstructure is nanoscale. These are

(1) the mechanical properties of nanostructured materials for a variety of potential structural applications, and

(2) ferromagnetic materials with nanoscale microstructures for potential applications as soft magnetic materials and permanent magnet materials, and for other special applications such as information storage, magnetoresistance spin valves, and magnetic nanocomposite refrigerants.

Structural Nanostructures Materials

The great interest in the mechanical behaviour of

nanostructured materials originates from the unique mechanical properties first observed and/or predicted for the materials prepared by the gas condensation method. Among these early observations were the following:

— lower elastic moduli than for conventional grain size materials-by as much as 30 - 50%

— very high hardness and strength-hardness values for nanocrystalline pure metals (~ 10 nm grain size) are 2 to 7 times higher than those of larger grained (>1 mm) metals

— a negative Hall-Petch slope, i.e., decreasing hardness with decreasing grain size in the nanoscale grain size regime

— ductility-perhaps superplastic behaviour-at low homologous temperatures in brittle ceramics or intermetallics with nanoscale grain sizes, believed due to diffusional deformation mechanisms.

Measurement of elastic constants

Early measurements of the elastic constants on nanocrystalline (nc) materials prepared by the inert gas condensation method gave values, for example for Young's Modulus, *E*, that were significantly lower than values for conventional grain size materials. While various reasons were given for the lower values of *E*, it was suggested by Krstic and coworkers that the presence of extrinsic defects-pores and cracks, for example-was responsible for the low values of E in nc materials compacted from powders. The observation that nc NiP produced by electroplating with negligible porosity levels had an *E* value comparable to fully dense conventional grain size Ni. Subsequent work on porosity-free materials has supported these conclusions, and it is now believed that the intrinsic elastic moduli of nanostructured materials are essentially the same as those for conventional grain size materials until the grain size becomes very small, e.g., < 5 nm, such that the number of atoms associated with the grain boundaries and triple junctions becomes very large.

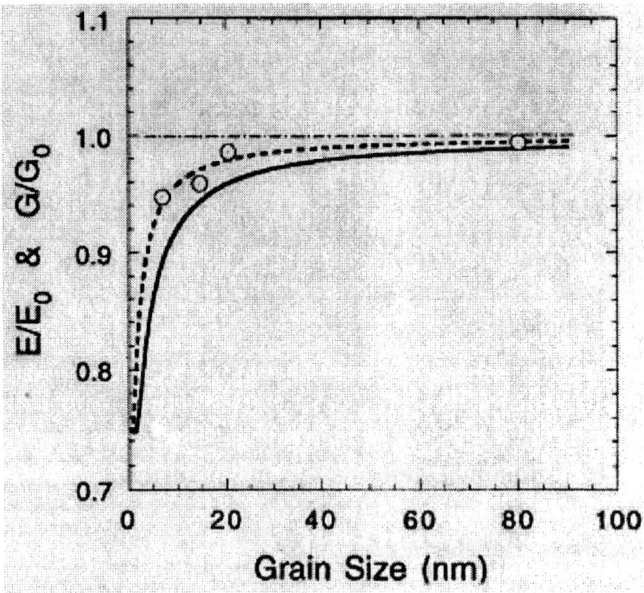

Figure 8. Ratio of the Young's (E) and shear (G) moduli of nanocrystalline materials to those of conventional grain size materials as a function of grain size

This is illustrated in Figure 8 for nanocrystalline Fe prepared by mechanical attrition and measured by a nano-indentation technique. Thus, for most nanostructured materials (grain size > 10 nm), the elastic moduli are not unique properties and not a "negative."

Superplastic behaviour

Superplasticity is the capability of some polycrystalline materials to exhibit very large tensile deformations without necking or fracture. Typically, elongations of 100% to > 1000% are considered the defining features of this phenomenon. As grain size is decreased it is found that the temperature is lowered at which superplasticity occurs, and the strain rate for its occurrence is increased. As discussed previously, Equation 1 suggests that creep rates might be enhanced by many orders of magnitude and superplastic behaviour might be observed in nc materials at temperatures much lower than 0.5 T_M. As mentioned above, actual creep experiments have not borne out this prediction, but instead have shown creep rates (Equation 1) comparable to or lower than those in coarse-grained samples of the same material. This is presumably why little enhancement in ductility or superplastic behaviour has been observed for nc materials at temperatures < 0.5 T_M. However, there is evidence of enhancement of superplastic behaviour in nc materials at temperatures > 0.5 T_M.

Superplasticity has been observed at somewhat lower temperatures and at higher strain rates in nc materials. The evidence for tensile superplasticity is limited and observed typically at temperatures greater than 0.5 T_M and in materials that exhibit superplasticity in coarser grain sizes (1-10 μm). For example, Mishra et al. observed superplastic behaviour in nc Pb-62%Sn at 0.64 T_M and nc Zn-22%Al at 0.52 to 0.60 T_M. However, Salishekev et al observed superplastic behaviour in submicron-200 nm-Ti and several Ti and Ni base alloys.

Here, superplasticity (190% elongation, m = 0.32) was observed in Ti at 0.42 T_M. This was at a temperature 50°C lower than for 10 μm grain size Ti. The flow stress for the 200 nm Ti at 550°C was 90 MPa, compared to 120 MPa for 10 μm Ti at 600°C. Very recently, Mishra and Mukherjee have observed superplastic behaviour in Ni3Al with a 50 nm grain size at temperatures of 0.56 to 0.60 TM to strains of 300 - 600%, but with unusual stress-strain behaviour and significant apparent strain-hardening. These new results suggest very different mechanisms may be causing superplastic behaviour in these nc materials.

While there are still only limited data on the mechanical behaviour-especially tensile properties-of nc materials, some generalisations may be made regarding the deformation mechanisms. It is likely that for the larger end of the nanoscale grain sizes, about 50 - 100 nm, dislocation activity dominates for test temperatures < 0.5 T_M. As grain size decreases, dislocation activity apparently decreases. The essential lack of dislocations at grain sizes below 50 nm is presumably the result of the image forces that act on dislocations near surfaces or interfaces. The lack of dislocations in small, confined spaces such as single-crystal whiskers has been known for many years. Creation of new dislocations is also made difficult as the grain size reaches the lower end of the nanoscale (< 10 nm). Stresses needed to activate dislocation sources, such as the Frank-Read source, are inversely proportional to the distance between dislocation pinning points.

Since nanoscale grains will limit the distance between such pinning points, the stresses to activate dislocation sources can reach the theoretical shear stress of a dislocation-free crystal at the smallest grain sizes (~ 2 nm). Thus, at the smallest grain sizes we may have new phenomena controlling deformation behaviour. It has been suggested that such phenomena may involve grain boundary sliding and/or grain rotation accompanied by short-range diffusion-assisted healing events. Several examples of deformation by shear banding have been reported for nc materials.

Carsley et al have studied nc Fe-10% Cu alloys with grain sizes ranging from 45 to 1,680 nm. In all cases, deformation in compression proceeds by intense localised shear banding. The stress-strain curves exhibited essentially elastic, perfectly plastic behaviour; that is, no measurable strain hardening was observed. Shear banding is also the deformation mode observed in amorphous metallic alloys and amorphous polymers. The deformation shear banding in nc Fe-10% Cu was compared to that for metallic glasses, amorphous polymers, and coarsegrained polycrystalline metals after significant plasticity and work hardening had taken place. While this suggests a close similarity between deformation in nc materials and amorphous materials, not all tensile data on nc materials exhibit a lack of strain hardening.

Applications for nc Materials

Of the present or near-term applications for nc materials, the hard material WC/Co is an example of several important trends. Nanostructured WC/Co composites have been prepared that can have the following characteristics:

— nanoscale grain sizes after consolidation of powder

— hardness values about twice that of conventional micrograined WC/Co

— enhanced wear resistance and cutting performance

Single-phase nanostructured materials studied to date have exhibited high strength and hardness but brittle behaviour at low homologous temperatures (< 0.5 TM). WC/Co two-phase nanostructured materials suggest that the combination of high hardness/strength and toughness/ductility may be possible in multiphase nanostructured materials. Inoue and coworkers have synthesised a variety of multiphase Al, Mg, and Ni-base alloys with nanoscale microstructures.

Many of these alloys consist of nanocrystallites in an amorphous matrix. Some Al-rich alloys contain nanoscale quasi-crystalline particles surrounded by crystalline face-centered cubic Al. The fascinating properties of these multiphase nanostructured alloys include extremely high strength coupled with some ductility. Ductility is high in compression, but uniform elongation in tension is limited.

Again, this behaviour is analogous to that exhibited by ductile amorphous alloys. These results again suggest the possibility for development of nanostructured multiphase composites that combine extremely high hardness and strength with toughness and ductility. Such materials could have many applications as unique structural materials. Multiphase ceramic nanocomposites are the focus of several efforts. While "low temperature" superplasticity has not been realised in nanostructured materials, enhanced superplastic behaviour has been observed at elevated temperatures in terms of a somewhat lower temperature range for superplasticity and, perhaps more significant, a higher strain rate regime. While much needs to be understood about superplastic behaviour of nanostructured materials, the possibility for using more conventional strain rates for forming has major industrial implications. This is of particular interest for near net shape forming of ceramics.

Opportunities and Challenges

The mechanical behaviour of nanostructured materials is the lack of understanding of the mechanisms for plastic deformation and fracture in these materials. An extensive experimental and theoretical research effort should be applied to solve these questions. Only with such understanding can the intelligent design of nanostructured materials with optimum mechanical properties be realised. Since many of the synthesis routes for nanostructured materials involve using powder or particulate products, compaction of such powders is needed to form bulk parts without coarsening the nanoscale microstructure. While there has been ongoing work on compaction and the thermal stability of nanocrystalline microstructures, more basic work is needed in this critical area.

If some unique properties are limited to the finest grain sizes, methods must be found to stabilise the grain size while attaining theoretical density and complete particulate bonding. Furthermore, conventional processing methods are desirable if realistic scaleup and economy are to be realised. Near-term opportunities for structural applications of nanostructured materials are in the form of coatings prepared by, for example, thermal spray deposition or electrodeposition. There is a significant effort in the United States on thermal spray deposition of nc materials. Several groups in Canada lead in deposition of nc materials by electrodeposition methods.

A spin-off company, Nanometals, formed under the auspices of Parteq Research and Development Innovations, has adopted a commercial electrodeposition method to produce nanostructured metals. Structural applications of nanostructured materials may be viewed as a focused approach to a long standing, well known design of materials with optimum mechanical properties. Use of nanoscale precipitates or dispersoids has been known for decades to improve mechanical behaviour. The "new" emphasis on using nanostructured materials comes from 2 significant factors:

1. the special processing methods to push microstructures to the limits of the nanoscale
2. the unique properties and phenomena-as yet not well understood-when this limit is approached

Ferromagnetic Nanostructured Materials

The discovery of nanocrystalline Fe-based soft magnetic materials is less than ten years old. The first class of such materials was the melt-spun Fe-Si-B alloys containing small amounts of Nb and Cu. The Fe-Si-B-Nb-Cu amorphous phase transforms to a body-centered cubic (bcc) Fe-Si solid solution with grain sizes of about 10 nm during annealing at temperatures above the crystallisation temperature.

The presence of small amounts of Cu helps increase the nucleation rate of the bcc phase while Nb retards the grain growth. These "Finemet" alloys provide low core losses (even lower than amorphous soft magnetic alloys such as Co-Fe-Si-B), exhibit saturation induction of about 1.2 T, and exhibit very good properties at high frequencies, comparable to the best Co-based amorphous alloys. These were first developed in Japan and have stimulated a large amount of research and development worldwide to optimise the magnetic properties. There has been relatively little work in the United States in this area, however.

While many of the soft magnetic properties of Finemet-type nanocrystalline alloys are superior, they exhibit lower saturation inductions than Fe-metalloid amorphous alloys, mainly because of the lower Fe content to attain amorphisation and because of the addition of Nb and Cu (or other elements to control the nucleation and growth kinetics). In order to remedy this problem, another class of Fe-based nanocrystalline alloys was developed by Inoue and coworkers at Tohoku University, which is commercialised by Alps Electric Co., Ltd., of Nagaoka, Japan. These "Nanoperm" alloys are based on the Fe-Zr-B system; they contain larger concentrations of Fe (83-89 at.%) compared to the Finemet alloys (~ 74 at.% Fe) and have higher values of saturation induction.

The Nanoperm nc alloys have very low energy losses at power frequencies (60 Hz), making them potentially interesting for electrical power distribution transformers.

While there has been extensive research on these alloys, particularly in Japan and Europe, most of the development has been carried out in Japan. The Finemet family of alloys is marketed by Hitachi Special Metals. Vacuumschmelze GmbH (Germany) and Impky (France) also market similar alloys. The Nanoperm alloys are being commercialised by Alps Electric Co. (Japan). No extensive research nor any commercialisation of these materials has been carried out in the United States.

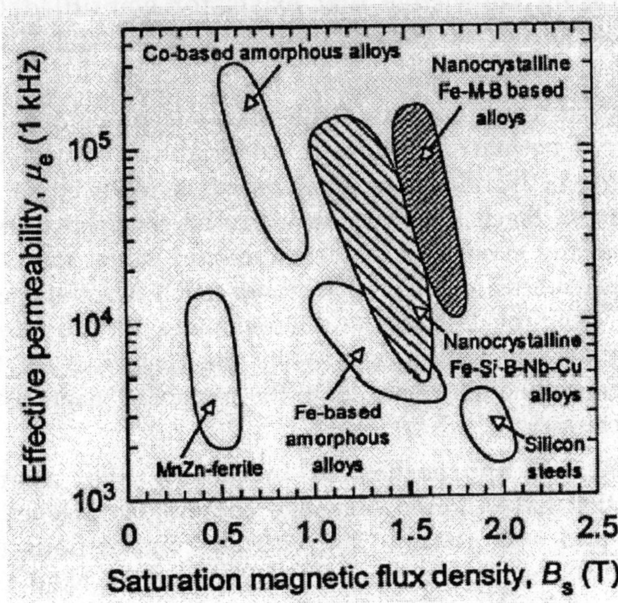

Figure 9. Effective permeability, μ_e, vs. saturation magnetic flux density, B_s, for soft ferromagnetic materials

The small single-domain nanocrystalline Fe particles in the amorphous matrix gives these alloys their unique magnetic behaviour, the most dramatic being the lowest energy losses (narrowest B/H hysteresis loop) of any known materials, along with very high permeabilities. These alloys can also exhibit nearly or exactly zero magnetostriction.

To date, these materials have been made by crystallisation of rapidly solidified amorphous ribbons. Other methods that might provide geometrically desirable products should be explored or developed. Electrodeposition is one such method that requires further work. Electrodeposited nc Fe-Ni soft magnetic alloys are being developed in Canada. The brittle nature of these materials is a problem for scaleup and transformer manufacture. The brittleness problem must be solved by finding less brittle materials or applying the handling and processing knowledge that exists for embrittled (after annealing) metallic glasses.

The first attempts to produce nanoscale microstructures to enhance the magnetic properties of the Nb-Fe-B permanent magnetic materials used mechanical alloying of blended elemental powders followed by heat treatment. Since the grain structure so obtained does not exhibit any crystallographic texture-and limits the energy product-special processing methods such as die-upsetting were used by Schultz and coworkers to provide the crystallographic anisotropy. While the .coercivities of these nanocrystalline alloys are high, the remanent magnetisation is decreased.

Recent approaches to increasing the magnetic induction have utilised exchange coupling in magnetically hard and soft phases. The Fe-rich compositions (e.g., $Fe_{90}Nd_7B_3$) result in a mixture of the hard $Fe_{14}Nd_2B$ phase and soft aFe phase. The nanoscale two-phase mixtures of a hard magnetic phase and a soft magnetic phase can exhibit values of remanent magnetisation, M_r, significantly greater than the isotropic value of 0.5 M_s. This "remanence enhancement" is associated with exchange coupling between the hard and soft phases, which forces the magnetisation vector of the soft phase to be rotated to that of the hard phase. Two important requirements for alloys to exhibit remanence enhancement are a nanocrystalline grain size and a degree of coherence across interphase boundaries sufficient to enable adjacent phases to be exchange-coupled.

The significant feature of the exchange coupling is that it allows crystallographically isotropic materials to exhibit remanence values approaching those achieved after full alignment. Such two-phase nanoscale ferromagnetic alloys have been prepared by nonequilibrium methods such as melt-spinning, mechanical alloying, and sputter deposition. Besides the high reduced remanence, the material cost is reduced by reduction in the content of the expensive hard rare earth-containing magnetic phase. The theoretical understanding of remanence enhancement appears to be developed to a degree enabling prediction of magnet performance; however, this performance, while a significant improvement over single-phase isotropic magnets, does not reach predicted values.

Work is required on optimising the orientation relationships between the hard and soft phases and the interphase properties (coherency) between them. Research on nanocrystalline hard magnetic alloys has received attention worldwide. While less research seems to be carried out in the world on these materials compared to the nanocrystalline soft magnetic alloys, some efforts exist in most countries. While the very low losses of the nc soft magnetic materials (Finemet or Nanoperm) are dependent on grain size for their properties, the hard magnetic nc alloys with remanence enhancement provide flexibility in processing, especially with powder materials. These remanence-enhanced nc hard magnetic alloys may find many applications as permanent magnet components.

Ferromagnetic Nanocrystalline Materials

Magnetic nanocomposite refrigerants, which have four times the magnetocaloric effects of the best low temperature magnetic refrigerant, were developed by NIST and described by R. Shull. The entropy change at a given (low) temperature for a system of magnetic spins is enhanced when the isolated spins are clustered. Shull et al. have shown that the nanocomposite $Gd_3Ga_{5-x}Fe_xO_{12}$ gives superior magnetocaloric effects, which increase with x up to x = 2.5 and can be extended to higher temperatures than conventional materials.

Magnetostrictive materials such as Terfonol-D ($Tb_{0.3}Dy_{0.7}Fe_2$) have been of scientific and technological interest in recent years. It is suggested by G.C. Hadjipanayis that nanostructured magnetostrictive materials can have improved properties, such as lower saturation fields, with reduced anisotropy and in multilayers with alternate layers of magnetostrictive and soft magnetic materials that are exchange-coupled. Nanocrystalline magnetic materials offer perhaps the nearest-term prospect of significant applications of bulk nanostructured materials.

The remanence enhancement in two-phase hard/soft magnetic materials can result in excellent energy products-comparable to those from rapid solidification processing routes-in powder composites. The flexibility in manufacturing this allows should provide many possible permanent magnet applications.Nanocrystalline soft magnetic materials have the lowest energy losses of any material. While problems such as mechanical brittleness remain, these materials promise to replace existing transformer core materials for power applications. The U.S. research and industrial effort in these materials lags the efforts in Japan.

8
Nanotechnology in Healthcare

Nanotechnology will bring a fundamental breakthrough in medicine. Physicians now rely chiefly on surgery and drugs to treat illness. Surgeons have advanced from stitching wounds and amputating limbs to repairing hearts and re-attaching limbs. Using microscopes and fine tools, they join delicate blood vessels and nerves. Yet even the best micro-surgeon cannot cut and stitch finer tissue structures. Modern scalpels and sutures are simply too coarse for repairing capillaries, cells, and molecules. Consider "delicate" surgery from a cell's perspective a huge blade sweeps down, chopping blindly past and through the molecular machinery of a crowd of cells, slaughtering thousands.

Later, a great obelisk plunges through the divided crowd, dragging a cable as wide as a freight train behind it to rope the crowd together again. From a cell's perspective, even the most delicate surgery, performed with exquisite knives and great skill, is still a butcher job. Only the ability of cells to abandon their dead, regroup, and multiply makes healing possible. Yet as many paralysed accident victims know too well, not all tissues heal. Drug therapy, unlike surgery, deals with the finest structures in cells. Drug molecules are simple molecular devices. Many affect specific molecules in cells. Morphine molecules, for example, bind to certain receptor molecules in brain cells, affecting the neural impulses that signal pain. Insulin, beta blockers, and other drugs fit other receptors. But drug molecules work without direction. Once dumped into the body, they tumble and bump around in solution haphazardly until they bump a target molecule, fit, and stick, affecting its function. Surgeons can see problems and plan actions, but they wield crude tools; drug molecules affect tissues at the molecular level, but they are too simple to sense, plan, and act. But molecular machines directed by nanocomputers will offer physicians another choice. They will combine sensors, programmes, and molecular tools to form systems able to examine and repair the ultimate components of individual cells. They will bring surgical control to the molecular domain.

These advanced molecular devices will be years in arriving, but researchers motivated by medical needs are already studying molecular machines and molecular engineering. The best drugs affect specific molecular machines in specific ways. Penicillin, for example, kills certain bacteria by jamming the nanomachinery they use to build their cell walls, yet it has little effect on human cells. Biochemists study molecular machines both to learn how to build them and to learn how to wreck them. Around the world (and especially the Third World) a disgusting variety of viruses, bacteria, protozoa, fungi, and worms parasitise human flesh. Like penicillin, safe, effective drugs for these diseases would jam the parasite's molecular machinery while leaving human molecular machinery unharmed. Dr. Seymour Cohen, professor of pharmacological science at SUN, argues that biochemists should systematically study the molecular machinery of these parasites. Once biochemists have determined the shape and function of a vital protein machine, they then could often design a molecule shaped to jam it and ruin it. Such drugs could free humanity from such ancient horrors as schistosomiasis and leprosy, and from new ones such as AIDS.

Drug companies are already redesigning molecules based on knowledge of how they work. Researchers at Upjohn Company have designed and made modified molecules of vasopressin, a hormone that consists of a short chain of amino acids. Vasopressin increases the work done by the heart and decreases the rate at which the kidneys produce urine; this increases blood pressure.

The researchers designed modified vasopressin molecules that affected receptor molecules in the kidney more than those in the heart, giving them more specific and controllable medical effects. More recently, they designed a modified vasopressin molecule that binds to the kidney's receptor molecules without direct effect, thus blocking and inhibiting the action of natural vasopressin. Medical needs will push this work forward, encouraging researchers to take further steps toward protein design and molecular engineering. Medical, military, and economic pressures all push us in the same direction.

Even before the assembler breakthrough, molecular technology will bring impressive advances in medicine; trends in biotechnology guarantee it. Still, these advances will generally be piecemeal and hard to predict, each exploiting some detail of biochemistry. Later, when we apply assemblers and technical AI systems to medicine, we will gain broader abilities that are easier to foresee. To understand these abilities, consider cells and their self-repair mechanisms. In the cells of your body, natural radiation and noxious chemicals split molecules, producing reactive molecular fragments. But evolution has favoured organisms with machinery able to do something about this problem. So long as a cell's DNA remains intact, it can make error-free tapes that direct ribosomes to assemble new protein machines. Unfortunately for us, DNA itself becomes damaged, resulting in mutations.

Repair enzymes compensate somewhat by detecting and repairing certain kinds of damage to DNA. These repairs help cells survive, but existing repair mechanisms are too simple to correct all problems, either in DNA or elsewhere. Errors mount, contributing to the aging and death of cells - and of people.

Since we are made of cells, this might seem to reduce human beings to "mere machines," conflicting with a holistic understanding of life. But a dictionary definition of holism is "the theory that reality is made up of organic or unified wholes that are greater than the simple sum of their parts." This certainly applies to people: one simpler sum of our parts would resemble hamburger, lacking both mind and life.

The human body includes some ten thousand billion protein parts, and no machine so complex deserves the label "mere." Any brief description of so complex a system cannot avoid being grossly incomplete, yet at the cellular level a description in terms of machinery makes sense. Molecules have simple moving parts, and many act like familiar types of machinery.

Cells considered as a whole may seem less mechanical, yet biologists find it useful to describe them in terms of molecular machinery. Biochemists have unravelled what were once the central mysteries of life, and have begun to fill in the details. They have traced how molecular machines break food molecules into their building blocks and then reassemble these parts to build and renew tissue. Many details of the structure of human cells remain unknown (single cells have billions of large molecules of thousands of different kinds), but biochemists have mapped every part of some viruses. Biochemical laboratories often sport a large wall chart showing how the chief molecular building blocks flow through bacteria. Biochemists understand much of the process of life in detail, and what they don't understand seems to operate on the same principles. The mystery of heredity has become the industry of genetic engineering. Even embryonic development and memory are being explained in terms of changes in biochemistry and cell structure. In recent decades, the very quality of our remaining ignorance has changed.

In many instances their studies have narrowed the competing explanations to a field of one. Certain biological processes - the coordination of cells to form growing embryos, learning brains, and reacting immune systems - still present a real challenge to the imagination. Yet this is not because of some deep mystery about how their parts work, but because of the immense complexity of how their many parts interact to form a whole. Cells obey the same natural laws that describe the rest of the world. Protein machines in the right molecular environment will work whether they remain in a functioning cell or whether the rest of the cell was ground up and washed away days before.

Molecular machines know nothing of "life" and "death." Biologists - when they bother - sometimes define life as the ability to grow, replicate, and respond to stimuli. But by this standard, a mindless system of replicating factories might qualify as life, while a conscious artificial intelligence modelled on the human brain might not. Biologists who work with viruses instead ask about viability.

Physicians once declared patients dead when the heart stopped; they now declare patients dead when they despair of restoring brain activity. Advances in cardiac medicine changed the definition once; advances in brain medicine will change it again. Just as some people feel uncomfortable with the idea of machines thinking, so some feel uncomfortable with the idea that machines underlie our own thinking.

The word "machine" again seems to conjure up the wrong image, a picture of gross, clanking metal, rather than signals flickering through a shifting weave of neural fibres, through a living tapestry more intricate than the mind it embodies can fully comprehend.

The brain's really machinelike machines are of molecular size, smaller than the finest fibres. A whole need not resemble its parts. A solid lump scarcely resembles a dancing fountain, yet a collection of solid, lumpy molecules forms fluid water. In a similar way, billions of molecular machines make up neural fibres and synapses, thousands of fibres and synapses make up a neural cell, billions of neural cells make up the brain, and the brain itself embodies the fluidity of thought. Being made of molecules, and having a human concern for our health, we will apply molecular machines to biomedical technology.

Biologists already use antibodies to tag proteins, enzymes to cut and splice DNA, and viral syringes (like the T4 phage) to inject edited DNA into bacteria. In the future, they will use assembler-built nanomachines to probe and modify cells. With tools like disassemblers, biologists will be able to study cell structures in ultimate, molecular detail. They then will catalogue the hundreds of thousands of kinds of molecules in the body and map the structure of the hundreds of kinds of cells. Much as engineers might compile a parts list and make engineering drawings for an automobile, so biologists will describe the parts and structures of healthy tissue. By that time, they will be aided by sophisticated technical AI systems. Physicians aim to make tissues healthy, but with drugs and surgery they can only encourage tissues to repair themselves.

Molecular machines will allow more direct repairs, bringing a new era in medicine. To repair a car, a mechanic first reaches the faulty assembly, then identifies and removes the bad parts, and finally rebuilds or replaces them. Cell repair will involve the same basic tasks - tasks that living systems already prove possible.

Access: White blood cells leave the bloodstream and move through tissue, and viruses enter cells. Biologists even poke needles into cells without killing them. These examples show that molecular machines can reach and enter cells.

Recognition: Antibodies and the tail fibres of the T4 phage - and indeed, all specific biochemical interactions - show that molecular systems can recognise other molecules by touch.

Disassembly: Digestive enzymes (and other, fiercer chemicals) show that molecular systems can disassemble damaged molecules.

Rebuilding: Replicating cells show that molecular systems can build or rebuild every molecule found in a cell. Reassembly. Nature also shows that separated molecules can be put back together again. The machinery of the T4 phage, for example, self-assembles from solution, apparently aided by a single enzyme. Replicating cells show that molecular systems can assemble every system found in a cell.

Thus, nature demonstrates all the basic operations that are needed to perform molecular-level repairs on cells. Natural systems show us only lower bounds to the possible, in cell repair as in everything else. In short, with molecular technology and technical AI we will compile complete, molecular-level descriptions of healthy tissue, and we will build machines able to enter cells and to sense and modify their structures.

Cell repair machines will be comparable in size to bacteria and viruses, but their more-compact parts will allow them to be more complex. They will travel through tissue as white blood cells do, and enter cells as viruses do - or they could open and close cell membranes with a surgeon's care. Inside a cell, a repair machine will first size up the situation by examining the cell's contents and activity, and then take action.

Early cell repair machines will be highly specialised, able to recognise and correct only a single type of molecular disorder, such as an enzyme deficiency or a form of DNA damage. Later machines (but not much later, with advanced technical AI systems doing the design work) will be programmed with more general abilities. Complex repair machines will need nanocomputers to guide them.

In a repair system, such computers will direct smaller, simpler computers, which will in turn direct machines to examine, take apart, and rebuild damaged molecular structures. By working along molecule by molecule and structure by structure, repair machines will be able to repair whole cells. By working along cell by cell and tissue by tissue, they will be able to repair whole organs. By working through a person organ by organ, they will restore health. Because molecular machines will be able to build molecules and cells from scratch, they will be able to repair even cells damaged to the point of complete inactivity.

Thus, cell repair machines will bring a fundamental breakthrough: they will free medicine from reliance on self-repair as the only path to healing. To visualise an advanced cell repair machine, imagine it - and a cell - enlarged until atoms are the size of small marbles. On this scale, the repair machine's smallest tools have tips about the size of your fingertips; a medium-sized protein, like hemoglobin, is the size of a typewriter; and a ribosome is the size of a washing machine.

A single repair device contains a simple computer the size of a small truck, along with many sensors of protein size, several manipulators of ribosome size, and provisions for memory and motive power. A total volume ten meters across, the size of a three-story house, holds all these parts and more. With parts the size of marbles packing this volume, the repair machine can do complex things. But this repair device does not work alone. It, like its many siblings, is connected to a larger computer by means of mechanical data links the diameter of your arm. On this scale, a cubic-micron computer with a large memory fills a volume thirty stories high and as wide as a football field.

The repair devices pass it information, and it passes back general instructions. Objects so large and complex are still small enough: on this scale, the cell itself is a kilometer across, holding one thousand times the volume of a cubic-micron computer, or a million times the volume of a single repair device. Cells are spacious. Existing molecular machines demonstrate the ability to travel through tissue, enter cells, recognise molecular structures, and so forth, but other requirements are also important.

The most extensive repairs cannot require vastly more work than building a cell from scratch. Yet molecular machinery working within a cellular volume routinely does just that, building a new cell in tens of minutes (in bacteria) to a few hours (in mammals). This indicates that repair machinery occupying a few percent of a cells volume will be able to complete even extensive repairs in a reasonable time—days or weeks at most.

Cells can spare this much room. Even brain cells can still function when an inert waste called lipofuscin fills over ten percent of their volume. Powering repair devices will be easy cells naturally contain chemicals that power nanomachinery. Nature also shows that repair machines can be cooled: the cells in your body rework themselves steadily, and young animals grow swiftly without cooking themselves.

Handling heat from a similar level of activity by repair machines will be no sweat—or at least not too much sweat, if a week of sweating is the price of health. All these comparisons of repair machines to existing biological mechanisms raise the question of whether repair machines will be able to improve on nature. Just as an illiterate "book-repair machine" could recognise and repair a torn page, so a cell's repair enzymes can recognise and repair breaks and cross-links in DNA. Correcting misspellings (or mutations), though, would require an ability to read. Nature lacks such repair machines, but they will be easy to build.

Imagine three identical DNA molecules, each with the same sequence of nucleotides. Now imagine each strand mutated to change a few scattered nucleotides. Each strand still seems normal, taken by itself.

Nonetheless, a repair machine could compare each strand to the others, one segment at a time, and could note when a nucleotide failed to match its mates. Changing the odd nucleotide to match the other two will then repair the damage. This method will fail if two strands mutate in the same spot. Imagine that the DNA of three human cells has been heavily damaged - after thousands of mutations, each cell has had one in every million nucleotides changed. The chance of our three-strand correction procedure failing at any given spot is then about one in a million. But compare five strands at once, and the odds become about one in a million million million, and so on.

A device that compares many strands will make the chance of an uncorrectable error effectively nil. In practice, repair machines will compare DNA molecules from several cells, make corrected copies, and use these as standards for proofreading and repairing DNA throughout a tissue. By comparing several strands, repair machines will dramatically improve on nature's repair enzymes.

Other repairs will require different information about healthy cells and about how a particular damaged cell differs from the norm. Antibodies identify proteins by touch, and properly chosen antibodies can generally distinguish any two proteins by their differing shapes and surface properties. Repair machines will identify molecules in a similar way. With a suitable computer and data base, they will be able to identify proteins by reading their amino acid sequences. Consider a complex and capable repair system. A volume of two cubic microns—about 2/1000 of the volume of a typical cell—will be enough to hold a central data base system able to:

— Swiftly identify any of the hundred thousand or so different human proteins by examining a short amino acid sequence.

— Identify all the other complex molecules normally found in cells.

— Record the type and position of every large molecule in the cell.

Each of the smaller repair devices (of perhaps thousands in a cell) will include a less capable computer. Each of these computers will be able to perform over a thousand computational steps in the time that a typical enzyme takes to change a single molecular bond, so the speed of computation possible seems more than adequate. Because each computer will be in communication with a larger computer and the central data base, the available memory seems adequate.

Cell repair machines will have both the molecular tools they need and "brains" enough to decide how to use them. Such sophistication will be overkill for many health problems. Devices that merely recognise and destroy a specific kind of cell, for example, will be enough to cure a cancer. Placing a computer network in every cell may seem like slicing butter with a chain saw, but having a chain saw available does provide assurance that even hard butter can be sliced. It seems better to show too much than too little, if one aims to describe the limits of the possible in medicine. The simplest medical applications of nanomachines will involve not repair but selective destruction.

Cancers provide one example; infectious diseases provide another. The goal is simple one need only recognise and destroy the dangerous replicators, whether they are bacteria, cancer cells, viruses, or worms. Similarly, abnormal growths and deposits on arterial walls cause much heart disease; machines that recognise, break down, and dispose of them will clear arteries for more normal blood flow.

Selective destruction will also cure diseases such as herpes in which a virus splices its genes into the DNA of a host cell.

A repair device will enter the cell, read its DNA, and remove the addition that spells "herpes." Repairing damaged, cross-linked molecules will also be fairly straightforward. Faced with a damaged, cross linked protein, a cell repair machine will first identify it by examining short amino acid sequences, then look up its correct structure in a data base. The machine will then compare the protein to this blueprint, one amino acid at a time. Like a proofreader finding misspellings and strange characters, it will find any changed amino acids or improper cross-links. By correcting these flaws, it will leave a normal protein, ready to do the work of the cell.

Repair machines will also aid healing. After a heart attack, scar tissue replaces dead muscle. Repair machines will stimulate the heart to grow fresh muscle by resetting cellular control mechanisms. By removing scar tissue and guiding fresh growth, they will direct the healing of the heart.This list could continue through problem after problem but the conclusion is easy to summarise. Physical disorders stem from mis-arranged atoms; repair machines will be able to return them to working order, restoring the body to health. Rather than compiling an endless list of curable diseases it makes sense to look for the limits to what cell repair machines can do.

Consider stroke, as one example of a problem that damages the brain. Then pull it back into shape and guide the growth of reinforcing fibres. Then dissolve the clots and normalise the blood and blood-vessel linings to prevent a recurrence. Moderate neural damage from stroke will also be repairable if reduced circulation has impaired function but left cell structures intact, then restore circulation and repair the cells, using their structures as a guide in restoring the tissue to its previous state. This will not only restore each cell's function, but will preserve the memories and skills embodied in the neural patterns in that part of the brain. Repair machines will be able to regenerate fresh brain tissue even where damage has obliterated these patterns.

But the patient would lose old memories and skills to the extent that they resided in that part of the brain. If unique neural patterns are truly obliterated, then cell repair machines could no more restore them than art conservators could restore a tapestry from stirred ash. Loss of information through obliteration of structure imposes the most important, fundamental limit to the repair of tissue. Other tasks are beyond cell repair machines for different reasons - maintaining mental health, for instance. Cell repair machines will be able to correct some problems, of course.

Deranged thinking sometimes has biochemical causes, as if the brain were drugging or poisoning itself, and other problems stem from tissue damage. But many problems have little to do with the health of nerve cells and everything to do with the health of the mind. Spilled ink or flood damage may harm the book, making the novel difficult to read. Book repair machines could nonetheless restore physical "health" by removing the foreign ink or by drying and repairing the damaged paper fibres. Such treatments would do nothing for the book's content, however, which in a real sense is nonphysical. If the book were a cheap romance with a moldy plot and empty characters, repairs would be needed not on the ink and paper, but on the novel. This would call not for physical repairs, but for more work by the author, perhaps with advice.

Similarly, removing poisons from the brain and repairing its nerve fibres will thin some mental fogs, but not revise the content of the mind. This can be changed by the patient, with effort; we are all authors of our minds. But because minds change themselves by changing their brains, having a healthy brain will aid sound thinking more than quality paper aids sound writing.

Readers familiar with computers may prefer to think in terms of hardware and software. A machine could repair a computer's hardware while neither understanding nor changing its software Such machines might stop the computer's activity but leave the patterns in memory intact and ready to work again. Physicians already stop and restart consciousness by interfering with the chemical activity that underlies the mind. Throughout active life, molecular machines in the brain process molecules. Some disassemble sugars, combine them with oxygen, and capture the energy this releases.

Some pump salt ions across cell membranes; others build small molecules and release them to signal other cells. Such processes make up the brain's metabolism, the sum total of its chemical activity. Together with its electrical effects, this metabolic activity underlies the changing patterns of thought. Surgeons cut people with knives. In the mid-1800s, they learned to use chemicals that interfere with brain metabolism, blocking conscious thought and preventing patients from objecting so vigorously to being cut. These chemicals are anesthetics. Their molecules freely enter and leave the brain, allowing anesthetists to interrupt and restart human consciousness. People have long dreamed of discovering a drug that interferes with the metabolism of the entire body, a drug able to interrupt metabolism completely for hours, days, or years. The result would be a condition of biostasis.

A method of producing reversible biostasis could help astronauts on long space voyages to save food and avoid boredom, or it could serve as a kind of one-way time travel. In medicine, biostasis would provide a deep anesthesia giving physicians more time to work. When emergencies occur far from medical help, a good biostasis procedure would provide a sort of universal first-aid treatment: it would stabilise a patient's condition and prevent molecular machines from running amok and damaging tissues. But no one has found a drug able to stop the entire metabolism the way anesthetics stop consciousness—that is, in a way that can be reversed by simply washing the drug out of the patient's tissues.

Nonetheless, reversible biostasis will be possible when repair machines become available. To see how one approach would work, imagine that the blood stream carries simple molecular devices to tissues, where they enter the cells. There they block the molecular machinery of metabolism—in the brain and elsewhere—and tie structures together with stabilising cross-links. Other molecular devices then move in, displacing water and packing themselves solidly around the molecules of the cell. These steps stop metabolism and preserve cell structures. Because cell repair machines will be used to reverse this process, it can cause moderate molecular damage and yet do no lasting harm.

With metabolism stopped and cell structures held firmly in place, the patient will rest quietly, dreamless and unchanging, until repair machines restore active life. If a patient in this condition were turned over to a present-day physician ignorant of the capabilities of cell repair machines, the consequences would likely be grim. Seeing no signs of life, the physician would likely conclude that the patient was dead, and then would make this judgment a reality by "prescribing" an autopsy, followed by burial or burning. The reversibility of biostasis and irreversibility of severe stroke damage help to show how cell repair machines will change medicine.

Today, physicians can only help tissues to heal themselves. Accordingly they must try to preserve the function of tissue. If tissues cannot function, they cannot heal. Worse, unless they are preserved, deterioration follows, ultimately obliterating structure. It is as if a mechanic's tools were able to work only on a running engine. Cell repair machines change the central requirement from preserving function to preserving structure. Biostasis involves preserving neural structure while deliberately blocking function. All this is a direct consequence of the molecular nature of the repairs. Physicians using scalpels and drugs can no more repair cells than someone using only a pickax and a can of oil can repair a fine watch.

Nanotechnology in Health Sector

Nanotechnology is the manipulation or self-assembly of individual atoms, molecules, or molecular clusters into structures to create materials and devices with new or vastly different properties. Nanotechnology can work from the top down (which means reducing the size of the smallest structures to the nanoscale e.g. photonics applications in nanoelectronics and nanoengineering) or the bottom up.

The medicine and healthcare markets are worth hundreds of billions of euros every year. Pharmaceuticals account for the vast majority of this with global sales amounting to $400.6 billion US in 2002. One of the largest sectors in global pharmaceuticals are the blockbuster drugs, which are unique entities each generating in excess of $1 billion US per annum. Generic drugs constitute a smaller but rapidly rising segment of the market (due to loss of patent rights) e.g. in Europe, generic drugs account for 50% of all prescriptions but this is forecast to reach 75% by 2007. Drug delivery systems account for $40 to 50 billion US of the global pharmaceutical sales and it is thought that by 2007 this share will have increased to 39% of total global sales.

Nanobiotechnology is a relatively new segment of these markets however it is expected to grow rapidly to reach over $3 billion US by 2008. The current estimated worldwide market breakdown is: U.S. at 65%, Europe at 20%, Japan at 10%, and the rest of the world at 5%. In terms of investment the medical device sector is smaller, e.g. in Europe, an average of 8.6% of GDP is spent on healthcare and of this, only 6.37% goes to medical technology (i.e. 0.54% of GDP).The sales generated in the medical device markets however, is more considerable and estimated at $55 billion US in 2003.This includes for example the wound closure devices market (which include sutures, staples, sealants and glues) which in Europe and the U.S. is valued at approximately $3.4 billion US, and the in vitro diagnostics market (which includes microarrays, sensors etc) which is predicted to grow to $25 billion by 2004. The main growth area is age-related health care. A poll of delegates at the annual 3i Healthcare CEO conference in Barcelona, revealed that over 70% felt that the increasing elderly population (and associated long-term care) would be the major impetus in the medical devices sector.

According to Jo Taylor, Director and Head of Technology for 3i in the UK: "We expect to see increased investment in the healthcare and biotechnology industry over the next three years, innovation will continue to fuel the sector and provide new opportunities for the market." Of these, nearer-the-patient testing is one of the fastest-growing segments.

Implementation Barriers

These barriers are fall into the following broad categories: cost, manufacturing scale and consumer perception. Cost is a major consideration for the exploitation of nanotechnology, e.g. high purity nanotubes (+95%) cost $400 per gram. Manufacturing advances however are decreasing these costs all the time e.g. five years ago, one gram of low-grade nanotubes cost $1 000, and nowadays the same nanotubes can be bought for $30.

In this respect the scaling up from lab to industry manufacturing processes must be taken into account when assessing time-to-market. This is an important consideration- many nanotechnologies can take years to develop to a marketable product, in which time patents can become invalid, which in turn will have a negative effect on initial venture capital.

Consumer perception is a key issue to the success of nanotechnologies and this is particularly true in the medical and healthcare sectors. There has been much discussion in the media of how nanotechnology may evolve in the future, some of which is fantastical. However the development of implantable smart medical devices that can respond to varying parameters within a patient, and for example alter drug dosage, monitor vital signs such as blood biochemistry, cardiac function and the presence of pathogens, and communicate remotely with a pc will soon be a reality. However, will people accept such implants? And who will govern access to such data, which potentially will be more comprehensive than that measured for most people at present, and ensure that it is used solely for medical treatment and not, for example, passed on to insurers? People in most countries are living longer.

According to European Commission forecasts, by 2020 there will be 40% more people aged 75 and above living in Europe than in 1990. According to the WHO "life expectancies equal or exceed 70 years in 24 countries, and 60 years in over half the Member States of WHO. At the other extreme are 32 countries where disability-adjusted life expectancy is estimated to be less than 40 years. Many of these are countries with major epidemics of HIV/AIDS, among other causes.

All of the bottom 10 countries were in sub-Saharan Africa, where the HIV-AIDS epidemic is rampant and the overall life expectancy has dropped precipitously over the past 10 years."It is important that the advances in nanotechnology that will bring great benefit to medicine and healthcare, do not do so at the expense of humankind and the environment.

The technology gap that may widen between developed and developing countries is a concern, nanotechnology will bring such improvements to healthcare that it should be available for all. Finally the environmental concerns of nanotechnology must be debated from an early stage to avoid such public rejection as was witnessed with GM crops and to address any potential long-term concerns from the breakdown of nanomaterials.

The ongoing miniaturisation of electrical components in the semiconductor industry has led to an enormous price-reduction, an increased performance and a strong dissemination of integrated circuits. The ability to control and to guide extremely small quantities of liquids may evoke a similar progress in biochemical analysis and clinical diagnosis.

Operating with tiny volumes results in an increased processing speed, reduced costs and thus a higher efficiency, especially when handling rare and expensive materials such as DNA samples. In this regard, microfluidic devices or biochips with analytical and functional capabilities and high sample throughput are receiving increased attention. Two different basic approaches can be distinguished for this "miniaturised" biochemical analysis. The first is based on a parallel processing technique, where a huge number of miniaturised test tubes or wells are placed side by side on a plate.

These plates or arrays are commonly named microarrays, for spot sizes below 200 micrometres. Microarrays can be used for diagnostic purposes such as DNA analysis (DNA array, DNA chip or genetic chip) and protein detection (protein array or chip). They offer a high sample throughput due to the simultaneous sample detection, but are limited in their functionality to a single chemical reaction / well. The other approach is based on a serial processing technique, with complex functions integrated on a miniaturised "lab" chip. According to their design, they offer a sequence of different chemical processing and analysis steps, such as mixing of different compounds, synthesis, electrophoreses or chromatography.

These systems are called Lab-on-a-chip devices (LOC) and they perform several processes with a minimum material usage. Furthermore, combinations of microarrays and LOC are possible. Besides the common concepts of miniaturised chemistry mentioned above, other microarray systems exist, such as the cell chip or tissue microarrays. These make use of living cells or tissues which are immobilised in discrete spots on an array and permit rapid drug testing or screening experiments. LOCs may be used for in vitro diagnostics (also called the near patient or Point-of-Care diagnostic) in the future. "Point-of-care" refers to a diagnosis, which is performed on the patient at the bedside in a clinical environment or at the patients home.

In the ideal case, the patient would benefit from this near patient diagnosis immediately, as the LOC, which is effectively a functional miniaturised laboratory, would enable the comprehensive analysis of bodily fluids and allow medical staff to determine the optimal therapy. Therefore, point-of-care biochips may help to reduce or even prevent problems arising from drug side-effects and from antibiotic resistance in individuals. In addition LOCs may reduce costs further by removing the need for sample handling and reporting. Taking more than a decade and a tremendous international effort, the decryption of the human genome (the human genome project, HGP) brought the field of genomics, the study of the functional dependency of genes, to the forefront of science.

This rapid development was based on the capability of processing biological data with high throughput and low costs. In this regard, it is believed that biochips will boost the scientific field of genomics in the future. The next step in understanding cellular biochemistry can be found in proteomics, the study of the functionality of all proteins in cells and tissues. The human genome is the "manual" for synthesising proteins, but it is proteins that provide functions, therefore a comprehensive analysis of disease requires a knowledge of both protein identity and function. Unfortunately, the human proteome is significantly larger than the human genome. A total of one million human proteins has been estimated, whereas the genome consists of about 30000 to 35000 genes. Thus, proteomics is dependent on the availability of high throughput protein-arrays or chips at moderate costs.

Arrays

Arrays and microarrays are used to perform a large number of different experiments simultaneously. They have microscopic and functionalised test tubes or spots, where each spot is designed to perform a distinct test. These reaction spots are arranged in arrays with up to several 100000 different spots on a single chip and a density of up to 100000 spots per cm^2. Microarrays can be used to perform several tasks including DNA sequencing, genetic disease diagnosis, drug efficiency tests (high-throughput screening) and gene expression studies.

DNA Microarrays

DNA functionalised microarrays represent one of the most prominent biochips exploiting the correlation of cell function and the expression of genes. Such DNA arrays are available for different genomes including human, mice, rats and micro-organisms, and are commonly referred to as DNA chips. The operation principle of such DNA-chips can be understood by considering the process of events within a cell that converts genetic information into protein, i.e. gene expression. The information to create a protein, which is stored in a sequence of base pairs in DNA, is copied first into messenger RNA (mRNA), a process called transcription.

The mRNA then acts as a template for the synthesis of the particular protein (a process called translation), which fulfils the functional role of the gene. The first stage of gene expression is exploited by gene chips to examine differences between healthy and morbid tissue. Each spot of a DNA chip contains a molecule of single-stranded DNA. Samples of mRNA to be tested are either labelled (usually with a fluorescent dye) before being applied to the chip or are first converted into cDNA (complementary DNA, i.e. DNA that has been copied from a mRNA) before being labelled and applied to the chip.

The location and the intensity of fluorescent spots provide information about which genes have been expressed by the cell and to what degree, respectively. In this scenario four different results can occur: i) the red-tagged molecules hybridise, ii) the green-tagged molecules hybridise, iii) both molecules hybridise, iv) no hybridisation takes place. By calculating the relative contribution from each dye, investigators can determine whether a gene from a diseased cell is being expressed to the same, higher or lower levels than in a normal, healthy cell. This allows the investigation of thousands of genes on a single chip and the identification of which genes are involved in specific diseases.

Microarrays are also being exploited for the study of DNA polymorphisms or mutations. Single nucleotide polymorphisms (SNP) are the most common variations in the human genome. These represent a difference of a single nucleotide at a defined point in the genome, for instance when AGGC changes to AGGT. A variation is termed a SNP when it occurs in more than 1 % of the human population. SNPs can be used as a marker in order to identify disease genes and occur on average every 1000 base pairs. Only 3-5% of the human genome has the potential to encode proteins i.e. are genes. Although most SNPs occur outwith these regions, it is believed that the comprehensive analysis of SNPs within genes will improve medication in the future.

If each patient has their own individual SNP map, this could provide detailed information about specific incompatibilities or possible side effects with a given drug. In this regard, a high-throughput method, as can be found in microarrays, is essential. The format of these arrays is similar to that for gene expression studies. A specific oligonucleotide (single-stranded DNA fragment) exhibiting a distinct SNP is immobilised at each reaction spot on the microarray. mRNA is extracted from the patient, introduced to the array where it hybridises to those spots on the microarray with a matching SNP, thus providing information about which SNPs are present in the patient's genome.

Protein microarrays

The exploitation of genomics has enormous capability, however proteomics- the study of proteins and their functionality, will be more powerful in the discovery of disease pathways. Despite the progress that has been made in the investigation of the human genome, little is known about proteins involved in pathogenesis. From the genomics perspective this can be attributed in part to the weak correlation between the concentration of mRNA and that of the corresponding protein. Thus, in order to illuminate the function of a given gene in the course of a certain disease, the protein(s) encoded by that gene have to be detected themselves. Considering the complexity and the tremendous number of proteins that are involved in human biology, proteomics seems to be a rather challenging task. The human proteome is more complex than the genome encoding it would suggest and has been estimated to consist of about 0.5 to 1 million proteins. Unlike the comparatively simple composition of DNA with its four basic building blocks, proteins consist of 20 different amino acids.

As a result of interactions between these amino acids, proteins adopt a specific 3-dimensional structure that is a major contribution to their functionality. Proteins can be further modified through the addition of carbohydrate and lipid groups, which adds to the variety issuing from a single gene.

Proteins with identical chemical composition but different spatial structures can evoke different reactions. The 3D structure of a protein can be changed when it interacts with other materials including other proteins. Furthermore, proteins are difficult to synthesise and there is no simple way of amplification as can be found in PCR (polymerase chain reaction) for DNA. At present, the quantitative analysis of proteins is achieved mainly with assistance of two-dimensional polyacrylamide gel electrophoresis (2D-PAGE).

Proteins are isolated from cells and initially separated based on charge (first dimension, this is called isoelectric focussing), followed by separation based on mass (second dimension, perpendicular to the first). This method can effectively separate thousands of different protein species on a single gel. Protein "spots" on the gel can be visualised using stains that can either be colourimetric or fluorescent, excised from the gel and analysed by mass spectrometry. Immunoassays, which are based on the specific interaction between an antibody and antigen, heralded the beginning of protein-detecting microarrays. Potential applications for protein chips can be found in diagnostics, drug screening, disease monitoring, drug discovery, and medical research. The market for protein chips is expected to grow to at least 500 million dollars by 2005.

Nanotechnology on arrays

The advantages of microarray technology emanate from their miniaturisation. In this regard, nanoscaled arrays or nanoarrays should have superior properties considering their processing speed and material consumption. Nevertheless, problems arise from the handling of ultra-small quantities of liquids. The reliable processing of volumes down to femtoliters ($1x10^{-15}$ l) is still a challanging task at present and cannot be performed on a routine base. One approach to miniaturise array size can be found in scanning or atomic force microscopy (SFM/AFM). The AFM is a prominent tool in nanotechnology allowing the visualisation and manipulation of surfaces at the nanometre scale.

The AFM can be used as a nanolithographic tool in order to modify the surface structure or chemistry. A common approach is based on the application of a voltage between tip and sample. A different method of AFM nanolithography can be used to produce arrays of nanometre dimensions by the deposition of molecules from the tip through a liquid meniscus (or "ink") onto the substrate during the scanning process.

This technique is called dip pen nanolithography (DPN)and can be used to functionalise surfaces in discrete spots with a user-defined chemistry. The smallest spot size which has been obtained by this method so far is about 100 nm and the ability of DPN to create protein nanoarrays has been demonstrated recently.

The inherent problem of all scanning techniques is low throughput which is a result of their serial nature. This can be overcome by intensive parallelisation using several thousands of ink-wetted tips. The advantage of this system can be seen in the label-free detection possibility, which can be done with the same instrument. A commercial DPN-writer was released in 2003 by NanoInk, Inc., Chicago.

Nanotechnology offers advantages not only for array production but also for sample detection on the array. The common approach of fluorescent staining suffers from the disadvantage of bleaching i.e. the fast degradation of fluorescent molecules. In contrast, nanoparticles exhibit improved stability and sensitivity for detection purposes, e.g. resonance light scattering (RLS) of distinct nanosised metal colloidal particles provides an ultra sensitive detection method.

A substantial 10-fold enhancement in sensitivity compared to common fluorescent markers has been accomplished through the use of gold and silver particles of uniform dimensions in the range of 40 nm to 120 nm. With regard to protein detection, a new strategy based on functionalised metal nanoparticles, in combination with a magnetic detection method, has been reported recently. This so-called bio-bar code method increases sensitivity and offers a strong multiplexing and simultaneous detection of many proteins. The current microarray technology is rather macroscopic.

Smaller spots can be achieved with scanning probe techniques as mentioned above, however these require a higher detection sensitivity due to the small number of molecules involved. With force spectroscopythe possibility of detecting single molecules by mechanical means can be realised. A conventional AFM with a functionalised tip can be used to measure specific interactions such as antibody/ antigen. Typical experiments probe the mechanical properties of single molecules and measure the energy needed to unfold molecular domains. The miniaturisation of DNA microarrays brought a significant progress in genomics, where the number of experiments covered by a single microarray has been steadily increased.

The ultimate gene chip has been produced recently by Affymetrix and has all human genes on a single chip. A better understanding of the functionality of proteins will have a strong impact on future diagnostics and therapies. The development of new drugs allows a more precise targeting with less side-effects. Highly specialised molecules offer an increased effectiveness in the therapy of cancer for example. Such intelligent active agents may require diagnostic tests to determine which patient is able to benefit from the drug e.g. due to the presence of a certain receptor. These tests can be performed using microarray technology in the future, bringing a new approach to diagnosis, the so called personalised medicine, where patients benefit from highly specific developed drugs, which have their effectiveness ensured through a diagnostic test. These molecular diagnostic tools, with precise targeting ability, are referred to as molecular medicine.

Lab-on-a-chip

In contrast to micro- and nanoarray technology, which allow the accomplishment of a single experiment, the basic idea of lab-on-a-chip (LOC) is the integration of an entire chemistry lab on a small substrate. Resembling the integrated circuits in the semiconductor industry, a LOC can perform sample isolation, mixing, separation, detection and data analysis on one highly integrated platform. In general, a LOC device is able to perform several different production steps, which can vary dependent on the purpose of the LOC, on a miniaturised base. This is achieved by a combination of microfluidic and microelectronic devices creating a small lab, which allows the realisation of a complete experiment with minimum material consumption, and provides data analysis in real-time. In the future, LOC devices may replace the expensive and time-consuming use of clinical laboratories. Therefore, LOCs are promising candidates for medical analysis at the point-of-care.

It was the advent of microfluidics that rendered the miniaturisation of fluid devices possible. Guiding fluids in micrometer-sized channels can be achieved in several ways such as electrohydrodynamic pumping, electroosmotic flow, electrowetting and thermocapillary pumping or temperature gradients.

Such an integrated LOC requires micro-engineered surface topographies or a chemical wetting contrast in combination with electronics, which are commonly referred to as micro electromechanical systems (MEMS). LOCs can be fabricated on glass, silicon or polymer substrates, which offers the advantage of a fast and inexpensive production of disposable LOCs. Polymer based microfluidic devices can be manufactured by replication methods such as casting, imprinting or embossing and injection molding, making the mass production of LOCs feasible. The first commercially available product was the Agilent 2100 Bioanalyzer, representing a versatile LOC platform for multiple forms of RNA, DNA and protein analysis.

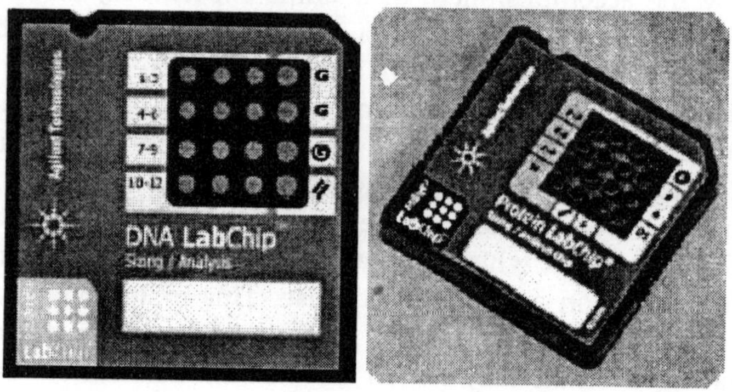

Figure 1. A DNA and a protein LabChipTM, AgilentTechnologies

Microfluidics and LOC devices represent a comparatively dynamic field of research. Over 2000 papers concerning LOCs have been published to date. The worldwide market for microarrays, microfluidic devices and other biochips is estimated to grow 65% per year and reach 3.3 billion dollar by 2004.

Nuclear imaging techniques (Figure 2) require the injection of a radioactive substance, which emits gamma rays. The absorption of radionuclides in tissues is dependent on metabolism and allows information about physiological processes, anatomy and organ function to be gathered. The main application areas are oncology and cardiology. However the disadvantage of nuclear imaging is that it delivers limited morphological information, which makes it difficult to precisely localise regions with higher metabolism.

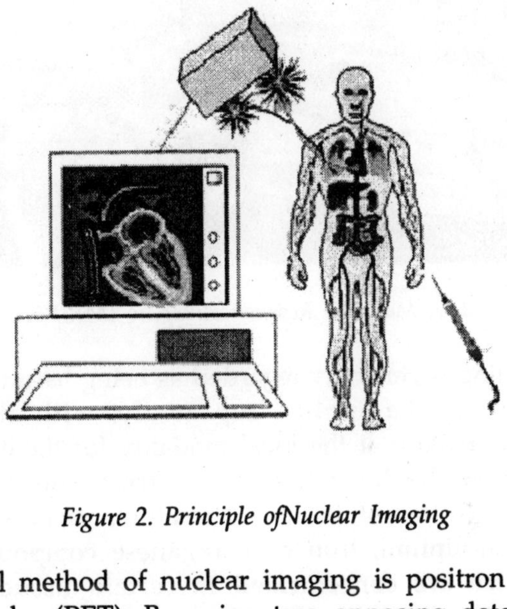

Figure 2. Principle ofNuclear Imaging

A special method of nuclear imaging is positron emission tomography (PET). By using two opposing detectors the sensitivity is increased strongly which makes PET a promising method for molecular imaging.

Magnetic Resonance Imaging (MRI)

Magnetic resonance imaging (MRI) scanners, as depicted in Figure 3, require strong magnets to align the nuclear spins of hydrogen atoms in tissue in one direction. High frequency coils excite the nuclear spins and analyse the weak signals of their relaxation process, with gradient coils used for further, local resolution. MRI is known for its ability to generate high-resolution images, displaying fine anatomical details at sub-millimeter dimensions.

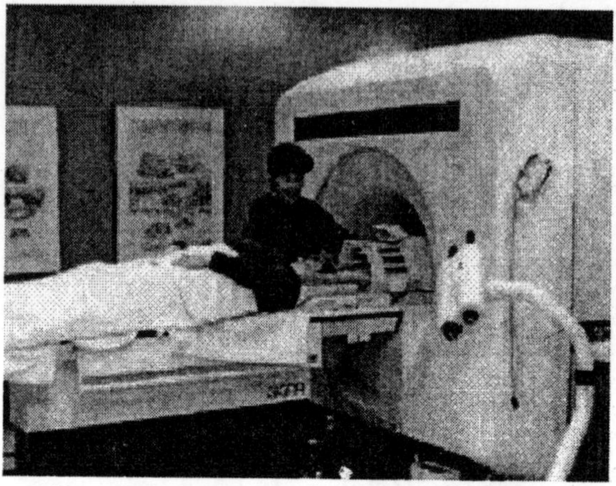

Figure 3. A Magnetic ResonanceImaging (MRI) Scanner

MRI scanning is generally regarded as being harmless to the body, and can be applied repeatedly, with almost no restrictions, making it the ideal modality for the evaluation of treatment. Its limitations arise from similar proton densities in different tissues. Therefore, various contrast agents (gadolinium, iron or manganese compounds) are used, which are concentrated in certain tissues. Smart design of the contrast agents allow molecular signatures to be visualised down to picomole levels. The 2003 Nobel prize in physiology or medicine was awarded to Paul C. Lauterbur (U.S.) and Sir Peter Mansfield (UK) for their discoveries concerning MRI.

Ultrasound (US)

In ultrasound diagnostics, the intensity of the ultrasound wave is reflected at tissue or organ boundaries. The reflected intensity is measured and displayed as an image on a monitor. The contrast between healthy and diseased tissues is usually weak. However, over the last two decades, several contrast agents have been developed, along with contrast-specific imaging methods, to enhance their discrimination. Current research is looking for contrast agents that bind to molecular markers. Traditional contrast agents consist of microscopic gas bubbles (microbubbles) surrounded by a stabilising coating to protect against dissolution. This well-established method offers a high sensitivity-it is even possible to detect a single microbubble. When the microbubbles are injected intravenously, they act as blood pool agents (i.e. remain within the vasculature), which limits their application to targets within the vascular system.

Electron Microscopy (EM)

Pathology represents a completely different field of diagnosis, e.g. where analytical methods are used to search for viruses in biopsy samples. Viruses have sizes of around 100 nm or less and therefore their detection is suited instruments such as the electron microscope (EM), which is used for analyses in the nanometre region. For example, polyomaviruses (PV) are pathogens which have tropism to the human urinary tract and have been reported with increasing frequency in renal transplant recipients.It is difficult to distinguish the effect of PV on graft rejection from patient immune responses against transplanted renal antigens. An accurate diagnosis is of great importance because the therapeutic approaches to both are very different.

PV appear as 40 to 50-nm, non-enveloped particles within epithelial cell nuclei and can be readily identified using EM. The EM was also the "first line of defence" during the SARS (Severe Acute Respiratory Syndrome) breakout. SARS is a viral respiratory illness that was first reported in Asia in November 2002. It is caused by a coronavirus, called SARS-associated coronavirus (SARS-CoV). The virus has a diameter of about 100 nanometers and was identified through an electron microscopic analysis.

Identification of Target

The first stage of drug discovery is the identification of a target that can be subsequently acted on by a future drug to bring about an improvement in disease. This can be achieved more quickly and reliably now through the use of array technologies.

DNA microarray technology

Up to 500000 oligos per square cm can be packed onto slides, allowing the detection of thousands of genes or mRNA species on a single chip. Differences in gene expression between normal and diseased cells can be determined by incubating microarrays with cDNA (mRNA which has been copied back into DNA) isolated from both sources that have been labelled with different fluorescent tags. As each spot is associated with an attached oligo of known sequence, the relative fluorescent intensities from each tag at each of these spots allows the determination of the relative expression of different genes in each source. By establishing whether the transcription levels of specific genes are the same, higher or lower in the diseased cell compared with normal, novel targets for drug intervention can be identified.

For example oestrogen has been known to play a key role in the development of breast cancer since it was observed that a side-effect of chemotherapy was inhibition of oestrogen production in the ovaries. Earlier this year Frasor and colleagues used DNA microarrays to identify oestrogen responsive genes in breast cancer cells, and therefore potential targets for drug intervention. According to analysts the market for DNA microarrays was $400-550 million in 2000, and this is expected to grow to $1-2.2 billion by 2005.

Protein chips

DNA microarrays provide a robust platform for the screening of multiple candidate drug targets, however as has been mentioned previously the diversity of proteins in any cell is not restricted to the number of genes that it expresses. Therefore to identify all possible targets, and in some cases to identify any targets, it is necessary to look at the protein complement of the cell.

Proteomics has been defined as "the branch of genetics that studies the full set of proteins encoded by a genome." Proteomic tools have been traditionally less robust and more time-consuming than those for DNA. However recent advances in protein chips and a fusion of DNA and protein technologies may change all that. 2D-polyacrylamide gel electrophoresis (2D-PAGE) separates proteins based on charge and mass, with it being possible to analyse two populations of proteins (e.g. from healthy and diseased tissue) stained with different fluorescent markers analysed on the same gel.

Following electrophoresis, protein "spots" are excised and identified by mass spectrometry. This technology has been bolstered recently through the production of protein chips. The identification of a protein(s) which is differentially expressed between diseased and normal tissues is the first step. If the protein has been previously characterised and its biological function is known, then perhaps intervening drugs are already available or can provide a starting point for the elaboration of more effective drugs. If however, the protein is unknown then its function must be either determined experimentally through expression and in vitro studies, or through the relatively new field of bioinformatics.

The "fusion" of DNA and protein technologies has come from the development and use of aptamers. Single-stranded DNA and RNA molecules can form complex 3D shapes through intramolecular interactions, and in some cases these formations (or aptamers) can interact specifically with proteins. Somalogic have incorporated bromodeoxyuridine into single-stranded nucleic acids to generate photoaptamers which can crosslink to proteins when irradiated. This provides a handle for the detection of specific proteins within a sample. Photoaptamers can be arranged in array format, different populations of proteins can be incubated on matching arrays, proteins UV-crosslinked and differences in individual protein expression levels determined by applying a universal protein fluorescent stain to the plates.

Target validation

The genomic and proteomic methods described above can identify differences gene expression and protein levels between normal and diseased cells. The use of DNA microarrays in particular has lead to an explosion in the number of candidate targets. But how do you tell whether these candidates are significant? How do you tell whether the target that has been identified will be amenable to intervention and whether it is the sole factor in the disease or is part of a complex pattern of differential protein expression? These questions must be answered by target validation. According to David Szymkowski, director of biotherapeutics at the biopharmaceutical company Xencor in Monrovia, California, drugs fail in the clinic for two basic reasons: they either don't work or they prove to be unsafe.

"Both of these are often the direct result of sloppy early target validation." It is important to ensure that the correct target is identified before candidate drugs are tested against it, as it can take 12 years and up to $1 billion dollars to bring a drug to market. Traditionally, target validation was achieved *in vivo,* however recently *in vitro* models have been developed which, although not available for more complex disease syndromes (e.g psychological diseases), offer a more ethical, quicker and cheaper alternative to animal models.

Target validation in vivo

The targets of many of the blockbuster drugs were validated using gene knockouts. Gene knockouts (KO) involve deleting or disrupting expression of a gene in early embryogenesis in an animal model. The rationale for this is that removing the gene encoding a protein that has been identified as a candidate will effectively mimic the application of a strong repressor for that protein, allowing investigators to determine the protein's normal cellular function.

For example KO mice for the histamine H_2 receptor (which is the target of Zantac) are unable to secrete gastric acid into the stomach in response to histamine, thereby preventing lowering of stomach pH and validating the receptor as a target for the treatment of gastric ulcers. KO animal models have to be taken in context. Some mutations may be lethal, some may have differential effects depending on developmental stage and others may have multiple effects.

Target validation in vitro

Using tissue culture systems is quicker and cheaper than animal models. Genomic approaches include antisense oligonucleotides and RNA interference. The principle of antisense technology is the binding of an oligonucleotide to complementary mRNA in the cell. This can prevent gene expression in one of 3 ways: 1) directed degradation of the DNA-RNA duplex by a cellular enzyme RNase H, 2) blocking protein translation or 3) preventing RNA processing, prior to translation of protein. BIOGNOSTIK manufacture phosphorothioate antisense oligonucleotides (ODN) that are capable of entering cells in tissue-culture and binding to complementary mRNAs preventing their translation. In the last few years RNA interference (RNAi) has received much attention for its ability to silence genes. This technology makes use of a natural cellular defence mechanism against double-stranded RNA (dsRNA) molecules, which can arise during virus replication for example.

Short dsRNA molecules that are identical in sequence to the target mRNA are transfected into cells where they are cleaved into smaller fragments by a cellular enzyme called Dicer. As a result of this recognition, Dicer also cleaves the cognate mRNA, silencing gene expression. It is estimated that the market for RNAi will be US $38 million by the end of 2003. There are many more proteins than genes, and so validating targets at the DNA or mRNA level may not always present an accurate physiological picture.

Proteomics approaches are now appearing in the form of solid phase and solution arrays. Xerion Pharmaceuticals use a novel procedure to functionally inactivate target proteins. First the target is "panned" against a phage display library that expresses single chain antibody fragments (scFv) which bind proteins with high specificity. Specific scFv's to the target are identified, enriched and labelled with UV-reactive dyes. These labelled scFv's are allowed to interact with the target protein within the cell and then irradiated using a laser. This causes the breakdown of the dyes into active compounds which in turn cause the inactivation of the target protein.

This procedure can also be used for a disease-based approach, combining target identification and validation. Proteins are isolated from healthy and diseased cells and scFv's identified that only bind proteins from diseased cells. These are used to validate the target as described above, and can then be used to isolate the target for identification by mass spectrometry.

Design and Validation

Following identification and validation of a target in a disease, drugs must be designed and validated that will affect that target (usually through inhibition) to alleviate disease symptoms. First of all lead compounds must be generated. This can be achieved through modelling or molecular manipulation. These then must be screened to confirm their efficacy and determine which compounds will be developed further into marketable drugs.

Structure guided discovery

In the 40 or so years since Perutz and Kendrow determined the 3D structure of haemoglobin and myoglobin, X-ray crystallography has proven invaluable in the generation of data on the 3D structure of proteins. It has become clear that proteins that perform similar functions but have different substrates (e.g. kinases, proteins which phosphorylate and thereby modify the activity of other proteins) have similar structures around their active sites. More recently, bioinformatics (defined as the merging of biology, computer science, and information technology into a single discipline) has been used to predict the 3D structures of targets and potential chemicals that could interact with them (ligands) and inhibit protein function, by comparing primary amino acid sequence of novel proteins with the determined 3D structure of known proteins. This approach has been heralded as the new way forward in drug discovery. It is estimated that only 1 out of 5000 screened compounds is approved as a new medicine. By using modelling systems many compounds can be eliminated from screening before they are synthesised. De Novo Pharmaceuticals uses complex algorithms in its Site Explorer™ software to characterise the active site of a target and determine potential structures of ligands which can interact with it.

Candidates are then screened "in silico" using the company's EasyDock programme to determine relative binding affinities. Using this approach thousands of compounds can be screened and only the best candidates synthesised for screening. A unique approach is employed by Momenta Pharmaceuticals. 80% of known proteins are modified through the addition of carbohydrate molecules, and it has been known for a long time that these "post-translational" modifications can influence protein function. Momenta Pharmaceuticals have developed a technology which allows the identification and functional characterisation of these sugar groups, which in turn can feed into the development of new therapeutics.

Libraries of drug candidates

As a result of research that has been undertaken in drug discovery there exists many libraries of potential drug candidates. Some of these are held privately by companies but some are available publicly. For example researchers at the Stockwell lab have compiled an annotated compound library (ACL) of some 2000 biologically active compounds which include 514 US FDA-approved drugs. By understanding the biological action of compounds pre-screening, it is possible to significantly increase the likelihood of success for those that enter validation. The Developmental Therapeutics Programme (DTP) is the drug discovery and development division of the US National Cancer Institute and acts as a repository of synthetic and natural products, which can be evaluated as anticancer and AIDS agents.

DTP provides information on more than 600000 compounds, which have been supplied from a variety of sources worldwide. Biofrontera Discovery offer an alternative based on natural compounds. This company specialises in screening compounds isolated from microorganisms, marine invertebrates and plants against protein targets. The potential for creating novel libraries of compounds to be screened against targets is immense: "Only a minute part (less than 5 %) of all naturally-occurring microorganisms have been successfully isolated and cultured...There is strong evidence that those microorganisms contain biosynthetic genes for unknown and innovative bioactive natural compounds."

Biofrontera Discovery uses chromatographic techniques to isolate compounds from different organisms and then characterises these via a number of methods including mass spectrometry and X-ray crystallography. The result is that they have approximately 140000 sub-fractions containing over 2 million compounds.

Models-validation

Ensuring that a drug can interact with the target protein of a disease and inhibit its function, may seem like the end-point for drug discovery. Unfortunately this is not the case. Taking a single target protein out of its cellular context and screening for compounds that have the desired effect on the target can result in the development of drugs that interact with other proteins and either become ineffectual or cause unwanted side-effects. It is essential to determine at the earliest stage whether a drug will be ineffectual (or dangerous) when administered to a patient.

This validation is summarised by the acronym ADMET, which stands for Absorption, Distribution, Metabolism, Excretion and Toxicity. This ensures that a drug will be absorbed into the body and penetrate the target tissue through the chosen route of administration (e.g. intravenous, nebulizer, enteric-coated pill), and that it will be metabolised and excreted from the body, without any toxic side-effects. Ultimately this must be determined in human volunteers, but prior to this all drugs are evaluated in animal models. New in vitro developments however, allow pre-animal testing of drugs and a further validation of lead candidates, and therefore earlier elimination of unsatisfactory compounds. To highlight the importance of this, it is worthwhile considering the impact of the cytochrome P450 (CYP450) family of enzymes on drug development.

CYP450 enzymes are key to the metabolism of many drugs, making them more water-soluble and therefore able to be excreted through the kidneys. In fact three family members CYP2D6, CYP2C9 and CYP3A4 are responsible for the metabolism of approximately 75% of all prescribed drugs. The family extends to 57 genes, which altogether encode more than 1000 different proteins. The structures of these proteins are similar, but the endogenous substrates of most are presently unknown.

Many potential drug candidates have been shown to have a higher affinity for the CYP450 family enzymes than for the target protein, making it essential that this is evaluated early on. A number of in vitro assays have been developed for pre-animal screening of drugs. These range from computational methods, to protein arrays, to cell-based systems.

Cell- and tissue-based assays

Although protein chips allow the interaction of the candidate drug with a number of proteins to be investigated, they cannot represent the complexity of real-life. Proteins are present in cells at massively different concentrations, they are restricted to sub-cellular compartments (e.g. the nucleus, cytoplasm and cell membrane) and some form complexes with others to exert a biological effect, any of which can have a direct bearing on the efficacy of a drug. To address this a number of companies have developed cell- and tissue-based systems which allow investigators to assay a candidate drug against the total cellular protein complement.

Cell-based systems are employed by a number of companies. Genesis workstations manufactured by TECAN allow the automation of many of drug validation tests including in vitro drug metabolism, cell permeability, toxicity and mutagenicity. Some of these tests can be combined on a single platform thus facilitating and accelerating the validation process. Cellomics have a high-content screening platform that combines fluorescent tagging of subcellular structures and different cell populations with an optical system that can detect morphological changes in cells in real-time. This allows the effects of a drug on the cell to be monitored and any adverse reactions to be detected early on.

In addition to manufacturing protein chips, Adaptive Screening manufacture the CytoFlux™ cell assay chip. This utilises integrated on-chip optics, electrical-field stimulation microelectrodes and electrical microsensors to evaluate the effects of drug compounds on cells. Advances in polymer chemistry and membranes have allowed the generation of synthetic 3D "tissues" which can be used for the evaluation of candidate drugs. For example the MatTek Corporation has synthesised in vitro models that mimic respiratory epithelium and skin, allowing researchers to investigate the effects of drugs in physiologically relevant systems.

An alternative to synthetic systems is to remove tissue from a patient to evaluate the efficacy of a drug. This is known as ex vivo and can be as straightforward as removing leukaemic white blood cells for investigating the effect of cytotoxic drugs on these cells or can involve transplanting human tissue into an animal model (which allows maintenance of tissue viability) as has been used for the investigation of cervical cancer.

In vivo testing

Ultimately all drugs must be tested in an animal model before they can enter clinical trials. Many human diseases have counterparts in the animal kingdom and this, to a large extent, dictates the model to be used.

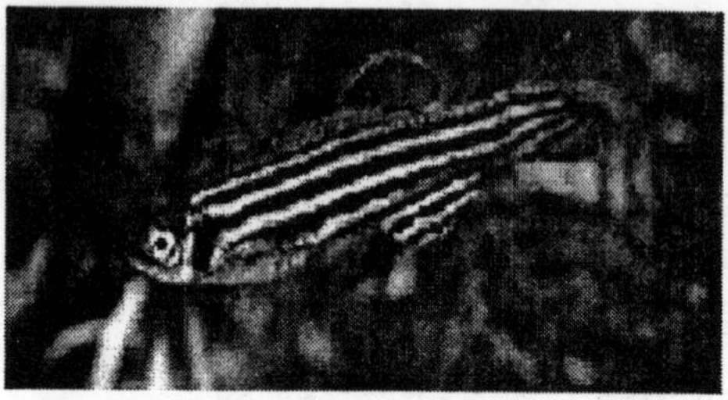

Figure 4. Zebrafish.

Zebrafish (Figure 4) have recently come into vogue as a model for many human diseases due to their relatively short reproductive cycle and ease of maintenance. Zygogen use zebrafish as a model for the investigation of cardiovascular and neurodegenerative disease, and are developing a high-content screening system based on zebrafish embryos.

Surgery

Surgery is one of the most physical and human dependent techniques within health care. In addition, it is one of the most emotive aspects of healthcare, as patients undergoing surgery are at their most vulnerable. Surgery has been practised for a long time, with surgical tools found from cultures as long ago as ancient Rome. With simple tools and techniques "surgeons" could provide critical help for injured persons. Of course this often created infection, toxicity and inflammatory problems due to the lack of sterile clinical conditions or of knowledge in how to prepare tools. However tools were developed for almost maximum effect and surprisingly enough some of the designs from back then can be found in present instruments.

The parallel research and development of tools and equipment on one side and surgery techniques on the other, has led to massive improvements in the surgery field. Tools are now very well developed and every factor for securing a patient's health is taken care of- including the provision of a sterile environment around and within the patient. Recent developments such as laser surgery have been used for the successful removal of cancerous tissue for example.

Laser surgery

Laser surgery uses concentrated beams of light of particular wavelengths instead of instruments for surgical procedures. Lasers were first developed in 1960. Since that time, many modifications have been made and a number of different types of lasers have been developed. These differ in emitted light wavelengths and power ranges, as well as in their ability to clot, cut, or vaporize tissue. The most commonly used are the pulsed dye laser, the Nd: YAG laser, the CO_2 (carbon dioxide) laser, the argon laser, and the KTP laser. Each works in a different manner and each is sometimes used as part of a treatment plan. The laser works as following; when the laser beam hits tissue such as skin, a certain amount of light is reflected. The remaining light is absorbed or transmitted through the tissue. Absorbed light has specific effects, creating physical, mechanical, chemical, or temperature changes that result in the desired surgical effect. Lasers permit highly localised precise surgery with reduced blood loss. Moreover, a relatively dry operative field affords better vision for the surgeon.

Minimally invasive surgery

In what is generally referred to as open surgery, surgeons have traditionally had to make an incision large enough to expose the internal organs being operated on, i.e. to gain access to the body cavity, normal, healthy tissue is cut. Within the last decade, however, new minimally invasive surgical techniques have revolutionised many surgical procedures by enabling surgeons to access body cavities for procedures while reducing the trauma to overlying skin, muscles, and nerves that occurs with traditional open surgery. Most minimally invasive surgical procedures are performed with small optical instruments, such as endoscopes, and instruments placed through the body. The benefits of minimal invasive surgery are a decreased injury to skin, muscle, and nerves, fewer wound complications, easier postoperative pain management and quicker recovery and return of the patient to normal functioning.

Surgical tools

All the surgical instruments available on the market today, varying from scalpels and knives to scissors and retractors. Usually these are made of stainless steel or tungsten but more recently titanium instruments have been introduced. Titanium benefits from its light weight and high tensile strength producing a much lighter instrument and giving the surgeon better handling during an operation. Sutures are another essential medical device and have been used since the beginnings of surgery to close up tissues or compress blood vessels and prevent bleeding. Historically hair, animal gut and various textiles were used, which understandably caused many problems for the patient, however these have now been replaced by synthetic materials such as polyethylene and polypropylene.

The driving force nowadays is to make surgery progressively less invasive. By producing a new set of tools on the nanoscale one can perhaps imagine a surgeon being able to make changes to and track individual cells. This could be very beneficial for neurosurgical aspects for example and, in addition, the patient will benefit from the reduced trauma of even smaller wounds. Gesellschaft für Diamantprodukte (GFD) have, through the application of nanotechnology, in a process termed "plasma polishing", created diamond scalpels with a cutting edge of only a few atoms (approximately 3 nm), that have applications in eye and minimal invasive surgery. The width of the scalpel blade is approximately one thousandth that of a metal blade and makes these scalpels officially the smallest in the world. Minimally invasive surgery will also answer another demand, not only from surgeons but also patients, which is to make the operation as short and minimally traumatic as possible and reduce the length of time spent in the hospital.

Another way to initiate this is to establish virtual surgical setups. The introduction of telepresence surgery has the potential to remove surgical limitations between countries and continents. However political, ethical and cultural differences between countries will need to be addressed to ensure that suitable procedures, acceptable to all parties, are established. When performing a surgical operation the surgeon works in a biological environment with corrosive or other effects.

As a result it is essential that instruments are thoroughly cleaned and rinsed with de-ionised water before sterilisation, to avoid corrosion and pitting. Corrosion of an instrument can lead to its failure (e.g. not opening or closing properly) and can visually mask contamination, which in turn can spread infection to patients who are operated on. The use of titanium alloyed with nano-composites of aluminium and/or vanadium in new surgical instruments addresses this.

Unfortunately such alloys are extremely difficult to machine and finish, currently making the prices for these products very high. Titanium is immune to corrosive attacks by laboratory saline solutions, blood and other bodily fluids, chlorides, oxidizing acids, alkalis etc., and it is 100% nonmagnetic, a great benefit when working with nerves, for example. Not all surgery techniques will be influenced through the production of better tools. For example sodium-2-mercaptoethane sulphonate (or MESNA) has been described recently as a "chemical dissection agent". This compound breaks disulphide bonds between proteins allowing tissue to be pulled apart more easily. As a result MESNA could potentially reduce surgery time, blood loss, trauma to local tissues and post-operative complications. Considerable efforts are being made in the creation of new tools for minimally invasive surgical instruments.

Over the past decade, a number of ingenious instruments have been developed for manipulating individual cells, macromolecules and even individual atoms. One prime example is the scanning probe microscope, developed originally at IBM Zurich Research Labs. These tools have contributed in significant ways to advances in several fields of research, such as electron transport in molecules, protein folding mechanics and dynamic processes at cell membranes. Such research provides novel insight into the structure and function of molecules relevant to biotechnology and the surgery field. Virtual Reality (VR) interfaces to experiments have also evolved rapidly over the past decade, a notable example being the nanomanipulator at the University of North Carolina, the leading U.S. academic VR research center, which provides a virtual interface to a scanning probe microscope.

This device has now been commercialised, and has been successfully used in teaching programmes. Another major development of the past decade has been the use of the Internet and PCs to control scientific equipment and analyse experimental data remotely. A prime example is the World Wide Web, which was originally developed by CERN for scientific purposes.

Today, researchers are developing the GRID, a next generation of network applications that will greatly facilitate internet-based distributed computing and remote visualisation, including VR applications. This will be particularly important for surgical operations as it requires a lot of computer power to interpret and display images and data to allow the surgeon to make the correct decisions. The surgeon uses a haptic display that delivers force feedback from the operation scene.

A simple example of how this works is the steering wheel found in some computer games, where a servo motor can make the wheel turn and vibrate just as a real wheel on a real car would do. In the nanomanipulator, the haptic device is a pen-like rod connected to several servos making the pen capable of 3D motion. When connected to a computer with appropriate software, the pen can be used as a probe to "feel" the outline of simulated objects. If the device and the software are advanced enough, texture and elasticity can also be included.

Instead of "feeling" a simulated landscape, the haptic device can be connected to an atomic force microscope (AFM). In this case, the AFM tip is moved in the same way as the pen, and the hand guiding the pen feels the surface magnified about a million times. If there are particles lying on the surface, the pen can be used to move them about. Once in a while, the AFM is run in tapping mode to image the surface so that the operator can see what has been created.

In metal-on-metal (MoM) hip resurfacing less of the femur is removed. This makes a future second replacement easier to carry out. As the name suggests, both the ball and the socket parts of the artificial joint are made of metal. MoM resurfacing is not suitable for people with a low bone density or osteoporosis.

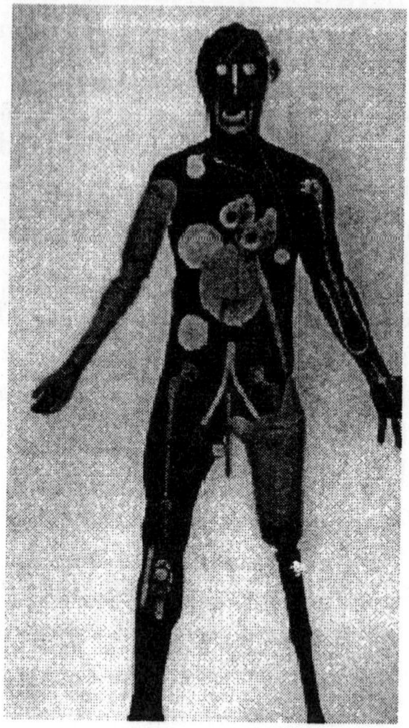

Figure 5. Various implants.

Knee-joints

When having a knee joint replacement the procedure is often to put in a whole new implant. The type of joints is made of metal (usually cobalt chrome, but also stainless steel or titanium). Plastics may be used as a cartilage replacement between the thigh and shin bones. Also "half knee" (uni-compartmental) joints are available, which are less surgery intensive. Usually knee joints are cemented to the bones, although some joints are non-cemented by design.

Spinal implants

Historically, spinal fusion has been performed with a bone graft without implants. However, the fusion rate with this technique is comparatively low, in the 50% range. Spinal implants consists of screws and axial connectors, which are usually made of stainless steel, however the use of titanium in spinal implants is on the increase.

Dental implants

Dental implants usually consist of metal (titanium, stainless steel) in combination with porcelain, ceramic or plastic.

Nanotechnology on Implants

The application of nanotechnology to implants allows the structure or surface of a biomaterial to be precisely defined thus improving biocompatibilty. Nanotechnology can also play a significant role in decreasing toxicity by creating a nano-coating on the implant, which reduces the effect of a corrosive environment. Optimising the coating not only avoids toxicity but also establishes a better interaction with the surrounding cells and tissue leading to a more stable and biocompatible implant. A nano-coated titanium or tantalum implant will therefore be better adapted to the human body and less likely to need to be subsequently removed and replaced by a new implant. It is however important that the coating does not itself cause problems by debonding.

Biomimetics technology

Biomimetics is the technology of biological growth of new bio-structures in a mould or directly in/on the injured bodypart. Researchers develop these structures from a single nano-physical or nano-chemical structure.

A nano-physical structure is developed from a single nano-crystal, whereas a nano-chemical structure is developed from an array of large reactive molecules attached to a surface. The idea is to use these nanostructures as seed molecules, or seed crystals, to drive materials to grow by themselves (*in vitro* or moulding). Researchers hope that this will lead to much better biomaterials for new and better implants. Other trends in the biomimetic field are the understanding of how specific body parts evolve and develop. Researchers are working on constructing replacement tissues such as muscle and bone using "tissue-engineering" techniques. Also the understanding of the biological functions of molecules e.g. biological motor proteins is now given lot of attention. The development of a molecular motor will aid the understanding of the biological process involved in muscle contraction and expansion.

Active Implants

Cochlear implants and retinal implants are examples of implants which aim to restore perception, by transforming an external signal into an electronic signal which is intelligible to the human brain. The cardiac pacemaker, bladder stimulator and other neural stimulator devices are examples of active implants whose purpose is to restore control over bodily functions. Finally, implantable insulin pumps and in vivo diagnostic devices are examples of medical therapies that are moving from the outside of the body to the inside. Not all of these active implants include nanotechnology, nanostructured materials or nano-components. Those active implants which do include nanotechnology, or for which nanotechnology improvements are being developed, e.g. in the form of bio-active coatings.

According to the European medical technology association, Eucomed, nanotechnology offers great potential for innovation in medical devices in general and some elements of (active) implants in particular. The nanotechnologies for (active) implants include advanced materials with nanostructured surface treatment. This surface treatment can enhance biocompatibility, promote tissue growth around the implant, and enhance the lifetime of the implants.

New smart materials incorporating slow release drugs can also be used in coatings for (active) implants to fight rejection or inflammation. Finally, nanotechnology can be applied in implanted lab-on-a-chip devices that can supply diagnostic data to active implanted medical devices. Eucomed therefore wants to stimulate networking between its members and the emerging nanotechnology industry in Europe. The European NEXUS Network of Excellence in Microsystems and nanotechnology has developed a roadmap for MEMS development for Medical Devices. They expect that by 2006, new MST pumps and valves implant development will be taken up in active implants such as pacemakers. After 2008, new power and data coupling methods will be taken up in active implants with internal electrodes and sensors. They do not explicitly mention nanotechnology, only the related biomaterials as expected technological developments.

Retinal Implants

Retinal implants are being developed to partially restore sight for blind patients suffering from diseases which destroy the photoreceptor cells of the retina at the back of the eye, but leave the visual nerve and visual cortex intact. These diseases include Retinitis Pigmentosa, Usher Syndrome, and Macular Degeneration. In the EU, there are 70-100,000 patients suffering from Retinitis Pigmentosa and 2.1 to 2.2 million patients with Macular Degeneration. Since the late 1990s there have been at least two fundamental retinal implant research projects in the USA and a further two in Germany, funded by the Federal Ministry for Education and Research. The German projects are the Epiret project, which aims to develop a retinal implant located at the back of the ganglion cells, that connects directly to the optic nerve; and the Subret project, which aims to develop a retinal implant located in place of the lost photoreceptor cells.

The projects have been running in two phases between 1995 and 2003. PD Dr. Marlies Dorlöchter, project leader for both projects at DLR in Bonn, Germany, explains: "In the current funding period prototypes of retinal implants have been developed and successfully tested in animal eyes. A third funding phase is planned but not yet realised. In this potential funding phase the clinical application of an implant will be the main goal." Currently at least one start up company in Germany, IIP-tec has started clinical trials of a retinal implant.

Nanotechnology on retinal implants

The artificial retina implant requires highly localised application of electrical stimuli, i.e. electrodes with a small geometric area. At the same time, charge transfer requires high capacitance, which requires a large surface area of the electrode. These opposite requirements can be reconciled by employing a nanoporous electrode material, which provides for an effective surface area which may be by as much as a factor of 100 higher than the geometric area of the electrode.

Cochlear Implants

Cochlear implants have been available for 25 years or so. These devices, which are implanted in the inner ear can restore partial hearing in profoundly deaf people in both ears, including children over two years old. The hearing ear consists of an outer, middle and inner ear. The outer ear picks up acoustic pressure waves, which are transformed via a series of small bones in the middle ear into mechanical vibrations. These vibrations are passed to the cochlea, a fluid-filled, snail-shaped cavity, in the inner ear. The resultant pressure waves cause movement of hairs on the basilar membrane of the cochlea. The frequency and amplitude of these movements are specific to the sounds picked up and causes the release of an electrochemical substance, which in turn stimulates neurons to fire and transmit an electrical signal to the brain. The electrical signal includes information about which neurones have fired, which is correlated to the sound heard.

The cochlear implant can partly restore hearing in profoundly deaf people if the cause of deafness is the absence of the hair cells. As long as there are enough neurones that can pick up and transmit an electrical signal, the cochlear implant can replace the missing link in the hearing chain of the absent hair cells.

There are different types of cochlear implants, however all consist of a microphone, a signal processor to convert the sound into electrical signals, a transmission system and a surgically implanted electrode or electrode array. Several companies manufacture different types of cochlear implants, including Ineraid, Nucleus, Clarion and Med-El. Most of the devices use transcutaneous connections between the outside microphone and the implanted device. Following surgical implantation of the inner part, the skin is re-closed to prevent infection. Both parts of the cochlear implant are held in place by a magnet, and the signal transmitted through a radio frequency link between external and internal coils. However, there are two downsides: removing the inner part requires another operation, and the system is incompatible with external magnetic fields such as those used in MRI scanners, which could expose the patient to risk.

The Ineraid device uses a percutaneous connection whereby the implanted electrodes are physically plugged into the outside part, without extra signal processing elements. However, the device is implanted through the skin, creating the possibility of infections. There is an ongoing debate about the pros and cons of cochlear implants. Proponents are optimistic about the health risks of operatively implanting the device and believe that deaf children have better chances of leading a normal life and acquiring language skills as a result.

Opponents highlight the risks of invasive surgery, which may cause dizziness and a mild form of eczema. They also point out hazards caused by strong magnetic fields such as applied in some jobs or involved in MRI scans. They also believe the implant and its associated medical care limit the ability of a child to lead a normal life with a high self-esteem. The risk of developing bacterial meningitis after a cochlear implant has received attention recently from regulators and industry.

A study published in the USA in mid 2002 by the Centre for Disease Control and Prevention and the FDA revealed that in a group of 4264 children, who had received cochlear implants before the age of six, 26 had contracted bacterial meningitis. Steps have been taken to mitigate this risk by ensuring prior vaccination of children, antibiotic treatment at the time of implant and removing from the market those devices that were associated with a higher probability of disease.

Nanotechnology on cochlear implants

It is apparent that the market for cochlear implants is already well established, however as described above, some problems with the technology remain. These include interference with strong magnetic fields, and the risk of infection, eczema or dizziness. According to Professor Helmut Schmidt of the Institute of Nanostructured Materials (INM) in Saarbrücken, Germany, nanotechnology can be applied in antimicrobial coatings on hearing aids including cochlear implants. His institute is developing nanostructured coatings including diffusable silver ions, which are released slowly from the coating and prevent infections in the ear.

There are two methods of administering antimicrobial remedies to the inner ear following cochlear implant operations: coatings or fluid-based drug delivery systems. Caroline Garnham and colleagues from Med-El have reviewed these alternatives. They favour fluid-based systems because these are less invasive and easier to control, as they can be switched off from outside the body.

Neural Implants

For neural implants which need to remain in the body for many years, long term stability of miniaturised systems is a major challenge. These active implants must be non-toxic and stable in a biological environment inside the body. They must also mimic the biological tissue near the implant to avoid irritation and rejection.

Nanotechnology on neural implants

Dr Thomas Stieglitz of the Fraunhofer Institute for Biomedical Technology, in Ingbert, Germany is working on micro and nanotechnology for neural prostheses. His Neuroprosthetics group works on a broad range of fundamental research topics including bladder stimulation, upper limb prostheses (grasp), implantable stimulators, neural prostheses, retinal-stimulator and a lower limb neuroprosthesis. According to him, "reactions between the artificial implant surface and the cells [of the human body] are mainly dependent on the material surface properties like surface energy, functional groups and on the nanostructure of the surface." His group has made topological surface modifications in the nanoscale range by Reactive Ion Etching, to change the cell adhesion on the implant. They are also focusing on other nanoscale surface modifications to improve the functionality of the electrical interfaces in neural prostheses, their fixation by biological means, and their long-term stability by defined topologies and cell-material interactions.

Dr Daryl R. Kipke, Department of Biomedical Engineering, University of Michigan is working on thin-film silicon and polymer neural probes for electrical and chemical interfaces to the central nervous system. "We have probe systems targeted for cortical, sub-cortical, and spinal cord targets. These are used actively in neuroscience research and we are beginning to translate the technology to medical applications." Nanotechnology aspects to this technology are nanostructured materials and nano-emulsions for bio-active coatings; micro-fluidics and device/tissue interface.

9

Nanotechnology in Electronics

Nanowires

Over the past twenty years, homogeneous nucleation in solution has proven to be an effective method for the synthesis of both metallic and semiconductor nanocrystals. Nearly isotropic, pseudospherical morphologies are typically produced. Other nanocrystalline morphologies are often desirable, and homogeneous nucleation has been adapted for the synthesis of rod-shaped morphologies. However, the growth of nanowires by homogeneous nucleation is apparently limited to materials having particularly favourable, highly anisotropic crystal structures.

How then might nanowire morphologies be generally prepared? The answer was uncovered by Wagner and Ellis in 1964, who discovered that micrometer-scale silicon whiskers (wires) could be grown from gold-droplet catalysts under Chemical Vapor Deposition (CVD) conditions at about 1000 °C. The process was named the "Vapor-Liquid-Solid" (VLS) mechanism after the three phases involved. VLS growth was extended to micrometer-scale whiskers of many inorganic materials and intensively studied for over a decade, before fading into relative obscurity. Many others made seminal contributions to nanowire growth by VLS adaptations, most notably Korgel (Supercritical Fluid-Liquid- Solid, SFLS, mechanism) and Yang.

We now routinely prepare soluble, III-V and II-VI semiconductor nanowires with controlled diameters in the strong-confinement regime of about 3-20 nm by bismuth-nanoparticle-catalysed SLS growth. The nanoparticle-catalysed VLS mechanism and its solution-phase variants have emerged as the popular, widely practiced, general methods for the synthesis of semiconductor nanowires. Gold nanoparticles are presently by far the most commonly employed catalysts.

The advantages of nanoparticle-catalysed nanowire growth include its general applicability to a wide variety of materials, the diameter control afforded, the uniformity of the wires (lack of significant diameter fluctuations) and their oriented, near-single crystallinity. The surface passivation, solubility and length of the wires may also be systematically varied.

Small-diameter "quantum" wires are ideal specimens for fundamental studies of two-dimensional (2D) quantum-confinement phenomena and for property comparisons to 3D-confined quantum dots, 1D-confined quantum wells and anisotropically 3D-confined quantum rods. Potential applications of semiconductor nanowires in nanophotonics and lasing, nanoelectronics, solar-energy conversion and chemical detection are under active development. Exciting progress and advances in the semiconductor-nanowire field, enabled by the emergence of nanoparticle-catalysed growth, are anticipated in the immediate future.

Organic Photovoltaic Devices

The ability to create high-efficiency solar cells is a key strategy to meeting growing world energy needs. Nanotechnology is currently enabling the production of high-efficiency organic photovoltaics (OPVs) to help meet this challenge. Organic photovoltaics are nanostructured thin films composed of layers of semiconducting organic materials (polymers or oligomers) that absorb photons from the solar spectrum. These devices will revolutionise solar energy harvesting, because they can be manufactured via solution-based methods, such as ink-jet or screen printing, enabling rapid mass-production and driving down cost. OPVs currently lag behind their "inorganic" counterparts because of low solar energy conversion efficiencies (approximately 1-3%)

Several research groups are addressing conversion efficiency by employing a combination of nanomaterials and unique nanoscale architectures. These hybrid organic-inorganic photovoltaics consist of light-absorbing polymers in contact with semiconductor nanocrystals, fullerenes or nanostructured metals. The nanomaterials affect electro-optical properties of the conducting polymer, which include assisting in absorption of red and near-IR photons, a significant portion of the solar spectrum. Examples of OPVs designs employing nanomaterials include:

— *Polymer-Fullerene Heterojunctions:* Cells where a chemically modified fullerene (C_{60}) layer, acting as electron acceptors, is in close physical contact with a polymeric organic electron donor. This contact improves efficiency by allowing charge transfer to take place at the sub 10-nanometer scale, on the order of the diffusion length of an exciton generated from organic semiconductors. The most recent cells exhibit conversion efficiencies of ~5%.

— *Organic-Nanocrytsal Solar Cells:* Blends of semiconducting polymers and semiconducting quantum dots or nanorods (CdSe or CdTe) are mixed in a manner similar to the polymer-fullerene blends. The polymers are modified to give rise to chemical bonding between the nanocrystal and polymer. The nanocrystals can be tailored to a wide variety of optical band gaps, which depend on the size of the nanocrystal (or the diameter of the nanorod).

— *Dye-Sensitised Cells:* These cells employ complex dye molecules attached to the surface of nanostructured oxides like titanium(IV) oxide (TiO_2) or niobium(V) oxide (Nb_2O_5). The dyes exhibit broad lightabsorption profiles and rapid photoinduced charge transfer of electrons to the nanocrystals. These cells show solar conversion efficiencies of ~4%.

— *Tandem Cells:* The tandem cell acts as a 2-1 cell, harvesting photons from the complete visible spectrum. These cells employ layers of C_{60} as a strong blue light absorber and copper-phthalocyanine (CuPc) as a red-yellow absorber. Nanosized silver particles act as a charge conduit between the cells but do not absorb photons traveling through the cell because of their nanosized dimensions. These cells have achieved conversion efficiencies of ~6%. Significant challenges exist to achieving OPV devices that can be mass-produced. Nanotechnology will assist in meeting the technical challenges of this rapidly evolving field. Nanopowders and nanoparticle dispersions have seen increasing applications in coatings. Due to their small size, very even coating can be achieved by painting nanoparticle dispersions onto a surface and baking off the residual solvent.

— *Optically Transparent Conductive Coatings:* Indium tin oxide (ITO) and antimony tin oxide (ATO) are well known, optically transparent, electrically conductive materials. Nanoparticles of these materials can be painted on surfaces such as interactive touch screens to create a conductive, transparent screen without relying on expensive sputtering techniques. In addition, ITO and ATO can be used as an antistatic coating, utilising their inherent conductivity to dissipate static charge.

— *Optically Transparent Abrasion-Resistant Coatings:* Nanoscale aluminum oxide and titanium oxide are optically transparent and greatly increase the abrasion resistance of traditional coatings. Titanium oxide is of particular interest in many optical applications, since it is highly reflective for most ultra-violet radiation. Zinc oxide and rare-earth oxides are also UV-reflective, but optically transparent and are therefore effective in protecting surfaces from degradation brought about by exposure to UV radiation.

Carbon Nanotube-Based Biosensors

Researchers developed near-infrared optical biosensors based on single-walled carbon nanotubes, which modulate their fluorescence emission in response to specific biomolecules. The viability of sensor techniques was demonstrated by creating a singlewalled carbon nanotube (SWNT) enzyme bio-conjugate that detects glucose concentrations. Carbon nanotubes fluoresce in a region of the near-infrared, where human tissue and biological fluids are particularly transparent to their emission. The important aspect of this technology is that the technique can be extended to many other chemical systems. New types of non-covalent functionalisation are developed, creating opportunities for nanoparticle sensors that operate in strong absorbing media of relevance to medicine or biology.

Layer-by-Layer Nano assembly

Researchers from Louisiana Tech University were among the pioneers of one of the novel nanotechnology methods: layer-by-layer (LbL) nanoassembly by alternate adsorption of oppositely charged polyelectrolytes, nanoparticles and proteins. With this technique, we can assemble ultrathin multilayers with nanometer precision and pre-determined composition across the film, and make nanocapsules from LbL films. Such nanocapsules for targeted drug delivery, biocompatible nanocoating and pulp microfiber processing. For this nanoarchitecture, we use nanoblocks, such as nanoparticles.

In the development of our research area, we successfully used nanoparticles, such as different diameter and surface-charged gold nanoparticles, silica, nanoclay-montmorillonite, alumina, titanium dioxide and other nanoparticles. Also, we investigated linear polyelectrolytes of different types and molecular weight (especially natural polyelectrolytes), which we used as electrostatic glue to assemble nanoparticle and protein arrays. As any architect, we nanoarchitects need a wide palette of nanoblocks with new properties and dimensions, ideally, monodispersed, stable in solution, charged nanoparticles of noble metals, metal oxides and ceramics with diameters of 5, 10, 20, 50 and 100 nm.

Antibacterial applications

Zinc oxide is an effective antibacterial and anti-odor agent. It has been used in deodorants, dental cleansers and diaper creams. The increased ease in dispersibility, optical transparence and smoothness make zinc oxide nanopowder an attractive antibacterial ingredient in many heath care products. Copper oxide nanopowder has also been proposed as an anti-microbial preservative for wood or food products.

Over the last two decades, general interest and research in fuel cells has increased, because they have the potential to be more energy efficient than conventional power generation methods. During this time period, researchers have begun using nanomaterials in the catalyst layer of fuel cell electrodes for a variety of reasons, including: increasing the active surface area of the anode and cathode catalyst, increasing the catalytic rate of oxidation or reduction and minimising the weight of platinum and other precious metals in the fuel cell.

The current generated at an electrode is proportional to the active surface of catalyst on the electrode surface, so higher power density fuel cells can be formed from nanomaterials, because nanomaterials have a higher surface area to volume ratio. Researchers have also shown that the electrocatalytic properties of the materials are sensitive to particle size, so increased catalytic activity can be observed for nanoparticles and nanomaterials. However, the most important goal has been to decrease the weight of platinum and other precious metals in the catalyst layer of the fuel cell, so that the fuel cell can be costeffective. This has been the main limitation to the widespread use of fuel cells.

Researchers have employed carbon nanomaterials as supports for dispersions of platinum nanomaterials. This allows for a decrease in the weight of platinum needed to produce the same surface area of active platinum catalyst. The nanomaterials could be carbon foams containing nanopores, different types of nanotubes or even singlewalled nanohorns. All of these materials can act as a support and a conductor for platinum nanomaterials, making strides toward cost-effective fuel cell catalysts.

Devising schemes to meet the world's growing energy demands while simultaneously reducing green house emissions and other pollutants, has become one of the major challenges facing materials scientists. Nanomaterials promise to help solve many of the problems associated with new and emerging energy technologies.

Fuel Cells: Solid oxide fuel cells (SOFCs) offer the advantage over other fuel cell designs in that they do not require expensive, precious metal catalysts and can operate effectively without extensive purification of fuel sources. The activity of doped rare-earth oxide electrodes such as yttrium stabilised zirconia (YSZ) is directly related to their surface areas. Nanoparticles exhibit the high surface required for developing SOFC technologies.

Cleaner Emissions: Catalytic converters on vehicles around the world have significantly reduced the amount of automotive pollution over the last three decades. These devices require large amounts of expensive metals such as platinum, palladium and rhodium. Doped rare-earth metal oxides offer the promise of increased catalytic activity without the heavy reliance on precious metals. In addition, the increased efficiency of the next-generation catalytic converters will result in cleaner emission of existing internal combustion and diesel engines.

Nanotube-Polymer Materials

Exceptional mechanical properties of single-walled carbon nanotubes (SWNT) have prompted intensive studies of SWNT-polymer composites. However, the composites made with nanotubes are still holding a substantial reserve of improvement of mechanical properties. The problem is that pristine SWNTs have very poor solubility in polymers, which leads to phase segregation of composites. Severe structural inhomogeneities result in the premature failure of the hybrid SWNT-polymer materials. The connectivity with the polymer matrix and uniform distribution within the matrix are essential structural requirements for strong SWNT composites. This problem is being solved by several approaches.

First, by using coatings from surfactants and polymers, such as sodium dodecyl sulfate or poly(styrenesulfonate). This enables formation of better dispersions in traditional solvents including water. Polymeric dispersion agents are strongly preferred for the composite preparation because of (a) tighter bonding with the graphene surface, (b) miscibility with polymer matrixes of composites and (c) substantially smaller concentration necessary for the preparation of SWNT dispersions. Among polymers, different poly(vinyl alcohols) work best as a host matrix for SWNTs, providing the composites with high tensile strength and excellent Young's modulus. An additional resource of SWNTs for improving the mechanical properties of composites is nanotube orientation.

Virtually complete alignment of nanotubes can be achieved in SWNT composite fibers. These composites display substantially better mechanical properties than any other SWNT-polymer hybrid. If one can find a simple and controllable method to produce not only fibers but also bulk materials and coatings with nanotubes oriented in a desirable direction, new technological vistas can be opened for various composites. Breakthroughs in this area can come both from the studies of fundamental properties of SWNTs and from development of methods for composite processing. In the past, magnetic field alignment with exceptionally powerful electromagnets and alignment in the flow was used for this purpose.

Metal Matrix Nanocomposites

Metal matrix composites (MMCs) such as continuous carbon or boron fiber reinforced aluminum and magnesium, and silicon carbide reinforced aluminum have been used for aerospace applications due to their lightweight and tailorable properties. There is much interest in producing metal matrix nanocomposites that incorporate nanoparticles and nanotubes for structural applications, as these materials exhibit even greater improvements in their physical, mechanical and tribological properties as compared to composites with micron-sized reinforcements. The incorporation of carbon nanotubes in particular, which have much higher strength, stiffness, and electrical conductivity as compared to metals, can significantly increase these properties of metal matrix composites. Nanocomposites are being explored for structural applications in the defense, aerospace and automotive sectors.

Concurrent with the interest in producing novel nanocomposite materials is the need to develop low cost means to produce these materials. Most of the prior work in synthesising nanocomposites involves the use of powder metallurgy techniques, which are not only high cost, but also result in the presence of porosity and contamination.

Solidification processing methods, such as stir mixing, squeeze casting and pressure infiltration are advantageous over other processes in rapidly and inexpensively producing large and complex near-net shape components, however, this area remains relatively unexplored in the synthesis of nanocomposites. Stir mixing techniques, widely utilised to mix micron size particles in metallic melts, have recently been modified for dispersing small volume percentages of nanosize reinforcement particles in metallic matrices. Although there are some difficulties in mixing nanosize particles in metallic melts resulting from their tendency to agglomerate, a research team in Japan has published research on dispersing nanosize particles in aluminum alloys using a stir mixing technique. Researchers at the Polish Academy of Science have recently demonstrated the incorporation of greater than 80 volume percent nanoparticles in metals using high-pressure infiltration with pressures in the GPa range. Composites produced by this method possess the unique properties of nanosize metallic grains.

Recently, metal matrix nanocomposites were synthesised at the University of Wisconsin, Milwaukee using aluminum alloy A206 and nanoparticles of alumina (Al_2O_3). TEM samples of the cast Al-A206/Al_2O_3 clearly show nanoparticles present within the metal matrix. SAD patterns show the pattern of the matrix as well as the nanoparticles.

EDX indicates that the grains are composed of aluminum, which contains nanosize alumina particles. The distribution of particles throughout the grains of the matrix with an absence of large concentrations at the grain boundaries suggests wetting of the alumina by the liquid metal. In this case the nanoparticles did not appear to act as nucleation sites for nanosized grains.

Nanoelectronic Systems

Self-assembly is not limited to the nanometer length scale. Strategies that are based on self-assembly are projected to have a major impact in the manufacturing of systems on both, the micro, and nanometer length scale. Programmable self-assembly involves the design of "intelligent" components that undergo self-assembly to form a desired device or microsystem. Programmable self-assembly has the potential to overcome the limitations of existing manufacturing concepts.

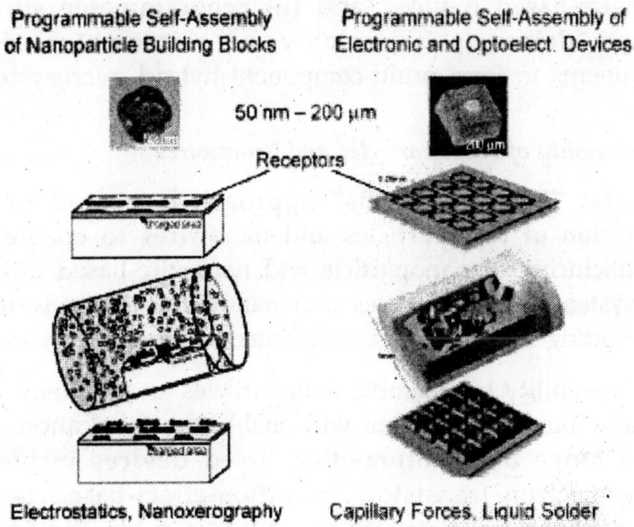

Figure 1. Concept of Programmable Self-Assembly; programmable/ reconfigurable receptors are used to direct the assembly of 50 nm - 200 µm sized components

Currently the incompatibility of Si, GaAs, GaN, InP, and III-VI semiconductor-based processes results in the assembly of systems that are connected with long interconnects on separate substrates. Such systems are typically assembled using robotic assembly. Conventional robotic methods and assembly lines, however, fail as components become smaller, because of the difficulty in building machines that can economically manipulate components in three dimensions. Programmable self-assembly has the potential to overcome these limitations and enable non-robotic manufacturing of hybrid micro and nanometer-sized systems with new functionalities, short interconnects, and superior performance.

Figure 1 illustrates the basic concept of the following two approaches: (i) electrostatically directed self-assembly of nanoparticles and nanowires to form nanoparticle and nanowire-based devices, and (ii) programmable surface tension driven self-assembly of micrometer sized components to form multi-component hybrid microsystems.

Self-assembly of Nanoparticles and Nanowires

The first "hybrid systems" approach is geared to the integration of nanoparticles and nanowires to enable the manufacturing of nanoparticle and nanowire-based devices and systems. Nanoparticles and nanowires are considered the building blocks of future nanotechnological devices.

The ability to assemble nanoparticles and nanowires in two and three dimensions will enable the fabrication of a whole range of quantum-effect-based devices including single electron transistors, quantum-effect-based lasers, photonic bandgap materials, filters, wave-guides, and high-density data storage devices. The use of nanoparticles and nanowires as building blocks, however, requires novel assembling strategies. Single particle/wire manipulation and random particle/wire depositioning have been used to fabricate first-device prototypes.

Strategies that use single particle manipulation and random particle deposition are considered as straightforward methods to fabricate and explore new device architectures. For example, a "nanorobot" would position nanoparticles with nm resolution to fabricate a certain device. Most commonly, such a "nanorobot" consists of a modified scanning probe microscope where the probe is used as a tool to position the nanoparticles or makes use of nanotweezers for pick and placement.

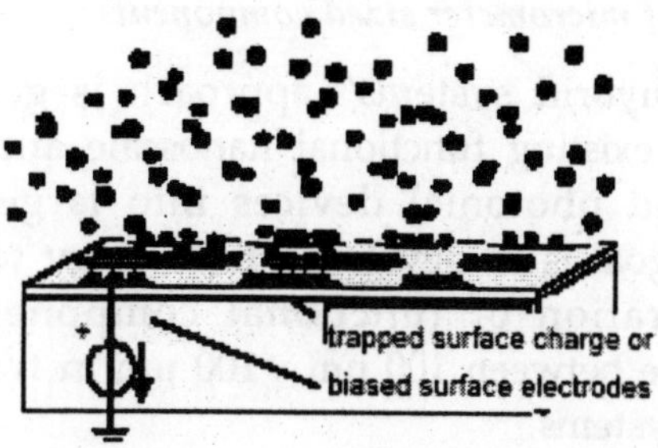

Figure 2. Principle of Electrostatic directed self-assembly.

Both single particle manipulation and random particle deposition enable the fabrication of device prototypes at an early stage and are therefore important strategies. However, inherent disadvantages such as the lag in yield and speed will have to be overcome to enable the manufacturing of nanotechnological devices. Fabrication strategies that rely on mechanisms of self-assembly may overcome these difficulties. Most actively investigated areas currently use protein recognition, DNA hybridisation, hydrophobicity/ hydrophilicit, and magnetic interactions. In the area of electrostatics, we have developed a method to pattern charge with sub 100 nm resolution and a number of different systems to enable the parallel integration of nanoparticles from a gas or liquid phase. The advantage of using electrostatic forces compared to other strategies is that it is long-range and non-material specific (any particle can be trapped). The basic principle of the electrostatically directed self-assembly process of nanoparticles is illustrated in Figure 2. Electric fields and charged areas are programmable by applying external bias voltages to surface electrodes. This process as electrostatically directed self-assembly or nanoxerographic type printing. We have developed a number of different systems to enable the parallel integration of nanoparticles from a gas or liquid phase.

Self-assembly of micrometer sized components

The second "hybrid systems" approach is geared to the integration of existing functional nanoscale and microscale (electronic and photonic) devices into large mesoscale systems. The goal is to develop a technology to enable the hybrid integration of functional components with a component size between 100 nm - 100 µm in two and three dimensional systems.

Previous demonstrations of directed self-assembly to generate functional electrical microsystems include the coplanar integration of segmented integrated circuit (IC) devices into 2D "superchips" using capillary forces, shapedirected fluidic methods that position electronic devices on planar surfaces using shape recognition and gravitational forces, liquid-solder-based self-assemblies that use the surface tension between pairs of molten solder drops to assemble three-dimensional electrical networks, ring oscillators, and shift registers, capillary force-directed self-assembly that uses hydrophobic-hydrophilic surfaces patterns and photo curable polymers to integrate micro-optical components, micromirrors and semiconductor chips on silicon substrates and solder-receptor-directed self-assembly to realise hybrid microsystems and flexible displays where metal contacts on segmented semiconductor devices bind to liquid-solderbased-receptors to assemble and electrically connect devices on planar and non-planar surfaces.

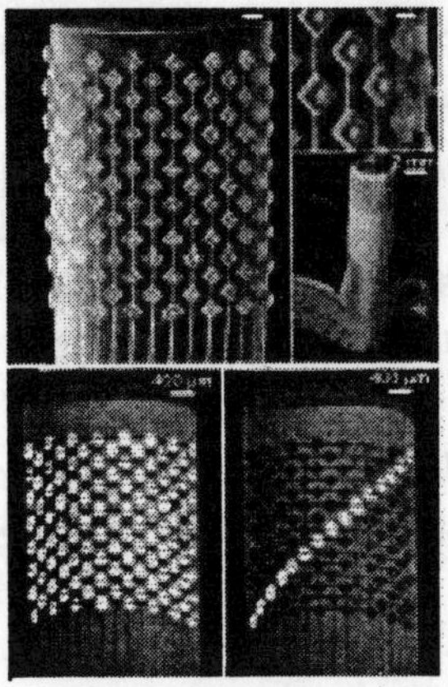

Figure 3. Self-Assembled Cylindrical Display.

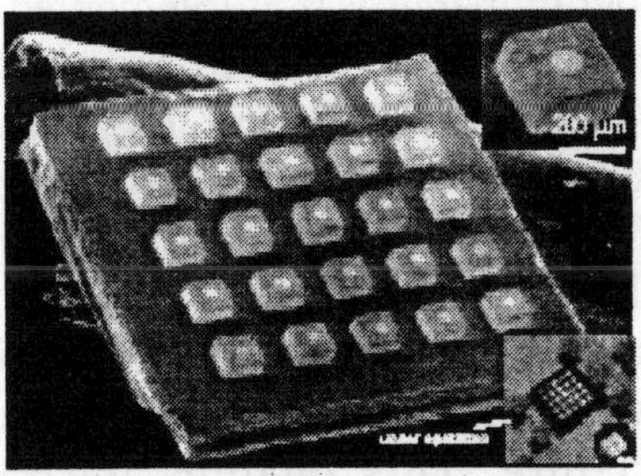

Figure 4. Hybrid Parallel Integration-Batch transfer of GaAs/GaAlAs LEDs on Si.

Metal contacts on segmented semiconductor devices bind to liquid-solder-based-receptors to assemble and electrically connect devices on planar and nonplanar surfaces. The liquid metal coated templates provide three key requirements: they can (i) act as receptors for subunits during the assembly (no manipulator is needed), (ii) they form rigid bonds upon solidification (no adhesive needed), and (iii) they provide electrical input/output-connectors to operate the final device (no wirebonder needed). We have used solder-receptor-directed self-assembly to realise flexible cylindrical displays and hybrid microsystems.

Hybrid Parallel Integration on Silicon: Figure 4 shows GaAs/GaAlAs light emitting diodes that have been assembled onto silicon wafers. A flexible copper-polyimide composite was used to connect the top contact to operate the assembly (inset).

Programmable Reconfigurable Liquid Solder-Directed Self-Assembly: Current self-assembly strategies are most suitable to handle large numbers of identical components. Their disadvantage is that they provide insufficient selectivity to assemble nonidentical components to form multicomponent hybrid systems. Programmable reconfigurable liquid solder directed self-assembly is a self-assembly concept that enables parallel hybrid integration of non-identical components. Programmability is implemented using solder-based receptors that can be switched on and off electrically using integrated heaters. The first biggest advantage of programmable liquid solder-directed self-assembly is that it enables reconfigurable self-assembly rather than static assemblies. The user can select the form of assembly without fabrication of a new structure. The second biggest advantage is that it forms electrical interconnects during the assembly procedure. This enables the fabrication of electrically functional assemblies. The third biggest advantage is that it allows the assembly of microsystems that contain non-identical parts—the integration of nonidentical devices to form multi-component microsystems is difficult to accomplish with existing self-assembly due to insufficient power of recognition.

Self-assembled Nanoparticle Clusters

Synthesis of a variety of Au nanoparticles with different coatings are needed to model a wide range of physical phenomena. Motivated by the limitations of the published nanoparticle synthesis methods, we have developed a strategy that would accommodate a broad range of ligands, similar to the Brust reaction, but which does not need a phase transfer catalyst to produce gold nanoparticles.

The desired ligand is then added to this solution. The core size of synthesised nanoparticle can be controlled at this point by varying the number of equivalents of thiol used with respect to the gold salt. Lithium borohydride is added followed by addition of toluene and removal of the tetrahydrofuran under reduced pressure. The gold nanoparticles solution is further diluted with toluene and washed with water to remove any reducing agent byproducts. The toluene is then removed and the crude product is collected on a fritted glass funnel and washed with acetonitrile and ethanol.

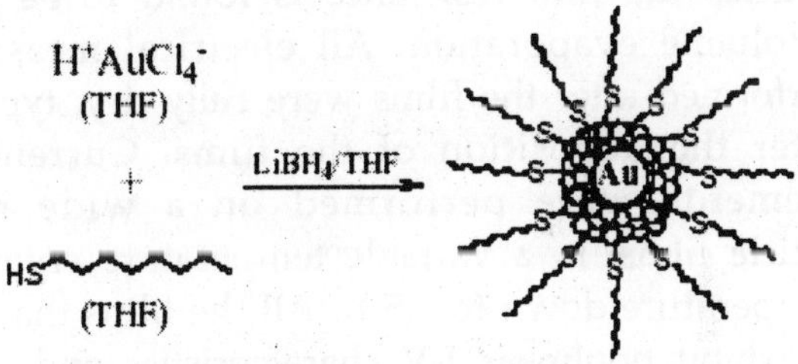

Figure 5. Reaction scheme of the homogeneous organic phase nanoparticle synthesis method.

The purified gold nanoparticles are collected with toluene to form a stable colloidal suspension. This procedure has proven to be a very versatile means for production of pure gold nanoparticles that are free of any ionic species capable of interfering with electronic measurements. Examples of products include the gold nanoparticles capped with 1-octanethiol (C8), 1-dodecanethiol (C12), 1-octadecanethiol (C18), 4-mercaptodiphenylacetylene (DPA), 4-nitro-4-

mercaptodiphenylacetylene (NDPA), and 3,5-dinitro-4-mercaptodiphenylacetylene (DNDPA). Sizewise this synthetic method reliably produces quite monodisperse nanoparticles. The average core size and the size dispersion of the nanoparticles were determined using TEM studies.

In most cases, due to the very high resistance of the Au nanoparticle films, interdigitated electrodes are needed to study transport properties of such films. 20 nm tall Au interdigitated electrodes with 50 fingers, with a finger length of 9 μm and electrode spacing of 100 nm, were fabricated on an insulating silicon oxide film by electron beam lithography. Au nanoparticles that were suspended in toluene are deposited on such interdigitated electrodes using an airbrush technique. The films prepared by this technique are found to be highly nonuniform in thickness.

In the first few hours after the deposition of the nanoparticles the film resistance is found to be changing due to toluene evaporation. All electrical measurements were performed after the films were fully dry, typically 1-2 days after the deposition of the films. Current-voltage measurements were performed on a wide range of nanoparticle films, in a variable temperature cryostat from room temperature down to 1.5 K. All the films that we have studied exhibit nonlinear I-V characteristics and insulating behaviour at low temperatures.

The insulating behaviour is evident in the non-linear I-V characteristics at low temperatures as well as the temperature dependence of the small-bias resistance. The insulating behaviour arises from the single electron effects; as the size of the particles becomes sufficiently small there is charging energy associated with electron tunnelling which can be larger than thermal energy and thus tunnelling is not allowed at low temperatures.

The size of the charging energy is given by $e^2/2C$ where C is the island capacitance. In real systems, there are trapped charges near the nanoparticles which would lead to a random offset charge disorder. In the presence of such disorder, current does not flow uniformly through the nanoparticle film. In fact it is possible that there may be a few energetically favourable paths that carry most of the current. Because of such kind of disorder, the charging energy extracted from the temperature dependent data is always smaller that the charging energy. The magnitude of the charging energy can be engineered by changing the size of the nanoparticles. To test this idea, we synthesised Au nanoparticles of different sizes.

The charging energy for 2.2 nm diameter Au nanoparticles is much larger than the thermal energy at room temperature. In fact, the small bias resistance of this film was unmeasurably large even at room temperature, consistent with a large Coulomb gap. In principle the size of the charging energy can also be engineered by changing the dielectric constant of the medium between the nanoparticles. In addition to charging energy we must also be ablc to engineer the tunnel coupling between the islands. There are two strategies to engineer the tunnel coupling. The first strategy is to change the distance between the nanoparticles by using different sized thiol coatings.

The second strategy is to control the energy barrier for tunnelling. For tunnelling of electrons the relevant energy barrier is given by the energy of the lowest unoccupied molecular orbitals (LUMO) of the thiol coating. To test these ideas we have synthesised Au nanoparticles with various coatings that had an approximate core diameter of 3-5 nm. These Au nanoparticle films showed activated behaviour with activation energies ranging from 26-45 meV.

The energies of the LUMOs for these three alkyl chains are expected to be similar. Thus, a difference in transport properties for these films is expected to arise from the different tunnel coupling. The trend from lowest to highest resistance for alkylthiol coated Au nanoparticles films is C8, C12, then C18, with C18 being immeasurably high. This is consistent with the thicker thiol coatings forming more resistive films. The second strategy is to control tunnel coupling by using thiol coatings with LUMOs with different energies. It is well known that there are conjugated ligands that have LUMO energies that are lower than that of alkyl chains.

10

Nanotechnology in Pollution Control

The classification and sources of pollutants of necessity have to be emitted to "traditional" contaminants. Not long ago, the nation's natural resources were exploited indiscriminately. Waterways served as industrial pollution sinks, skies dispersed smoke from factories and power plants, and the land proved to be a cheap and convenient place to dump industrial and urban wastes. However, society is now more aware of the environment and the need to protect it. The American people have been involved in a great social movement known broadly as "environmentalism." Society has been concerned with the quality of the air one breathes, the water one drinks, and the land on which one lives and works. While economic growth and prosperity are still important goals, opinion polls show overwhelming public support for pollution controls and a pronounced willingness to pay for them.

Since the Clean Air Act was passed in 1970, the United States has made impressive strides in improving and protecting air quality. As directed by this Act, the EPA set National Ambient Air Quality Standards (NAAQS) for those pollutants commonly found throughout the country that posed the greatest overall threats to air quality. These pollutants, termed criteria pollutants under the act, include: ozone, carbon monoxide, airborne particulates, sulphur dioxide, lead, and nitrogen oxide. Although the EPA has made considerable progress in controlling air pollution, all of the six criteria except lead and nitrogen oxide are currently a major concern in a number of areas in the country.

The following are the most significant air quality challenges: ozone and carbon monoxide, airborne particulates, airborne toxics, sulphur dioxide, acid deposition, and indoor air pollutants.

Ozone and Carbon Monoxide: Ozone is one of the most intractable and widespread environmental problems. Chemically, ozone is a form of oxygen with three oxygen atoms instead of the two found in regular oxygen. This makes it very reactive, so that it combines with practically every material with which it comes in contact. In the upper atmosphere, where ozone is needed to protect people from ultraviolet radiation, the ozone is being destroyed by manmade chemicals, but at ground level, ozone can be a harmful pollutant. Ozone is produced in the atmosphere when sunlight triggers chemical reactions between naturally occurring atmospheric gases and pollutants such as volatile organic compounds (VOCs) and nitrogen oxides.

The main source of VOCs and nitrogen oxides is combustion sources such as motor vehicle traffic. Carbon monoxide is an invisible, odorless product of incomplete fuel combustion. As with ozone, motor vehicles are the main contributor to carbon monoxide formation. Other sources include wood-burning stoves, incinerators, and industrial processes. Since auto travel and the number of small sources of VOCs are expected to increase, even strenuous efforts may not sufficiently reduce emissions of ozone and carbon monoxide.

Airborne Particulates: Particulates in the air traditionally include dust, smoke, metals, and aerosols. Major sources include steel mills, power plants, cotton gins, cement plants, smelters, and diesel engines. Other sources are grain storage elevators, industrial haul roads, construction work, and demolition. Wood-burning stoves and fireplaces can also be significant sources of particulates. Urban areas are likely to have wind-blown dust from roads, parking lots, and construction work.

Airborne Toxics: Toxic pollutants are one of today's most serious emerging problems and found in all media. Many sources emit toxic chemicals into the atmosphere: industrial and manufacturing processes, solvent use, sewage treatment plants, hazardous waste handling and disposal sites, municipal waste sites, incinerators, and motor vehicles. Smelters, metal refiners, manufacturing processes, and stationary fuel combustion sources emit such toxic metals as cadmium, lead, arsenic, chromium, mercury, and beryllium. Toxic organics, such as vinyl chloride and benzene, are released by a variety of sources, such as plastics and chemical manufacturing plants, and gas stations. Chlorinated dioxins and furans are emitted by some chemical processes and the high-temperature burning of plastics in incinerators.

Sulphur Dioxide: Sulphur dioxide can be transported long distances in the atmosphere because of its ability to bond to particulates. After travelling, sulphur dioxide combines with water vapour to form acid rain. Sulphur dioxide is released into the air primarily through the burning of coal and fuel oils. Today, two-thirds of all national sulphur dioxide emissions come from electric power plants. Other sources of sulphur dioxide include refiners, pulp and paper mills, smelters, steel and chemical plants, and energy facilities related to oil shale, syn (synthetic) fuels, and oil and gas production. Home furnaces and coal-burning stoves are sources that directly affect residential neighbourhoods.

Acid Deposition: Acid deposition is a serious environmental concern in many parts of the country. The process of acid deposition begins with the emissions of sulphur dioxide (primarily from coal-burning power plants) and nitrogen oxides (primarily from motor vehicles and coal-burning power plants). During a storm, these compounds fall to Earth as acid rain or snow; the compounds may also join dust or other dry airborne particles and fall as "dry deposition."

Indoor Pollutants

Indoor air pollution is rapidly becoming a major health issue in the United States. Indoor pollutant levels are quite often higher than outdoors, particularly where buildings are tightly constructed to save energy. Since most people spend 90 percent of their time indoors, exposure to unhealthy concentrations of indoor air pollutants is often inevitable. The degree of risk associated with exposure to indoor pollutants depends on how well buildings are ventilated and the type, mixture, and amounts of pollutants in the building. Indoor air pollutants of special concern are described below.

Radon: Radon is a unique environmental problem because it occurs naturally. Radon results from the radioactive decay of radium-226, found in many types of rocks and soils. Most indoor radon comes from the rock and soil around a building and enters structures through cracks or openings in the foundation or basement. Secondary sources of indoor radon are well water and building materials. Environmental Tobacco Smoke Environmental tobacco smoke is smoke that nonsmokers are exposed to from smokers. This smoke has been judged by the Surgeon General, the National Research Council, and the International Agency for Research on Cancer to pose a risk of lung cancer to nonsmokers. Tobacco smoke contains a number of pollutants, including inorganic gases, heavy metals, particulates, VOCs, and products of incomplete combustion (PICs), such as polynuclear aromatic hydrocarbons.

Asbestos: Asbestos has been used in the past in a variety of building materials, including many types of insulation, fireproofing, wallboard, ceiling tiles, and floor tiles. The remodelling or demolition of buildings with asbestos-containing materials frees tiny asbestos fibers in clumps or clouds of dust. Even with normal aging, materials may deteriorate and release asbestos fibers. Once released, these asbestos fibers can be inhaled into the lungs and can accumulate.

Formaldehyde and Other Volatile Organic Compounds: The EPA has found formaldehyde to be a probable human carcinogen. The use of formaldehyde in furniture, foam insulation, and pressed wood products, such as some plywood, particle board, and fiberboard, makes formaldehyde a major indoor air pollutant. The VOCs commonly found indoors include benzene from tobacco smoke and perchlorethylene emitted by dry-cleaned clothes. Paints and stored chemicals, including certain cleaning compounds, are also major sources of VOCs. VOCs can also be emitted from drinking water; 20 percent of water supply systems have detectable amounts of VOCs.

Pesticides: Indoor and outdoor use of pesticides, including termiticides and wood preservatives, are another cause of concern. Even when used as directed, pesticides may release VOCs. In addition, there are about 1200 inert ingredients added to pesticide products for a variety of purposes. While not "active" in attacking the particular pest, some inert ingredients are chemically or biologically active and may cause health problems. EPA researchers are presently investigating whether indoor use of insecticides and subsurface soil injection of termiticides can lead to hazardous exposure.

The EPA, in partnership with state and local governments, is responsible for improving and maintaining water quality. These efforts are organised around three themes. The first is maintaining the quality of drinking water. This is addressed by monitoring and treating drinking water prior to consumption and by minimising the contamination of the surface water and protecting against contamination of groundwater needed for human consumption.

The second is preventing the degradation and destruction of critical aquatic habitats, including wetlands, nearshore coastal waters, oceans, and lakes. The third is reducing the pollution of free-flowing surface waters and protecting their uses. The following is a discussion of various pollutants categorized by these themes.

Drinking Water Pollutants: The most severe and acute public health effects from contaminated drinking water, such as cholera and typhoid, have been eliminated in America. However, some less acute and immediate hazards remain in the nation's tap water. These hazards are associated with a number of specific contaminants in drinking water. Contaminants of special concern to the EPA are lead, radionuclides, microbiological contaminants, and disinfection by-products. The primary source of lead in drinking water is corrosion of plumbing materials, such as lead service lines and lead solders, in water distribution systems and in houses and larger buildings. Virtually all public water systems serve households with lead solders of varying ages, and most faucets are made of materials that can contribute some lead to drinking water.

Radionuclides are radioactive isotopes that emit radiation as they decay. The most significant radionuclides in drinking water are radium, uranium, and radon, all of which occur in the natural environment. While radium and uranium enter the body by ingestion, radon is usually inhaled after being released into the air during showers, baths, and other activities, such as washing clothes or dishes.

Radionuclides in drinking water occur primarily in those systems that use groundwater. Naturally occurring radionuclides seldom are found in surface waters (such as rivers, lakes, and streams). Water contains many microbes-bacteria, viruses, and protozoa. Although some organisms are harmless, others can cause disease. The Centers for Disease Control reported 112 waterborne disease outbreaks from 1981 to 1983. Microbiological contamination continues to be a national concern because contaminated drinking water systems can rapidly spread disease. Disinfection by-products are produced during water treatment by the chemical reactions of disinfectants with naturally occurring or synthetic organic materials present in untreated water.

Since these disinfectants are essential to safe drinking water, the EPA is presently looking at ways to minimise the risks from by-products. Critical Aquatic Habitat Pollutants Critical aquatic habitats that need special management attention include the nation's wetlands, near coastal waters, oceans, and lakes. In recent years, the EPA has been focusing on addressing the special problems of these areas. The following is a discussion of pollutants categorised by the habitats they affect. Wetlands in urban areas frequently represent the last large tracts of open space and are often a final haven for wildlife.

Not surprisingly, as suitable upland development sites become exhausted, urban wetlands are under increasing pressure for residential housing, industry, and commercial facilities. Increasing evidence exists that the nation's wetlands, in addition to being destroyed by physical threats, also are being degraded by chemical contamination. The problem of wetland contamination received national attention in 1985 due to reports of waterfowl deaths and deformities caused by selenium contamination. Selenium is a trace element that occurs naturally in soil and is needed in small amounts to sustain life. However, for years it was being leached out of the soil and carried in agricultural drainwater used to flood the wildlife refuge's wetlands, where it accumulated to dangerously high levels. Coastal water environments are particularly susceptible to contamination because they act as sinks for the large quantities of pollution discharged from municipal sewage treatment plants, industrial facilities, and hazardous waste disposal sites.

In many coastal areas, non-point-source runoff from agricultural lands, suburban developments, city streets, and combined sewer and stormwater overflows poses an even more significant problem than point sources. This is due to the difficulty of identifying and then controlling the source of the pollution. Physical and hydrological modifications from such activities as dredging channels, draining and filling wetlands, constructing dams, and building shorefront houses may further degrade near coastal environments.

In addition, growing population pressures will continue to subject these sensitive coastal ecosystems to further stress. The Great Lakes provide an inestimable resource to the 45 million people living in the surrounding basin. A 1970 study by the International Joint Commission identified nutrients and toxic problems in the lakes. They suffered from eutrophication problems caused by excessive nutrient inputs.

Since then the United States and Canada have made joint efforts to reduce nutrient loadings, particularly phosphorus. However, contamination of the water and fish by toxics from pesticide runoff, land-fill leachates, and in-place sediments remains a major problem.

Ocean dumping of dredged material, sewage sludge, and industrial wastes is a major source of ocean pollution. Sediments dredged from industrialised urban harbors are often highly contaminated with heavy metals and toxic synthetic organic chemicals like PCBs and petroleum hydrocarbons. Although ocean dumping of dredged material, sludge, and industrial wastes is now less of a threat, persistent disposal of plastics from land and ships at sea has become a serious problem. Debris on beaches from sewer and storm drain overflows or mismanagement of trash poses public safety and aesthetic concerns.

Surface Water Pollutants: Pollutants in waterways come from industries or treatment plants discharging wastewater into streams or from waters running across urban and agricultural areas, carrying the surface pollution with them (nonpoint sources). The following is a discussion of surface water pollutants categorised by their main sources. Raw or insufficiently treated wastewater from municipal and industrial treatment plants still threatens water resources in many parts of the country. In addition to harmful nutrients, poorly treated wastewater may contain bacteria and chemicals.

Sludge, the residue left from wastewater treatment plants, is a growing problem. Although some sludges are relatively "clean," or free from toxic substances, other sludges may contain organic, inorganic, or toxic pollutants and pathogens. An important source of toxic pollution is industrial wastewater discharged directly into waterways or indirectly through municipal wastewater treatment plants.

Industrial wastes discharged indirectly are treated to remove toxic pollutants. It is important that those wastes be treated because toxics may end up in sludge, making them harder to dispose of safely. Nonpoint sources present continuing problems for achieving national water quality in many parts of the country. Sediment and nutrients are the two largest contributors to non-point-source problems. Nonpoint sources are also a major source of toxics, among them pesticide runoff from agricultural areas, metals from active or abandoned mines, gasoline, and asbestos from urban areas. In addition, the atmosphere is a source of toxics since many toxics can attach themselves to dust, later to be deposited in surface waters hundreds of miles away through precipitation.

Land Pollutants

Historically, land has been used as the dumping ground for wastes, including those removed from the air and water. Early environmental protection efforts focused on cleaning up air and water pollution. It was not until the 1970s that there was much public concern about pollution of the land. It is now recognised that contamination of the land threatens not only future uses of the land itself, but also the quality of the surrounding air, surface water, and groundwater. There are five different forms of land pollutants. These include:

1. Industrial hazardous wastes
2. Municipal wastes
3. Mining wastes
4. Radioactive wastes
5. Underground storage tanks

Industrial Hazardous Wastes: The chemical, petroleum, and transportation industries are major producers of hazardous industrial waste. Ninety-nine percent of the hazardous waste is produced by facilities that generate large quantities (more than 2200 lb) of hazardous waste each month. A much smaller amount of hazardous waste, about one million tons per year, comes from small quantity generators (between 220 and 2200 lb of waste each month). These include automotive repair shops, construction firms, laundromats, dry cleaners, printing operations, and equipment repair shops. Over 60 percent of the these wastes are derived from lead batteries. The remainder includes acids, solvents, photographic wastes, and dry cleaning residue.

Municipal Wastes: Municipal wastes include household and commercial wastes, demolition materials, and sewage sludge. Solvents and other harmful household and commercial wastes are generally so intermingled with other materials that specific control of each is virtually impossible. Sewage sludge is the solid, semisolid, or liquid residue produced from treating municipal wastewater. Some sewage sludges contain high levels of disease-carrying microorganisms, toxic metals, or toxic organic chemicals. Because of the large quantities generated, sewage sludge is a major waste management problem in a number of municipalities.

Mining Wastes: A large volume of all waste generated in the United States is from mining coal, phosphates, copper, iron, uranium, other minerals, and from ore processing and milling. These wastes consist primarily of overburden, the soil and rock cleared away before mining, and tailings, the material discarded during ore processing. Runoff from these wastes increases the acidity of streams and pollutes them with toxic metals.

Radioactive Wastes: Radioactive materials are used in a wide variety of applications, from generating electricity to medical research. The United States has produced large quantities of radioactive wastes that can pose environmental and health problems for many generations.

Underground Storage Tanks: Leaking underground storage tanks are another source of land contamination that can contribute to groundwater contamination. The majority of these tanks do not store waste but instead store petroleum products and some hazardous substances. Most of the tanks are bare steel and subject to corrosion. Many are old and near the end of their useful lives. Hundreds of thousands of these tanks are presently thought to be leaking, with more expected to develop leaks in the next few years.

Before the early 1970s, the nation paid little attention to industrial production and the disposal of the waste it generated, particularly hazardous waste. As a result, billions of dollars must now be spent to clean up disposal sites neglected through years of mismanagement. The EPA often identifies a waste as hazardous if it poses a fire hazard (ignitable), dissolves materials or is acidic (corrosive), is explosive (reactive), or otherwise poses danger to human health or the environment (toxic). Most hazardous waste results from the production of widely used goods such as polyester and other synthetic fibers, kitchen appliances, and plastic milk jugs.

A small percentage of hazardous waste (less than 1 percent) is comprised of the used commercial products themselves, including household cleaning fluids or battery acid. Definitions of hazardous substances are not as straightforward as they appear. For purposes of regulation, Congress and the EPA have defined terms to describe wastes and other substances that fall under regulation. The definitions below show the complexity of the EPA's regulatory task.

1. *Hazardous Substances [Comprehensive Environmental Response, Compensation and Liability Act (CERCLA), or "Superfund"]*: Any substance that, when released into the environment, may cause substantial danger to public health, welfare, or the environment. Designation as a hazardous substance grows out of the statutory definitions in several environmental laws: CERCLA, RCRA, CWA, CAA, and TSCA. Currently there are 717 CERCLA hazardous substances.
2. *Extremely Hazardous Substance (CERCLA as amended)*: Substances that could cause serious, irreversible health effects from a single exposure. For purposes of chemical emergency planning, EPA has designated 366 substances extremely hazardous. If not already so designated, these also will be listed as hazardous substances.
3. *Solid Waste (RCRA)*: Any garbage, refuse, sludge, or other discarded material. All solid waste is not solid; it can be liquid, semisolid, or contained gaseous material. Solid waste results from industrial, commercial,

mining, and agricultural operations from community activities. Solid waste can be either hazardous or nonhazardous. However, it does not include solid or dissolved material in domestic sewage, certain nuclear material, or certain agricultural wastes.

4. *Hazardous Waste (RCRA)*: Solid waste, or combinations of solid waste, that because of its quantity, concentration, or physical, chemical, or infectious characteristics, may pose a hazard to human health or the environment.
5. *Nonhazardous Waste (RCRA)*: Solid waste, including municipal wastes, household hazardous waste, municipal sludge, and industrial and commercial wastes that are not hazardous.

Today's high standard of living would not be possible without the thousands of different chemicals produced. Most of these chemicals are not harmful if used properly. Others can be extremely harmful if people are exposed to them, even in minute amounts. The following is a discussion of four toxic chemicals under control of the Toxic Substance Control Act of 1976. Polychlorinated biphenyls (PCBs) provide an example of the problems that toxic substances can present. PCBs were used in many commercial activities, especially in heat transfer fluids in electrical transformers and capacitors. They also were used in hydraulic fluids, lubricants, and dye carriers in carbonless copy paper, and in paints, inks, and dyes.

Over time, PCBs accumulated in the environment, either from leaking electrical equipment or from other materials such as inks. Like PCBs, asbestos was widely used for many purposes, such as fireproofing and pipe and boiler insulation in schools and other buildings. Asbestos was often mixed with a cementlike material and sprayed or plastered on ceilings and other surfaces. Now these materials are deteriorating, releasing the asbestos.

Dioxins refer to a family of chemicals with similar structure, although it is common to refer to the most toxic of these-2,3,7,8-tetrachlorodinitro-p-dioxin, or TCDD-as dioxin. Dioxin is an inadvertent contaminant of the chlorinated herbicides 2,4,5-T and silvex, which were used until recently in agriculture, forest management, and lawn care. It is also a contaminant of certain wood preservatives and the defoliant Agent Orange used in Vietnam. Dioxins and the related chemicals known as furans also are formed during the combustion of PCBs. Several other sources of dioxin contamination have been identified in recent years. These include pulp and paper production and the burning of municipal wastes containing certain plastics or wood preserved by certain chlorinated chemicals. In 1978, the use of chlorofluorocarbons (CFCs) as a propellent in aerosol cans and other nonessential uses were prohibited by the EPA. The EPA took this action as a result of evidence that CFCs caused a decrease in stratopsheric ozone.

Influence of Pollutants

The material that follows, therefore, primarily addresses "traditional" pollutants. Pollutants are various noxious chemicals and refuse materials that impair the purity of the water, soil, and the atmosphere. The area most affected by pollutants is the atmosphere or air. Air pollution occurs when wastes pollute the air. Artificially or synthetically created wastes are the main sources of air pollution. They can be in the form of gases or particulates, which result from the burning of fuel to power motor vehicles and to heat buildings. More air pollution can be found in densely populated areas. The air over largely populated cities often becomes so filled with pollutants that it not only harms the health of humans, plants, and animals but also adversely affects materials of construction.

Water pollution occurs when wastes are dumped into the water. This polluted water can spread typhoid fever and other diseases. In the United States, water supplies are disinfected to kill disease-causing germs. The disinfection, in some instances, does not remove all the chemicals and metals that may cause health problems in the distant future. Wastes that are dumped into the soil are a form of land pollution, which damages the thin layer of fertile soil that is essential for agriculture. In nature, cycles work to keep soil fertile. Wastes, including dead plants and wastes from animals, form a substance in the soil called humus. Bacteria then decays the humus and breaks it down into nitrates, phosphates, and other nutrients that feed growing plants.

Air Pollution

Humans: Humans are in constant contact with pollutants, whether they are indoors or outdoors. The pollutants, primarily air pollutants, may have negative effects on human health. In some instances humans adapt and do not realise that they are being affected. For example, people living in smog-covered cities know that smog is bad for their health but just consider it "normal." There are still some who do not think that there is anything that can be done about it. Indoors, which includes the home and the workplace, a definite correlation seems to exist between some of the most important indoor activities and the resulting pollutants that are generated. Some examples of these are smoking, the use of personal products, cleaning, cooking, heating, maintenance of hair and facial care, hobbies, and electrical appliances such as washing machines and dryers.

Fumes from these activities can get trapped in the home or workplace, and the buildup of these over time will cause health problems in the short- and long-term future. When people go outside, they usually say they are going to "get some fresh air." This "fresh air" to them usually means breathing in the air from a different location. Although the common term for the air outside is "fresh air." The air may not necessarily be very "fresh." The outside air can be full of air pollutants that can cause negative effects on the health of humans.

The influence of air pollution on human productivity has not been firmly established. In addition, a number of authorities suspect (and some are convinced) that air pollution is associated with an increasing incidence of lung and respiratory ailments and heart disease. Table 1 shows some of the health effects of the regulated air pollutants. "Air toxics" is the term generally used to describe cancer-causing chemicals, radioactive materials, and other toxic chemicals not covered by the National Ambient Air Quality Standards for conventional pollutants.

Air toxics result from many activities of modem society, including driving a car, burning fossil fuel, and producing and usirg industrial chemicals or radioactive materials. The latter is one of the highest health risk problems with which the EPA is wrestling. Some major contributors to pollution that affect human health are: sulphur dioxide, carbon monoxide, nitrogen oxides, ozone, carcinogens, fluorides, aeroallergens, radon, smoking, asbestos, and noise.

Sulphur dioxide (SO_2) is a source of serious discomfort and in excessive amounts is a health hazard, especially to people with respiratory ailments. In the United States alone, the estimated amount of SO_2, emitted into the atmosphere is 23 million tons per year. SO_2 causes irritation of the respiratory tract; it damages lung tissue and promotes respiratory diseases. The taste threshold limit is 0.3 ppm and SO_2 produces an unpleasant smell at 0.5 ppm concentration. In fact, sulphur dioxides in general have been considered as prime candidates for an air pollution index. Such an index would be a measure reflecting the presence and action of harmful environmental conditions. This would aid in rendering meaningful analyses of the effect of air pollutants on human health, especially since health effects are most probably due to the complementing action of pollutants and meteorological variables.

SO_2 is more harmful in a dusty atmosphere. This effect may be explained as follows: The respiratory tract is lined with hairlike cilia, which by means of regular sweeping action force out foreign substances entering the respiratory tract through the mouth.

SO_2 and H_2SO_4 (sulfuric acid) molecules paralyse the cilia, rendering it ineffective in rejecting these particulates, causing them to penetrate deeper into the lungs. Alone, these molecules are too small to remain in the lungs; but, some SO_2 molecules are absorbed on larger particles, which penetrate into the lungs and settle there, bringing concentrated amounts of the irritant SO_2 into prolonged contact with the fine lung tissues. SO_2 and the other sulphur dioxide-particulate combinations are serious irritants of the respiratory tract.

In high-pollution intervals they can cause death. Their action of severely irritating the respiratory tract may cause heart failure due to the excessive labouring of the heart in its pumping action to circulate oxygen through the body. Carbon monoxide (CO) levels have declined in most parts of the United States since 1970, but the standards are still exceeded in many cities throughout the country. Carbon monoxide pollution is the basic concern in most large cities of the world where traffic is usually congested and heavy. CO cannot be detected by smell or sight, and this adds to its danger. It forms a complex with hemoglobin, called carboxy-hemoglobin (COHb).

The formation of this complex reduces the capability of the bloodstream to carry oxygen by interfering with the release of the oxygen carried by remaining hemoglobin. Also, since the affinity of human hemoglobin is 210 times higher for CO than it is for oxygen, a small concentration of CO markedly reduces the capacity of the blood to act as an oxygen carrier. The threshold limit value (TLV), or maximum allowable concentration (MAC), of CO for industrial exposure is 50 ppm; concentrations of CO as low as 10 ppm produce effects on the nervous system and give an equilibrium level of COHb larger than 2 percent. A concentration of 30 ppm produces a level greater than 5 percent COHb, which affects the nervous system and causes impairment of visual acuity, brightness discrimination, and other psychomotor functions.

Carbon monoxide concentrations of 50 to 100 ppm are commonly encountered in the atmosphere of crowded cities, especially at heavy-traffic rush hours. Such high concentrations adversely affect driving ability and cause accidents. In addition, an estimate of the average concentration of CO inhaled into the lungs from cigarette smoking is 400 ppm. Two major pollutants among nitrogen oxides (NO_x) are nitric oxide (NO), and nitrogen dioxide (NO_2). Emissions from stationary sources are estimated to be 16 million tons of NO_x per year. Mobile sources of NO_x pollution are automobiles emitting an estimated average of 10.7 million tons per year.

NO is colourless, but it is photochemically converted to nitrogen dioxide, which is one of the components of smog. Nitrogen dioxide also contributes to the formation of aldehydes and ketones through the photochemical reaction with hydrocarbons of the atmosphere. Nitrogen dioxide is an irritant; it damages lung tissues, especially through the formation of nitric acid. Breathing nitrogen dioxide at 25 ppm for 8 hours could cause spoilage of lung tissues, while breathing it for one-half hour at 100 to 150 ppm could produce serious pulmonary edema, or swelling of lung tissues. A few breaths at 200 to 700 ppm may cause fatal pulmonary edema. Ozone (O_3) is produced from the activation of sunlight on nitrogen dioxide, pollutants such as volatile organic compounds (VOCs), and atmospheric gases such as oxygen. It is an irritant to the eyes and lungs, penetrating deeper into the lungs than sulphur dioxide. In air it forms complex organic compounds; dominant among these are aldehydes and peroxyacetyl nitrate (PAN), which also causes eye and lung irritation. Rural areas have concentrations of 2 to 5 parts per hundred million (pphm) of ozone, which is distinguished by an odor of electrical shorting.

A few good smells and the individual's sensitivity for this odor disappears. At 5 to 10 pphm, the odor is unpleasant and pungent. Exposure to ozone for 30 min at 10 to 15 pphm, which is normally encountered in large cities, causes serious irritation of the mucous membranes and reduces their ability to fight infection. At 20 to 30 pphm it affects vision, and exposure to concentrations of 30 pphm for a few minutes brings a marked respiratory distress with severe fatigue, coughing, and choking. When volunteers were exposed intermittently for 2 weeks to a 30-pphm ozone atmosphere, they experienced severe headaches, fatigue, wheezing, chest pains, and difficulty in breathing. It reduces the activity of individuals, especially those with previous heart conditions. Even young athletes tire on smoggy days.

Carcinogens, which are often polycyclic hydrocarbons inducing cancer in susceptible individuals, are present in the exhaust emissions of the internal combustion engine, be it diesel or gasoline. Two major carcinogens are benzopyrene, which is a strong cancer-inducing agent, and benzanthracene, which is a weak one. They are essentially nonvolatile organic compounds associated with solids or polymeric substances in the air. These compounds are not very stable, and they are destroyed at varying rates by other air pollutants and by sunlight. However, as a result of industrialisation and urbanisation, these substances are discharged into the atmosphere in significant quantities, reportedly causing a steady increase in the frequency of human lung cancer in the world.

Aeroallergens are airborne substances causing allergies. These are predominantly of natural origin, but some are industrial. Allergic reactions in sensitive persons are caused by allergens such as pollens, spores, and rusts. A large percentage of the population is affected by hay fever and asthma each year; ragweed pollen may be the worst offender-it is about 20 mm in diameter, and under normal conditions, nearly all of it will be deposited near the source. Organic allergens come from plants, yeasts, molds, and animal hair, fur, or feathers. Fine industrial materials in the air cause allergies; for example, the powdered material given off in the extraction of oil from castor beans causes bronchial asthma in people living near the factory.

Radon is a radioactive, colourless, odorless, naturally occurring gas that is found everywhere at very low levels. It seeps through the soil and collects in homes. Radon problems have been identified in every state, and millions of homes throughout the country have elevated radon levels. Radon in high concentrations has been determined to cause lung cancer in humans. Smoking can be categorised as voluntary pollution. The smokers not only create a health hazard for themselves but also for the nonsmokers in their company. Cigarette smoke causes lung cancer, and in pregnant women it may cause premature birth and low birthweight in newborns.

Asbestos is a mineral fiber that has been used commonly in a variety of building construction materials for insulation as a fire retardant. The EPA and other organisations have banned several asbestos products. Manufacturers have also voluntarily limited the use of asbestos. Today asbestos is most commonly found in older homes in pipe and furnace insulation materials, asbestos shingles, millboard, textured paints, and floor tiles.

The most dangerous asbestos fibers are too small to see. After the fibers are inhaled, they can remain and accumulate in the lungs. Asbestos can cause lung cancer,

cancer of the chest and abdominal linings, and asbestosis (irreversible lung scarring that can be fatal). Symptoms of these diseases do not show up until many years after exposure. Most people with asbestos-related disease were exposed to elevated concentrations on the job, and some developed disease from clothing and equipment brought home from job sites. Noise pollution is not usually placed among the top environmental problems facing the nation; however, it is one of the more frequently encountered sources of pollution in everyday life.

Recent scientific evidence shows that relatively continuous exposures to sound exceeding 70 dB can be harmful to hearing. Noise can also cause stress reactions that include: (1) increases in heart rate, blood pressure, and blood cholesterol levels, and (2) negative effects on the digestive and respiratory systems. With persistent, unrelenting noise exposure, it is possible that these reactions will become chronic stress diseases such as high blood pressure or ulcers. Plants Pollutants, especially in the air, cover a wide spectrum of particulate and gaseous matter, damaging and effecting the growth of many types of vegetation.

Whether particulate matter is harmful to vegetation depends upon the type of particulate matter predominating, upon the concentration of particulate matter versus time, the type of vegetation under consideration, climatic conditions, the duration of exposure, and similar factors. Different types of plants are affected differently by pollutants. The three major types of plants are trees, vegetative plants (crops), and flowers. Only a few kinds of trees can live in the polluted air of a big city.

Sycamores and Norway maples seem to resist air pollution best. That is why those trees are planted among most city streets. However, air pollution can kill even sycamores and Norway maples. The danger to the trees is greatest at street corners. That is where cars and buses may have to stop and wait for traffic lights to change. While they are waiting, exhaust pours out of their tailpipes, resulting in tree kills. Pine trees do not resist air pollution as well as sycamores and Norway maples. Air pollutants, even in small amounts, are very harmful to pine trees. The major contributors to plant pollution are sulphur dioxide, ethylene, acid deposition, smog, ozone, and fluoride.

Metallurgical smelting processes emit substantial quantities of sulphur dioxide, and they are in, general associated with a good degree of defoliation. Serious damage from sulphur dioxide is usually characterised by loss of chlorophyll and suppression of growth. Leaf and needle tissues are damaged, and die as the time of exposure increases. The attack starts at the edges, moving progressively toward the main body of the leaf or needle. A concentration as low as 2 pphm could suppress growth. Cereal crops, especially barley, are readily damaged at concentrations less than 50 pphm.

The presence of soot particles in the air can increase the damage because sulphur dioxide and sulfuric acid mist are enriched at the surface of particles. It has been determined that pine trees cannot survive the damage when the mean annual concentrations of sulphur dioxide exceed 0.07 to 0.08 ppm. Ethylene in the air causes injury to many flowers, whether they are orchids, lilacs, tulips, or roses. The first symptom of ethylene damage is the drying of the sepals, which are leaflike formations located at the bottom of the flower bloom. This attack destroys the beauty of the flowers and contributes to extensive economic losses to growers. In addition, accidental escape of ethylene from a polyethylene plant caused 100 percent damage to cotton fields a mile away.

The process of acid deposition begins with emissions of SO_2 and NO_X. These pollutants interact with sunlight and water vapour in the upper atmosphere to form acidic compounds. When it rains (or snows), these compounds fall to the Earth. Forests and agriculture may be vulnerable because acid deposition can leach nutrients from the ground, killing nitrogen-fixing microorganisms that nourish plants and release toxic metals. Smog damage to vegetation is serious, especially in locations such as Los Angeles; the lower leaf surfaces of petunias and spinach become silvery or bronze in colour.

The most toxic substance of the Los Angeles air has been identified as peroxyacetyl nitrate (PAN), formed by photochemical reactions of hydrocarbons and nitrogen oxides emanating mostly from automobile exhausts. Ozone is a major component of the Los Angeles smog; it is phytotoxic at concentrations of 0.2 ppm, even when exposure time is only a few hours. Its effect on spinach is strong and destructive, causing whitening or bleaching of the leaves. Certain tobaccos are damaged by concentrations as small as 5 to 6 ppm. Ozone hinders plant growth even if bleaching or other distinctive marks are not found. Fluorides are given off by factories that make aluminum, iron, and fertiliser.

Due to these factories, growers have complained about the damage to fruits and leaves of peach, plum, apple, fig, and apricot trees. Fluorides also damage grapes, cherries, and citrus. It has been observed that the average yield of fruit per tree decreases 27 percent for every increase of 50 ppm of fluoride in the leaves. Animals Animals are also affected by pollutants in the air. There are many similarities between the effects on humans and the effects on animals. For example, animals in zoos suffer the same effects of air pollution as humans. They also are beset with lung disease, cancer, and heart disease. Their babies have more birth defects than those of wild animals.

Air that is polluted with fluorides can be deadly for sheep, cows, and some other animals. However, inhaling the polluted air is not what causes the damage. Some plants that are eaten by the animals store up the fluoride that they have taken from the air, and after a while contain dangerous amounts of fluoride. Animals become ill and even die after eating these plants. The bald eagle is the U.S. national bird, but it is being killed mainly with insecticides. The eagles are not killed by breathing the polluted air but are dying because they cannot reproduce. When an insecticide is sprayed on plants, some of it misses the plants and gets into the air as a pollutant.

Certain kinds of insecticides do not change into harmless substances; they are referred to as "persistent" insecticides because they remain harmful for years. Rain washes these insecticides out of the air and into the water. Small animals bioaccumulate the insecticides, and these animals are often eaten by larger animals, who also have absorbed the insecticide, thereby doubling their insecticide intake. Bald eagles eat large animals (fish), and they may store enough insecticide to kill them. Even if they do not die, the insecticide prevents the bird from reproducing. The eggs that the females lay either have very thin shells or no shells at all, causing the inability of baby eagles to hatch. Materials of Construction Air pollution has long been a significant source of economic loss in urban areas. Damage to nonliving materials may be exhibited in many ways, such as corrosion of metal, rubber cracking, soiling and eroding of building surfaces, deterioration of works of art, and fading of dyed materials and paints.

Water Pollution

Pollution in waterways impairs or destroys aquatic life, threatens human health, and simply fouls the water such that recreational and aesthetic potential are lost. There are several different types of water pollution and there are several different ways in which water can be polluted.

Half of all Americans and 95 percent of rural Americans use groundwater for drinking water. Through testing water in different areas and at different times, pollutants were found in the drinking water. Several public water supplies using groundwater exceeded EPA's drinking water standards for inorganic substances (fluorides and nitrates).

Major problems were reported from toxic organics in some wells in almost all states east of the Mississippi River. Trichloroethylene, a suspected carcinogen, was the most frequent contaminant found. The EPA's Ground Water Supply Survey showed that 20 percent of all public water supply wells and 29 percent in urban areas had detectable levels of at least one VOC. At least 13 organic chemicals that are confirmed animal or human carcinogens have been detected in drinking water wells.

The most severe and acute public health effects from contaminated drinking water from the tap, such as cholera and typhoid, have been eliminated in America. However, some less acute and immediate hazards still remain in the nation's tap water. Contaminants of special concern to the EPA are lead, radionuclides, microbiological contaminants, and disinfection by-products.

Lead in drinking water is due primarily to the corrosion of plumbing materials. The health effects related to the ingestion of too much lead are very serious and can lead to impaired blood formation, brain damage, increased blood pressure, premature birth, low birth weight, and nervous system disorders. Young children are especially at high risk.

Radionuclides are radioactive isotopes that emit radiation as they decay. The most significant radionuclides in drinking water are radium, uranium, and radon, all of which occur in nature. Ingestion of uranium and radium in drinking water can cause cancer of the bone and kidney. Radon can be ingested and inhaled. The main health risk due to inhalation is lung cancer. Microbiological contaminants such as bacteria, viruses, and protozoa may be found in water. Although some organisms are harmless, others may cause disease. Microbiological contamination continues to be a national concern because contaminated drinking water systems can rapidly spread disease.

Disinfection by-products are produced during water treatment by chemical reactions of disinfectants with naturally occurring or synthetic materials. These by-products may pose health risks, and these risks are related to long-term exposure to low levels of contaminants.

Wetlands are the most productive of all ecosystems, but the United States is slowly losing them. There are many positive effects of wetlands: converts sunlight into plant material or biomass that serve as food for aquatic animals that form the base of the food chain, habitats for fish and wildlife, and spawning grounds; maintains and improves water quality in adjacent water bodies; removes nutrients to prevent eutrophication; filters harmful chemicals; traps suspended sediments; controls floods; prevents shoreline erosion with vegetation; and contributes $20 to 40 billion annually to the economy.

Coastal waters are home to many ecologically and commercially valuable species of fish, birds, and other wildlife. Coastal waters are susceptible to contamination because they act as sinks for the large quantities of pollution discharged from industry. The effects include toxic contamination, eutrophication, pathogen contamination, habitat loss and alteration, and changes in living resources. Coastal fisheries, wildlife, and bird populations have been declining, with fewer species being represented.

The Great Lakes are all being affected by toxics that are contaminating fish and the water. Lake Ontario and Lake Erie are also being affected by eutrophication. Oceans are being polluted with sediments dredged from industrialised urban harbors that are often highly contaminated with heavy metals and toxic synthetic organic chemicals. The contaminants can be taken up by marine organisms. In addition, persistent disposal of plastics from land and sea have become serious problems. The most severe effect of the debris floating in the ocean is injury and death of fish, marine animals, and birds. Debris on beaches can affect the public safety, the beauty of the beach, and the economy.

Municipal wastewater and industrial discharges produce nutrients in sewage that foster excessive growth of algae and other aquatic plants. Plants then die and decay, depleting the dissolved oxygen needed by fish. Wastewater that is poorly treated may contain chemicals harmful to human and aquatic life. Non-point-source pollution consists of sediment, nutrients, pesticides, and herbicides.

Sediment causes decreased light transmission through water resulting in decreased plant reproduction, interference with feeding and mating patterns, decreased viability of aquatic life, decreased recreational and commercial values, and increased drinking water costs.

Nutrients promote the premature aging of lakes and estuaries. Pesticides and herbicides hinder photosynthesis in aquatic plants, affect aquatic reproduction, increase organism susceptibility to environmental stress, accumulate in fish tissues, and present a human health hazard through fish and water consumption.

Humans are not affected similarly by the presence of water pollution as they may be by the presence of polluted air. Humans are affected by water pollution through consuming contaminated water or animals (fish). Due to contaminated drinking water, lakes, and oceans, humans are inflicted with diseases, impaired blood formation, brain damage, increased blood pressure, premature birth, low birth weight, nervous system disorders, and cancer (bone, kidney, and lung).

Plants are affected by wastewater, sewage, sediments, pesticides, and herbicides found mainly in surface water. Effects on plants in these areas are:

1. Decreased plant reproduction
2. Hinderance of photosynthesis in aquatic plants
3. Excessive growth of algae and other aquatic plants
4. Ultimate death of plants

Animals, especially those that live in or near the water, are directly affected by water pollution. Chemical and solid waste disposal in water can affect animals in many ways, varying from waste/pollutant accumulation effects to death. Animals such as fish, marine mammals, and birds can be injured or killed due to floating debris in the ocean. Contaminants can be taken up by marine organisms and accumulate there. The accumulations increase as the larger fish consume contaminated smaller fish. This cycle interferes with animals feeding and mating patterns, affects aquatic reproduction, and decreases the viability of aquatic life.

Land has been used as dumping grounds for wastes. Improper handling, storage, and disposal of chemicals can cause serious problems. Several types of wastes that are placed in the land are:

1. Industrial hazardous wastes
2. Municipal wastes
3. Mining wastes
4. Radioactive wastes
5. Leakage from underground storage tanks

Humans: Potential health effects in humans range from headaches, nausea, and rashes to acid burns, serious impairment of kidney and liver functions, cancer, and genetic damage. Underground storage tank leaks may contaminate local drinking water systems or may lead to explosions and fires causing harm and injury to the people in the vicinity.

Plants: Trees are usually not planted around landfills, and if they were they would have difficulty growing due to the contaminated soil in the vicinity of the landfill. Vegetative plants also have difficulty growing around landfills. This is due to the fact that the hazardous wastes from industry are usually dumped in the landfills. Flowers also do not normally grow near landfills for similar reasons.

Animals: Animals are essentially affected in the same ways as humans. They may experience the effects of drinking contaminated water and suffer from acid burns, kidney, liver, and genetic damage, and cancer.

Several different dimensions can account for the universe of potential chemical toxicants. From each of these dimensions comes a different perspective in terms of how the continuum of the chemical universe "pie" is sliced. Previously unrecognised, unexpected, or unanticipated scenarios for exposure to chemicals can be viewed from a number of different perspectives. Discussions regarding "emerging" pollutants often get confused because of the failure to define (i) what is meant by "emerging" and (ii) the dimension of the chemical universe around which the discussion is focused.

The dimensions include chemical classes (according to chemical functionality; chemicals of totally new structure), type of use (new uses in either the industrial or consumer realms), type of effect (newly discovered but prior-existing effects or totally new receptor targets or ligand-receptor interactions), mechanism of action, source (new types of sources or previously unknown origins for existing chemicals), and exposure route (pathways that had not been anticipated or previously discounted as not possible). Each dimension can intersect with the others to various degrees. These different perspectives often inject confusion into discussions oriented to anticipating future risks or uncovering existing, but previously unrecognised, risks. For example, discussions regarding endocrine disrupting compounds (EDCs) are sometimes equated with discussions concerning PPCPs. But the former is defined according to type of biological effect or mechanism of action, while the latter is defined by chemical classes and types of use; and the two intersect only to a limited extent.

Chemical Pollutants

Countless galaxies of chemical classes have continual presence in waters-regardless of the water's purity. A water's "purity," a concept that breeds much confusion in its own right, is merely a reflection of the types and concentrations of these chemicals. The number of chemical contaminants at trace levels can exceed those present at higher levels.

As the power of analytical chemistry increases, the types of chemicals that can be detected increase, and the limits of concentration at which they can be measured are continually lowered; analytical chemistry plays a key role in expanding and refining our ever-changing perspective of water purity. These chemicals comprise the broad spectrum of anthropogenic chemicals (those purposefully synthesised and indirectly produced by human activities-drinking water disinfection by-products are one example) as well as "natural products" (those created both by natural physicochemical or biological processes-an example being geosmin, the off-flavour bicyclic alcohol produced by certain algae and fungi). Anthropogenic pollutants gain entry to surface and groundwater as a result of manufacturing emissions, waste disposal (e.g., incineration, landfills), accidental releases (e.g., spills), purposeful introduction (e.g., pesticides, groundwater recharge, sewage sludge application to land), and consumer activity (which includes both the excretion and purposeful disposal of a wide range of naturally occurring and anthropogenic chemicals such as PPCPs).

All of these sources but the last have long been recognised as major potential routes of pollutant release.

Consumer activities have only recently been recognised as a potentially major, long-standing source of uncontrolled nonpoint, disperse pollution. As of March 2004, nearly 23 million organic and inorganic substances (excluding biosequences such as proteins and nucleotides) had been indexed by the American Chemical Society's Chemical Abstracts Service in their CAS Registry. Roughly one-third of these (over 7 million) were commercially available, representing a 23% increase over the prior 9-month period.

In contrast, only about a quarter million (230,000) of these are inventoried or regulated by numerous government bodies worldwide. While the known universe of organic chemicals might seem large, the universe of potential organic chemicals (those that could possibly be synthesised and those that already exist but which have not yet been identified) is unimaginably large. To get an idea as to the numbers of distinct organic chemical entities that could hypothetically be synthesised and added to a limitless, ever-expanding known chemical universe, consider the back-of-the-envelope calculations of Bohacek et al., which yielded over 106° distinct structures that are possible with a total of merely 30 atoms of just C, N, O, or S! Far more than 106° structures would be possible if the wide spectrum of other heteroatoms (including common ones such as P or the halogens) was included, or even larger numbers of C, N, O, and S. Clearly, there are essentially no limits to the types of possible organic chemicals. The possibilities are only beginning to emerge from the efforts of synthetic organic chemists or combinatorial chemistry.

The high potential for the continued proliferation of new PPCPs (as well as myriads of other anthropogenic chemicals) poses substantial (and perhaps insurmountable) challenges to the evolution and design of viable systems based on a chemical-by-chemical approach for regulating (or monitoring) the occurrence of pollutants in the environment. Just as an example, as of March 2004, more than 140,000 bioactive compounds were in various phases of drug research and development.

The rapid evolution of the "omics" revolution will undoubtedly feed an expansion of new drug entities that has already been underway. New drug entities, many with mechanisms of action never before encountered by biological systems, can be expected to enjoy continued introduction to commerce-while others are retired or withdrawn from market. For any sample collected from the environment, a large (but unknown) portion of its organic constituents are not (or cannot) be identified.

Toxicity can be associated with constituents from both groups of chemicals-those that can be identified, as well as from those that cannot be identified. Attempts to fully characterise the chemical composition of an environmental sample are rare because they are very demanding of time and resources; historically, they have been attempted most frequently for the easiest environmental "matrix," ambient air. Such studies attempt to identify and quantify every organic chemical (necessarily limited to those present above detection limits) and seek to achieve a mass balance around total organic carbon. But even after thorough analysis, a portion of the organic carbon will remain unaccounted for (comprising those solutes that cannot be detected for any number of reasons).

Significantly, almost always these unidentified compounds comprise an unknown fraction of all those present (unless carbon balances are calculated-a very onerous task), so it is rarely known how significant their presence is. These unidentified chemicals are neglected, ignored, omitted, or overlooked because of any number of limitations or idiosyncrasies of the many tools that compose the repertoire of the analytical chemist.

As an example of chemical pollution from consumer activities (in contrast to the origins for most "conventional" regulated pollutants), the U.S. EPA and other federal agencies such as the USGS in the late 1990s began to examine the occurrence, sources, fate, and potential for environmental and human health effects of pharmaceuticals and personal care products (PPCPs) as environmental pollutants.

These diverse galaxies of chemicals comprise potentially thousands of distinct parent structures, each of which can gain entry to the environment merely by consumer end use (such as excretion and bathing) and by disposal of expired or otherwise unwanted materials to waste drains. The numbers of these chemical entities are then susceptible to amplification simply by the action of biological and physicochemical transformation processes, which can create cascades of other modified structures (such as chains of metabolites), some of which possess biological activity of their own.

While PPCPs are considered by many to be "emerging" pollutants, one can safely assume that any consumer chemical has the potential to enter the environment from the first day it is introduced to commerce. In this sense, PPCPs (except for those just introduced to commerce) are not examples of emerging pollutants (that is, those that are just beginning to occur), but rather, it is the recognition of their potential significance or environmental ramifications that is actually emerging. In this sense, they are emerging concerns rather than emerging pollutants. Although PPCPs comprise a very large and diverse spectrum of pollutants, most of which have received little' attention, there are possibly numerous others, many of which environmental scientists undoubtedly are not yet even aware.

Some examples of more recently recognised pollutants (many of which have origins from multitudes of consumer products) include brominated flame retardants and the multiuse perfluoroalkylated synthesis/transformation chemicals such as, the fluorotelomer alcohols (FTOHs) and the interrelated perfluoroalkyl sulfonates and carboxylates; in general, fluorinated chemicals can have enhanced environmental persistence, and their transformation pathways are poorly understood.

Future Trends

While it is not possible to predict the future regarding the many dimensions of chemical pollution, one can hypothesise new paradigms that could develop from now-emerging industries or practices.

Sources of water pollutants

Two examples are totally new pollutants, never before encountered by biological systems, and totally new sources for substances that never had a significant presence in the environment [such as the transgenic production of proteinaceous therapeutics by genetically altered plants, also known as plant-made pharmaceuticals (PMPs) from "molecular farming" or "biopharming". With regard to new sources, continued advancements in combinatorial chemistry, coupled with less-costly and more sophisticated robotics, could expand the user-base for the mass synthesis of untold numbers of chemicals for myriads of possible uses. The disposal and escape to the environment of these chemicals from multitudes of dispersed point sources holds the potential for a significant new source of pollutants.

Evaluation of monitor undefinable pollutants

Nanomaterials comprise particles with diameters ranging roughly from 1 nm (10 Angstroms, about the size of 10 hydrogen atoms) to 100 nm. Naturally occurring and certain anthropogenic nanoparticles have long posed toxicological concerns; examples include the inhalation of soot from the pyrolysis or combustion of fuels or even from cooking. Indeed, nanoparticles have been used since antiquity for various purposes, such as in artwork (where the colour of certain particles can be dictated solely by controlling their size). The emergence of specially designed and manufactured nanomaterials (which by definition would be "manufactured" from the "bottom-up," atom by atom) via a multitude of industries could contribute greatly to the load and distribution of nanoparticles in the environment.

In contrast to "conventional" pollutants, the properties of these materials are dictated more by their molecular or particle size and shape than by their chemical structures or compositions, many of which can be expected to be ill-defined and varied in terms of both composition and conformation. A host of currently unanswerable questions quickly arise regarding the environmental chemistry and environmental toxicology of these newly created xenobiotics, which could quickly achieve worldwide distribution via wide-spread use in consumer products.

Natural weathering/aging or environmental transformation of nanomaterials from consumer items could hold the potential for creating nearly universal, continual, inadvertent exposure to a large spectrum of additional ill-defined materials (via respiratory, dermal, and ingestion routes). Many currently unforeseeable environmental and human health ramifications could be posed by re-inventing the material world. Both the parent nanoparticles and their associated transformation products can be referred to as structurally undefinable ubiquitous xenobiotics (SUDUX). Inherent to the ill-defined structural nature of SUDUX may be its propensity to thwart our chemical analysis wherewithal to monitor environmental occurrence or to measure exposure; currently, these types of potential pollutants can be analysed only with sophisticated approaches such as single-particle mass spectrometry.

Inadequate water infrastructure

Conventional municipal sewage treatment facilities were

never designed to remove exotic anthropogenic chemicals with structures and mechanisms of biological action that are foreign to biological degradative/transformation systems. Indeed, the ubiquitous, albeit low level, presence of PPCPs in treated sewage effluent reflects this limitation. Even if existing waste treatment and water treatment facilities together with the associated conveyance distribution networks functioned according to original specifications, the types and quantities of xenobiotics in treated water could continue to rise, partly as a result of the introduction of new chemicals to the marketplace and partly because the nation's water infrastructure requires considerable investment for repair and upgrading. An additional infrastructure need is to reduce the occurrence of un-permitted straight-piping, septic systems, and privies, which serve to maximise the release of xenobiotics to the environment (to both surface waters and groundwaters).

Recharge of groundwater

The diminishing quantity and quality of potable source waters are pressures serving to heighten interest in reusing water. Just as with the historic practice of treating domestic wastewaters for discharge to surface waters (which, after sufficient spatial and temporal disconnect, is eventually recycled for drinking), the long-practiced purposeful recharge of groundwater (both indirect and direct) is a major route to achieving water reuse. But the ever-shortening spatial and temporal hydraulic connectivity between the point of wastewater discharge and the point of use for drinking will pose serious challenges for ensuring human safety and for framing how risk is perceived by the consumer. These challenges will be magnified as the levels of micropollutant residues are reduced and as new pollutants continually emerge.

Decentralised water re-use

The growing shortage of freshwater could drive a transition

from centralised municipal water treatment and distribution to truly distributed water reuse-where wastewater is both treated and reused at its origin-on site (the ultimate extension of so-called "toilet-to-tap" programmes). Such distributed water reuse systems pose unique challenges regarding public acceptance and effective communication of risk. But they also offer advantages regarding independence and the inherent design advantage of ultimate security from large-scale sabotage. Another advantage of recycling water generated directly from the point of original use (as opposed to collective water from domestic, municipal, and industrial generators) is that the universe of microcontaminants that need to be removed is vastly reduced.

Pollution Prevention

Depending on the source or the end-use exposure for each "class" of anthropogenic xenobiotics in water supplies, their overall environmental loads could be reduced by instituting any of seemingly unlimited means of pollution prevention strategies. Long practiced at the manufacturing level, pollution prevention has only begun to be implemented or contemplated at the many stages leading up to and including consumer consumption or end use. Successfully engaging the public is critical for making meaningful progress toward sustainability.

The extreme diversity of actions that can be designed or implemented to reduce the introduction of PPCPs to the environment serves as but one example for minimising consumer chemicals as pollutants. Of the many approaches for reducing the introduction of drugs to the environment are consumer-level "take-back" programmes. While several countries have implemented these programmes, the U.S. is only beginning to consider such an approach. As an example, the State of Maine has been particularly proactive in this regard, with a proposal to implement an innovative "mail-back" programme. An ultimate objective of any programme focused on "emerging pollutants" should be to create a mechanism for identifying new environmental pollutants as early as possible-well before their becoming pervasive in the environment.

A mechanism for the real-time detection of the presence of new pollutants in water is important not just for protecting the environment and public health from the effects of inadvertent pollution. It would also serve double duty in protecting water supplies from chemical sabotage. The sheer numbers of potential new contaminants would clearly pose insurmountable obstacles for conventional target-based monitoring approaches.

A straightforward way to sidestep this limitation would be to design an early-warning system around the simple approach of detecting "change"-where any perturbation in a water's normal chemical "fingerprint" (distribution pattern of types and quantities of solutes) would trigger an immediate in-depth chemical analysis to determine the cause (identify the chemicals responsible for the change). Such a nationwide change-detection approach was proposed in 2001. The timely elucidation of newly emerging (or previously unrecognised) pollutants is also critical to uncovering trends in geographic pollutant distribution, prevalence, and loads. Having available long-term change-detection data could greatly assist epidemiological studies, especially those involving cancer clusters, which have long been a bane of toxicologists.

Another approach is to leverage the involvement of amateur observers to report unusual phenomena in nature that are possibly the result of chemical stressors; one such proposal was noted by the Royal Commission on Environmental Pollution.

Sabotage of water supplies currently presents a major un-addressed problem with respect to Homeland Security. Traditional target-based monitoring schemes applied to detecting chemical sabotage (monitoring based on pre-defined lists of potential sabotage agents) could easily be circumvented simply with the use of chemical agents that are not included on such pre-defined lists. Furthermore, the use of sabotage agents having mechanisms of action that yield symptoms only after delayed periods of time (delayed-onset of action) can easily circumvent any real-time detection device based on the more inclusive (but still not universal) monitoring approaches using biological assays. In contrast, early-warning systems based on chemical-fingerprint "change-detection" could prove essential for protecting water supplies.

Certain pollutants can be used as tools (probes or tracers) for providing ready indication of the presence of other types of pollutants that are more difficult, costly, or time consuming to measure directly. For example, PPCPs can be used as sentinels of sewage intrusion (to trace sewage plumes or determine the source of groundwater contamination). Monitoring for select PPCPs could also be used for heightening community or societal awareness of adverse behaviour or of the connection between personal activities and the environment.

The quality of source waters depends in part on the diffuse impacts of the collective actions, activities, and behaviours of multitudes of individuals-from each of whom minuscule (and seemingly insignificant) contributions combine to yield detectable levels of certain pollutants that otherwise have little origin from industrial activities. Scientists need to better leverage opportunities for providing the public a greater understanding for how its actions are immediately, intimately, and inseparably linked to the environment. The fact that PPCPs occur as environmental pollutants (with still poorly understood ramifications) can be used as an excellent teaching tool. Societies worldwide are depending increasingly on rapid and complex advances in science and technology. With this in mind, arguments have long been made that optimal, rational, sociopolitical decisions cannot be made without a widespread public grounding in how science works: "It is suicidal to create a society dependent on science and technology in which hardly anybody knows anything about science and technology". Effective communication of science is also critically important to ensure the continued support of science by the public and to ensure that science plays its due role in the development of policy and the broader social agenda.

A major factor that limits the advancement of science and technology is public acceptance, which is largely driven by the perception of risk and the way in which it is communicated by scientists. Effective risk communication will prove particularly important with regard to the future of water resources for two reasons. First, the numbers of water pollutants newly introduced and newly discovered will continue to expand. Second, as freshwater supplies diminish, the pressure to recycle water will continue to grow.

The ultimate culmination of water recycling will probably be the so-called "toilet-to-tap" programmes (eventually those that rely on on-site treatment/recycling) for turning wastewater (e.g., sewage) into drinking water. The occurrence of even minute traces of drugs in certain drinking waters can foster the formation of negative mental images for the consumer (regardless of the water's overall purity), being that the origin of these drugs often derives solely from human excretion. It could prove critical that the public understand the ramifications of these programmes.

It might also prove useful that more resources be devoted to studying and improving the communication of risk to the general public. A better understanding is needed of the origins of the chasm existing between hazard/risk communication and how the public perceives risk. This will prove especially important with the growing need to recycle water for drinking, as maintenance of public trust in water supplies will prove critical to sustainable societies-the erosion of public trust in government and industry increases public resistance to adopting change. Regardless of the thoroughness and soundness of the science that will continue to be developed, it might all be for naught without integrating -the cognitive sciences (e.g., psychology) into the environmental sciences to develop a better communications interface between science and the public.

Public education is particularly important for minimising the incidence of the so-called "nocebo" response, which could possibly play a larger role in the chasm separating hazard assessment and risk perception than previously realised.

The nocebo effect (the opposite of the placebo effect) is a real, physiologically adverse outcome caused simply by the suggestion or belief that something (such as a chemical) is harmful, regardless of any inherent toxicity. The nocebo effect could play a key role in the development of adverse health consequences from exposure even to trace levels of contaminants-simply by the power of suggestion.

Hypothetical future advances often amplify our anticipation to the point where the future cannot come soon enough. Dr. Kristen Kulinowski coined the term "wow index" -,to describe this phenomenon. In certain instances, however, when the public is not properly informed of the potential ramifications of emerging technologies or insufficiently involved in considerations of its adoption, early anticipation can melt away to anxiety or fear. Dr. Kulinowski refers to this as the "wow-to-yuck trajectory".

The widespread public resistance to genetically modified food crops, after an "advertising" period that touted countless benefits, is one example of wow quickly transforming to yuck. The traditional way of addressing emerging pollutants or long-recognised pollutants that "resurface" (with new concerns), regardless of how timely, is at best a reactive approach. The fact that corrective reactions are required long after chemicals achieve commercial footholds leads to discussions of the controversies surrounding the Precautionary Principle.

Bibliography

Bonard, J. M., Chauvin, P. & Klinke, C. "Monodisperse multiwall carbon nanotubes obtained with ferritin as catalyst". *Nano Lett.* 2, 2002.

Goldstein A. N. (Ed.), "Handbook of Nanophase Materials". Marcel Dekker, New York, 1997.

Hammond, C. "The Basics of Crystallography and Diffraction" Oxford University Press. 1997.

Hiemenz, P. C.; Rajagopalan, R. *Principles of Colloid and Surface Chemistry*. Marcel Dekker Inc.: New York, 1997.

Israelchvili, J. N. *Intermolecular and Surface Forces*. Second Edition ed.; Academic Press: London, 1992.

Koch, C. C. "Nanostructured Materials: Processing, Properties and Applications". Institute of Physics, 2002.

Kohler M. and W. Fritzsche, "Nanotechnology: An Introduction to Nanostructuring Techniques". Wiley-VCH, Weinheim, 2004.

Kolasinski, K. W. "Surface Science: Foundations of Catalysis and Nanoscience". Wiley, Chichester, 2002.

Leopold, J. G., Zik, O., Cheifetz, E. & Rosenblatt, D. "Carbon nanotube-based electron gun for electron microscopy". J. Vac. Sci. Technol. A19. 2001

Paulmier, T., Balat-Pichelin, M., Le Queau, D., Berjoan, R. & Robert, J. F. "Physicochemical behavior of carbon materials under high temperature and ion radiation". *Appl. Surf. Sci.* 2001

Pirio, G., Legagneux, P., Pribat, D., Teo, K. B., Chhowalla, M., Amaratunga, G. A. J. & Milne, W. I. "Fabrication and electrical characteristics of carbon nanotube field emission microcathodes with an integrated gate electrode". *Nanotechnology*. 2002

Poole C. P. and F. J. Owens, "Introduction to Nanotechnology". Wiley, New Jersey, 2003.

Purcell, S. T., Vincent, P., Journet, C. & Binh, V. T. "Tuning of nanotube mechanical resonances by electric field pulling". *Phys. Rev. Lett.* 2002.

Roco, M. C. R. S. Williams and P. Alivisatos, "Nanotechnology Research Directions". Kluwer, Dordecht, 2000.

Suryanarayana, C., J. Singh and F. H. Froes (Eds), "Processing and Properties of Nanocrystalline Materials". TMS, Warrendale, PA, 1996.

Timp G. (Ed.), *Nanotechnology.* Springer-Verlag, New York, 1999.

Wang Z. L. (Ed.) "Characterisation of Nanophase Materials". Wiley-VCH, Weinheim, 2000.

Index

सामान्य मनोविज्ञान